CHARLIE GALLAGHER? WHAT A PLAYER!

David Potter

Forewords by Willie Wallace and Tommy Gemmell

CQN BOOKS

Published by CQN Books, Scotland.

First published in the United Kingdom in 2016 by CQN Books
ISBN 978-0-9934360-5-5

A catalogue for this book is available from the British Library and the Irish Library in Dublin.

Cover & page design and typesetting
by Stephen Cameron for CQN Books.

Edited by David Faulds, Publisher, CQN Books (email david@cqnpublishing.co.uk)

Printed by Gutenberg Press, Malta.

A special thank you to everyone in the

Celtic Quick News community and the wider Celtic family.
CQN has published books on Lisbon Lions Willie Wallace, Tommy Gemmell and John Hughes alongside Caesar & The Assassin and The Winds of Change by Alex Gordon.

Please visit
www.celticquicknews.co.uk and www.cqnbookstore.com

ACKNOWLEDGEMENTS

I owe a debt of gratitude to many people for the completion of this book, but I really must single out at the start Pat Woods for the magnificent work that he has done in the past in collating photographs, newspaper reports and ephemera on Charlie Gallagher, and for his co-operation in allowing me to use the results of his research.

Others who have helped, encouraged or co-operated in this venture include Tom Campbell, Willie Wallace, Tommy Gemmell, Danny McGrain, John Fallon, John McLauchlan, Marie Rowan, George Sheridan, Andrew Milne, Jamie Fox, Mike Maher, Maureen Andrew, Peter Marshall, Charlie McGinley and many others to whom I apologise for not mentioning by name. My own Supporters Bus, the Joseph Rafferty of Kirkcaldy, has always been very supportive as well.

Charlie himself, his wife Mary and daughter Claire have been very co-operative, and I hope they enjoy reading this book of a worthy subject. My thanks too must go to CQN for publishing this work.

David Potter

Kirkcaldy, March 2016

CONTENTS

WILLIE WALLACE

Honours: 7 caps for Scotland. 1 European Cup medal, 5 Scottish League medals, 3 Scottish Cup medals, 3 Scottish League Cup medals (one with Hearts, two with Celtic)

My fondest recollections of Charlie playing was shortly after I joined the club from Hearts in late 1966. For some reason or other Celtic's application for me to play against Vojvodina Novi Sad in the quarter final of the European Cup was not submitted on time so I was a spectator that night.

Charlie played that night and was one of the best players on the field. Late on in the game Charlie took a superb corner kick from which Billy McNeill scored with a great header. This made the score 2-1 for Celtic which meant that they had qualified for the semi-finals. Thanks to Charlie's skill and accuracy I was to benefit from this as progression to the semi-final meant I would be available to play if chosen.

Charlie is a very quiet and modest man and this was not the only occasion when Charlie's skill and football ability contributed to Celtic's many significant wins. Charlie and I went on to play together at Dumbarton Football Club with another ex Celtic squad member John Cushley. Charlie was a strong and reliable part of the Dumbarton club and an excellent role model for the youngsters on and off the field.

I am proud to have played with Charlie with both Celtic and Dumbarton. I wish Charlie and his family good health and every success with the book.

TOMMY GEMMELL

Honours: 18 caps for Scotland. 1 European Cup medal, 6 Scottish League medals, 3 Scottish Cup medals, 5 Scottish League Cup medals (four with Celtic, one with Dundee)

Charlie Gallagher was a great passer of the ball. He was a very skillful player even in the context of the Celtic team that he played in – he really did stand out.

He'd be the first to admit that he wasn't the hardest working player at Parkhead at the time but when you're that good on the ball you will be forgiven for that by your fellow players and the Celtic supporters, who always liked Charlie.

It was a pleasure to play alongside Charlie Gallagher and I wish him all the very best with his new biography. It's about time he got round to writing a book as I've done three!

CHAPTER ONE
THE BEGINNING

Charles Gallagher was born on November 3 1940 in the Gorbals in Glasgow, the middle of three children born to Dan and Annie (nee Duffy) Gallagher both of whom had been born in Donegal. The family hailed from near Megaraclogher and Gweedore area of Donegal near Mount Errigal, and Charlie was frequently taken there for his summer holidays. His brother was called Dannie and his sister Eileen. There would be no lack of Gallaghers in that part of Donegal. Everyone seemed to bear that name!

The spelling is Gallagher, not Gallacher which is considered the Scottish spelling. Gallacher was the name of the great Wembley Wizard and ultimately very tragic figure Hughie Gallacher of Airdrie and Newcastle United. Patsy Gallacher of Celtic, on the other hand, really should have his name spelt Gallagher. He was born Gallagher in Donegal in 1891, but when the family moved to Clydebank a few years later, the name was changed, almost by accident, to Gallacher. The story goes that when they arrived and a nameplate had to be put on the door, it was Gallacher. Either Patsy's parents (they were illiterate) did not notice the mistake made by the Scottish workmen, or they chose deliberately to become Scottish by calling themselves Gallacher.

Charlie however is undeniably Gallagher. The Second World War had been going on for 14 months when Charlie was born. Great Britain had just been saved, temporarily at least, from invasion by the RAF in the skies over Kent in what history has named the Battle of Britain, but the blitz was in full swing in London with the Londoners subjected to nightly bombing raids in an attempt to force the country into submission. It was widely believed that it would only be a matter of time before similar treatment was meted out to Glasgow, although Glasgow was just a little out of range for any sustained assault. This did not, however, save Clydebank in 1941.

Charlie's father Dan was a general labourer, what is called with a touch of condescension perhaps a "navvy". He worked all over Scotland working on roads in the Highlands, for example, and in the chaotic circumstances of World War II it was never easy to predict where he would be or what he would be doing at any given time. Charlie's mother Annie was, like many women of the time, a housewife, feeling that when her children were young, she had enough on her plate to keep them well clad and well fed. She did on occasion do cleaning jobs on a part-time basis, and for a spell was a cleaner in West Nile Street in the offices of Fred Donovan, Secretary of the Scottish Football League. The young Charlie would sometimes go with her and read his books!

The Gorbals is in central Glasgow to the south of the River Clyde. In recent decades, there has been much redevelopment of the area, although some would argue that still more redevelopment is required. It would be fair to say that when Charlie was born there and for a long time after, the Gorbals had a bad reputation, being looked upon in polite genteel society as almost a byword for crime. The 1930s until the early 1950s was the heyday (if that is an appropriate term) for the razor gangs which thrived in the Gorbals and indeed in other parts of Glasgow as well, until the stern policing of Percy Sillitoe, aided by the draconian Scottish justice system, managed to get on top of that particular crime, if not wipe it out altogether.

It was in the 1950s and 1960s no uncommon experience to find oneself beside a man at Parkhead or Hampden with a huge scar running down his face. Some of these were war wounds honourably sustained at Anzio or El Alamein, or even at the Somme or Loos if the man were a little older, but most were the victims of the razor gang culture so prevalent in the Gorbals and other areas of Glasgow.

The Gorbals teemed with humanity. It was described as one gigantic slum, and that description is often acknowledged as being none too wide of the mark. Large families would live in one or two rooms of a flat or sometimes even a "single end" which was only one room! There were no indoor toilets, just outside ones shared by many families, and not even running water in most flats. In these scarcely believable living conditions, the wonder was that people actually put up with it without any great political movements demanding extreme measures like revolutions as for example happened in Russia in 1917.

It is no surprise that every social evil that can be imagined could be found in the Gorbals. Filth, illness, childhood mortality, drunkenness and crime all thrived. In vain did the Churches and other moral guardians thunder against "the demon drink". Alcohol, readily available, for there were very few streets which did not have at least one public house, was there for those who wished to forget the pointlessness of their existence or the sheer squalor which surrounded them.

The phrase "The Boy from the Gorbals" was frequently used of Benny Lynch, the boxer who was born in the Gorbals in 1913 and became World Flyweight Champion in 1936 before lapsing into alcoholism and drinking himself to death in 1946. He had been a strong Celtic supporter and had always been welcomed at Parkhead by Willie Maley, the Celtic Manager. But there was also a play called "The Boy From The Gorbals" screened by STV in August 1959 about a well-meaning but naïve middle class family who took a boy from the Gorbals with them on holiday. The boy stole from them, got drunk, seduced the daughter and fought with the son and the play was about how the family coped with this intruder into their cosy, sheltered lives. It stigmatised the Gorbals even more than previously, and did the image of the place no good.

And yet, that is not the whole story either. The stereotypes in drama and literature, particularly the classic novel No Mean City by H Kingsley Long and Alexander McArthur, did exist but were not universally true. Many respectable families grew up in the Gorbals and survived. It was a major benefit if the man of the household did not drink. For one thing, there was more money and for another, there was a great deal less of the violent behaviour towards the women and children. Many organisations made a determined effort to help – this was, after all, one of the raisons d'etre of Celtic football club in its early days – and religion too flourished, giving the lie to the commonly held belief that Churches, whether Roman Catholic or Protestant, were the province of the well-to-do or the middle class.

The other good thing about the Gorbals at the time of Charlie's birth and early childhood was that it was definitely multi-racial and multi-ethnic with people of Irish, Lithuanian, Russian, Polish, Italian and Jewish extraction all living there in reasonable social harmony. The Clyde with all its jobs had meant that Glasgow, even as early as the 18th century had been a cosmopolitan city. It was to Scotland's credit that there has never been documented any large scale or organised persecution of its Jewish minority – and that could not be said of very many European countries – but of course the two historical events that caused the massive population invasions of Glasgow were the Highland Clearances of the 1820s and the Irish Potato Famine of the 1840s.

The Potato Famine in Ireland was a catastrophe of unimaginable magnitude and severity. And yet, although the actual disease of the potatoes could not have been foreseen or forestalled, its consequences could have been greatly lessened if prompt and effective action had been taken by the two bodies to whom the Irish would have reasonably looked to for succour, coincidentally the two richest organisations on earth at the time, the British Empire and the Roman Catholic Church. Little if anything was forthcoming from the Vatican, and the Great Britain (of which Ireland was a part since the Act of Union in 1801) saw only a belated and half-hearted effort by Prime Minister Robert Peel (a man with some sort of conscience) who repealed the Corn Laws in 1846 but was thrown out of office by his own party for so doing!

As large areas of west Ireland, particularly Donegal, starved, the Irish had little recourse other than emigration. Some tried the long and dangerous crossing of the Atlantic, a few even went further to Australia, (some, like the fictitious Michael in The Fields of Athenry were forced to go there!) but many came to Liverpool, London and Glasgow. There was usually a job for them in Scotland – ill-paid, filthy, difficult jobs in Scotland's burgeoning Industrial Revolution for which they had been ill-prepared by their agricultural background in Ireland – but it was at least a job, and provided some kind or relief from starvation. Many of them found a home of sorts in the Gorbals.

Their religion, that of the Roman Catholic Church, set them apart of course to a certain extent but there were some benefits of living in Scotland and Glasgow. Scotland had always been strong on education and children usually went to some kind of school even before 1872 when the Education Act made it compulsory, and thus illiteracy was gradually addressed. And of course from 1888, they had their own football time to provide a rallying point for the community and to give them something to cheer about. Frequently they needed it, for as late as 1900 we find an outbreak of medieval plague in the Gorbals! In the same year, large numbers of young men would try to enlist for service in the Boer War, but were rejected simply because they were not fit enough or well enough fed! Such was the malnutrition and lack of proper nourishment in many areas of Glasgow.

Charlie grew up in Salisbury Street with loads of people of Irish descent around him. The Second World War was obviously a difficult time for anyone, with an added dimension for the Irish, who had only recently, 20 years ago and as a by-product of another war, gained some sort of independence in the Irish Free State which defied Great Britain in 1939 and announced its neutrality. It is to the credit of De Valera that he managed to do that without provoking a violent reaction from either the Allies or the Axis powers. In particular, he might have been tempted to follow the old adage of "England's difficulty is Ireland's opportunity" and to make an ill-advised attempt to seize the Six Counties while Britain was otherwise engaged, but he resisted that as well.

Indeed, on two occasions, De Valera was, if we may believe some historians and biographers, offered the Six Counties by Churchill in return for full participation in the Second World War. The second such offer was accompanied by the emotive phrase "a nation once again" and was made in the wake of the entry of the USA into the war in December 1941, something that would have struck a personal chord with De Valera, for he himself had been born in the USA. (Indeed some think that he owed his reprieve from execution in 1916 to this very fact.) But De Valera would not take the bait, and continued to stay neutral during what was known in Ireland as "the emergency".

For the Irish community in Glasgow and indeed throughout the Irish diaspora, it was of course very tempting to "enjoy" the discomfiture of Great Britain, so often the tyrants and bullies in Ireland. On the other hand, there could be little doubt that in comparison with the odious Adolf Hitler and his grizzly henchmen, Winston Churchill and the British Empire were undeniably the lesser of the two evils. Support for the British war effort may have been grudging in the Glasgow Irish community, but it was real. In Dublin, de Valera himself had come to the same conclusion that he wanted the Allies to win, but he did not announce it publicly until the war was virtually over. Even then he tried to sign a Book of Condolences at the death of Adolf Hitler!

Indeed, historians are often surprised at the lack of any opposition to the Second World War in Glasgow – something that was in stark contrast to the Great War where there had been a Rent Strike, many labour problems on the Clyde ("Red Clydeside" as it was called) involving men like John McLean, Jimmy Maxton and Manny Shinwell, l and of course a major disturbance in George Square in January 1919. The Second World War contained very little of this, possibly for two main reasons – one was that the Labour Party happily in 1940 joined Churchill's coalition government, and the other was that everyone realised that the Nazis were irreconcilably evil and simply had to be removed from the face of the earth, no matter what the cost would be.

Glaswegians, of course, are famously cheerful and supportive people. They helped each other get through it all. And in addition, the horrors of war with its rationing, the nightly fear of aerial bombing (although Glasgow itself escaped virtually unscathed) and the depressing news of casualties were alleviated to a certain extent by the three traditional Glasgow forms of entertainment – dancing, cinema and football. Charlie recalls that even from an early age he played football in the streets and the backyards of the Gorbals.

Every boy loved football. It had the great advantage of not being too difficult to organise as long as one had a ball. Goalposts, pitch markings, referees were all superfluous luxuries which one might graduate to at a later stage, and even injuries were things to be despised. Anyone who didn't want to play because of a "sore leg" or some weak excuse like that would be rightly mocked and scoffed at. Scottish football never has been a place for softies and certainly was not in Glasgow in the 1940s.

Even in the war years and certainly in the years immediately afterwards, football boomed in Glasgow. Junior football was not really affected too much by the war and continued unabated, and even senior football, although unofficial and without tournaments like the Scottish Cup, provided much needed solace for the population who needed something to take their minds off the horrors of war. There were of course many young men around Glasgow at the time – soldiers on leave, men in the munitions industry and loads of English servicemen based temporarily on the Clyde – so that the availability of players and spectators was not a problem. The only real problem was transport. Celtic could not, for example, play against Aberdeen or Dundee very easily, but there was no problem with teams in the Glasgow area.

It is a major mistake to assume that war-time football was not taken seriously. It most certainly continued to be the major pre-occupation of the Scottish working class , although it had to compete for attention in the newspapers, and was subject to so many limitations and problems including, for example, the basic ones of finding equipment, in particular the ball! The impression is often given by historians that people didn't really care about football during the Second World War. They most certainly did!

There were of course a few people who objected to football being played at this dire time of history when civilization itself was in the balance, but they were countered very easily by the beneficial effect that the game had on morale. In any case after 1942 it became more and more obvious that that the war was going in the right direction and that the nation was going to survive. War time International games between Scotland and England, in particular, were looked forward to with great anticipation both at home and overseas.

The problem for the Irish community in Glasgow was that their team was going through a prolonged slump with the suspicion that the Directors of the club were not really interested in war-time football. Yet in 1938, Celtic had quite clearly been the best team in Great Britain when they won the Empire Exhibition Trophy at Ibrox beating Everton 1-0 in the final with Johnny Crum's Highland Fling of celebration after he scored the only goal of the game, much talked about and indeed imitated by the support.

But Celtic had a poor season after that in spite of having some great players like Jimmy Delaney and Malky MacDonald, and in early 1940 after a particularly poor run in the wartime regional League, Willie Maley "the man who made Celtic" resigned, retired or was sacked, depending on one's take of the situation. Maley, now in his 70s had in a real sense created and maintained Celtic, and his loss was not easily repaired. Jimmy McStay was Manager but was never given a chance by the Directors who did not work as hard as their Rangers equivalents did to keep their men out of the forces, nor as hard as Maley himself had done in the Great War for the same purpose. Nor did they take advantage of the "loaning" or "guesting" of players which was very prevalent at the time. Matt Busby, for example, the Celtic-daft star of Manchester City was frequently in Scotland and awaited the call. It never happened. As a result Celtic won only two Glasgow trophies in World War II, and one particular game at Ibrox on New Year's Day 1943 saw Celtic go down 8-1. It was perhaps just as well that wartime football was considered unofficial!

The drought continued for a long time after the war, even though Jimmy McGrory took over in 1945. Relegation came perilously close in 1948 and it would be 1951 before a national trophy was won. Thus Gallagher's formative years were spent with Celtic in the doldrums. The problem was that Celtic never really EXPECTED to win very much. They seemed to be content to play second fiddle to Rangers, and there was even a time in the early 1950s when Hibs seemed to be taking over as the main rivals with many Celtic supporters not afraid to sing the praises of the "famous five" forward line of Smith, Johnstone, Reilly, Turnbull and Ormond, comparing them favourably with what was happening (or not happening) at Celtic Park. At least if Hibs won the Scottish League, Rangers didn't!

This may well have had an effect on talented youngsters like Charlie Gallagher who would naturally have expected to gravitate to Celtic Park. "Many are called but few are chosen" was as applicable to Celtic Park in the 1950s as it was to the New Testament, but eager youngsters would go to the ground in awe of men like Jimmy McGrory, but with no great expectation of the team becoming consistently successful. There had been triumphs "isolated but spectacular"- not least the Coronation

Cup of 1953 - and there had been no lack of superbly talented players like Bobby Evans, Willie Fernie, Bobby Collins, Charlie Tully and Bertie Peacock, but the sad fact remained that until 1966, Celtic had won the Scottish League only once since 1938 – and that was in 1954. They had a superb captain that year in centre half Jock Stein.

Mediocre Rangers teams were allowed to rule the roost with such challenges as there were coming from the east, for both Hibs and Hearts did Edinburgh proud in the 1950s, but when Gallagher arrived at Celtic Park, consistent success from Celtic (of the type that had been seen by Celtic fans in the distant days of before the Great War) seemed a long way off, and there did not seem to be any great hope that it would arrive any time soon. Leadership was lacking.

But talented players were arriving, one of them a relative (in a sense) of Charlie. Clydebank was badly bombed in March 1941, and in that blitz, Pat Crerand's father was killed. Pat's mother subsequently married Charlie's uncle, and thus Charlie and Pat became cousins through marriage. Pat of course grew up to be a brilliant right half, arguably one of the best that Celtic have ever had, but grew frustrated by the lack of progress made by the club in the early 1960s, had an argument with those in authority and departed to Manchester United in the middle of the big freeze-up of February 1963.

All this was in the future though for Charlie as he went to school at St John's Primary in 1945 and then on to Holyrood Secondary. This has nothing to do with the Palace or indeed the Scottish Parliament in Edinburgh, but was a well-established Catholic school not all that far from Hampden Park on the south side of Glasgow. It had been founded in 1936, and was, when Charlie went there, considered to be one of the better schools in the city. One of his teachers there was Bob Crampsey who would become a TV presenter, pundit and general football expert in later years. Another teacher was called John Murphy, and he was the loudspeaker announcer at Celtic Park. Both these men would have a great effect on Charlie.

Crampsey in particular knew what he was talking about. Keen on cricket, music and many other things like the American Civil War, he won the Brain of Britain radio quiz in 1965 and became Headmaster of St Ambrose High School, but was best known for being one of the three anchors of STV's Scotsport when it started in 1957. Alec Cameron and Arthur Montford were the other two. Crampsey was a true polymath and became an excellent writer and commentator on the Scottish game. While he was at Holyrood, football flourished and was much talked about. Charlie Gallagher, a bright boy who did well enough academically as well, took to playing football in the same way as a duck takes to water.

Schools Football in the 1950s was big. It is a shame that the teachers' pay dispute of 1984-86 severely curtailed teachers' involvement with their pupils on a Saturday morning. Not only that, but such is society's obsession with child abuse these days, that teachers must sign so many forms and jump through so many hoops before they are ALLOWED to help with sports like football on a Saturday morning. Schools Football has taken a huge dip, and this is a great shame for so many young players used to learn their craft at school under the guidance of enthusiastic and dedicated teachers who were doing it all for the love of the game.

In Charlie's day, more or less every blade of grass in Glasgow (sometimes not even grass, more often sand!) would be covered by a school football match on a Saturday morning. The games would be played at all levels from 1st year to 6th year, and for every youngster it was a great honour to be playing for the school team. The "home" school would supply the referee, and every game would attract a fair amount of parents, some of them fiercely committed to the cause of their son's school.

Occasionally, hysterical things happened. A father of a goalkeeper was standing behind his son's goal. The son was beaten and the ball was trickling slowly, held back by the mud, but inevitably to the goal line. There was no goal net, however, and suddenly the father ran out and kicked the ball clear! At another game, a mother (an even more hysterical breed of people than fathers) saw fit to criticise the referee and was not shy of using foul language. At one point, when the referee awarded a throw-in in what she saw was the wrong way, she exploded and said "F*** me!". The referee, who was only a couple of yards away replied "No thanks, ma'am, I'm rather particular" and charged up the field.

A teacher of a defeated team in a Scottish School Cup game objected on the grounds that one set of goalposts was smaller by 3 inches than the other. The Headmaster went out one wet Thursday afternoon with a tape measure and discovered that both sets were exactly the same! On another occasion, a real thug of a boy was being excluded by the Headmaster for a rather nasty piece of violence and vandalism in the toilets. The teacher in charge of football, realising that the suspension would rule the boy out of a vital Cup tie, intervened on his behalf, using the immortal phrase that on the field he was "a gentle giant".

More seriously, Schools Football was an avenue for a talented boy to earn himself a chance to play a Schools representative game at the ground of a top team. There were even Schoolboy Internationals against the other three British nations, and these games were great showpieces for the youngsters to show off their talents and attract the attention of top teams. Even the run of the mill Saturday morning games were covered by the Press now and again – annoyingly not comprehensively for you could not guarantee that any given game would get a mention, nor necessarily always very accurately – by reporters calling themselves scholastic names like "Prefect" or "Inspector" who used educational imagery like "six of the best" or "teaching lessons in the football classroom of the field" and so on.

In Glasgow and the surrounding district, there was the added element of religion. Everyone knew which school was a "Catholic" school, and what was not. There is the true story of a Rangers scout who turned up to watch a Lanarkshire School Cup final in the hope of spotting some talent. On discovering that the final would be contested by two Roman Catholic schools, he went way home, knowing that his club would not be interested in signing any of the 22 players, no matter how good they were!

Charlie would often find himself playing two games on a Saturday – for the school in the morning and the Boys Guild in the afternoon. This left very little time for him to go and watch the team that he loved and whom everyone in the Gorbals talked about. In any case Celtic Park was a little too far from his house, but he does recall occasionally going to see Clyde or Third Lanark whose grounds were nearer. Clyde played at Shawfield, the dog track, before they moved to Broadwood in Cumbernauld, and Third Lanark went bankrupt and folded in 1967. Their ground was called Cathkin Park and was situated not far from Hampden. Indeed until 1903, Cathkin had been Hampden until the new Hampden was built.

Charlie does remember however the great occasion in his childhood on May 20 1953 when Celtic won the Coronation Cup and when there was dancing in the streets of the Gorbals on a fine spring evening. They had beaten Hibs in the final, the heroes being goalkeeper John Bonnar and centre half Jock Stein. This had been an all-British tournament to celebrate the Coronation of Queen Elizabeth II, and it remains a source of great irony that the two finalists were not the establishment teams of Rangers and Arsenal, but the two Scottish teams of Irish origins, Celtic and Hibs! Celtic scored first, then survived a momentous barrage as Hibs "Famous Five" of Smith, Johnstone, Reilly, Turnbull and Ormond threw everything at them but simply could not get one past "that bugger Bonnar" as he was lyrically described by Willie Ormond.

Charlie was only 12 at the time. The Celtic open-topped team bus was driven through the streets to show off the Cup to their adoring fans (it was only their second major trophy since World War II, along with the Scottish Cup of 1951) and Charlie recalls everyone rushing to see the bus passing the pub now called The Brazen Head, (it was then called incongruously The Granite City!) which was near where he lived. Little did he think that less than 12 years later he himself would be on a bus showing off a trophy to a similar bunch of delighted fans!

He also recalls being a ball boy at Celtic Park on April 16 1956 in a game played between Celtic and Manchester United in a benefit games for Cheshire Homes. The game finished 2-2 in pouring rain. Manchester United, for whom Duncan Edwards was outstanding, had just won the English League and were given a great reception from the Parkhead crowd that Monday evening. Matt Busby was of course the Manager of Manchester United and an unashamed lover of Celtic as well. Celtic, for their part played well, but it was possibly a blessing that the Parkhead crowd, eagerly looking forward to the Scottish Cup final against Hearts on Saturday, did not know what horrors lay in store for them in that particular game.

The fact that he was given the job as ball boy made Charlie think that Celtic had their eye on him and it was at Holyrood Secondary School that people first noticed that there was something special about this lad who played at inside left. He had a certain control of the ball which was by no means usual at that age, and certainly passed with astonishing accuracy and knew exactly the amount of "weight" to put on a pass. On one occasion he inspired Holyrood to beat Greenock High School 12-1, and he played a series of good games against teams like St Gerards and Govan High School. Such performances drew the attention of selectors and on Wednesday January 4 1956, we find him playing for Glasgow Schools against Edinburgh Schools at Tynecastle before a huge crowd of 4,000, and it was largely due to the talented Gallagher that Glasgow beat Edinburgh 6-2.

The Daily Record goes into overdrive about his performance talking about a "young man with a famous football name" (a reference to Patsy of Celtic and Hughie of Airdrie and Newcastle United) who "walked jauntily out of Tynecastle with a big beam on his face...Charlie Gallagher a dark-haired handsome youngster with golden feet. In the school-boys inter-city match, Charlie showed like a twinkle-toed beacon" Praise indeed! The Daily Record, one has to admit has been known to practice more than a little rhetorical exaggeration from time to time and to "lay things on thick", but other papers agreed with their assessment, albeit a little less lavishly. He scored one goal and played a part in all of the other five, and heads were turned. But he was still only 15.

On another occasion when he was still eligible for the Under 15 team, he was moved up to play for Holyrood's Under 18 team against Govan High School. Against him was another chap in a similar situation, also playing for the bigger boys. This fellow was called Alex Ferguson! Sir Alex recalled this game at a Dinner once when he was the guest speaker and Charlie was in the audience. His recollection was correct but perhaps for understandable reasons, he failed to add that the game was won 4-1 by Holyrood, the game was played at Dixon Park and that Charlie Gallagher scored all four goals for Holyrood. Details are sparse, but the first goal was from a penalty kick and the second is singled out as being a “magnificent second goal” and Gallagher is the “personality of the match”.

The teams were:

Holyrood: Duffy, Connolly and McCoy: Connelly, Hoey and Burke: O’Donnell, Cuddihy, Murphy, Gallagher and Mallan

Govan High: Barron, McLean and Wood: Jardine, Crichton and Reid: Bowie, Cullen, Murray, Ferguson and Burt.

CHAPTER TWO
HIS PRE-CELTIC CAREER

Charlie left school in 1956 and began an apprenticeship as an electrician in a firm in London Road, but he was determined that he would like a career in professional football. Which young boy does not entertain fantasies of that sort? The difference was that Charlie was good. Some felt that he lacked the "devil" for the tough world of professional football, but no-one could deny his skill, in particular his passing ability and his tremendous shot. In the meantime, while he naturally hoped that he could make the grade as a professional and play for the team that he and the rest of the Irish community adored, he would continue to play football as often as he could, for he possessed the one thing that is more essential than anything else – namely the desire to play the game

There was a team called the Rancel. Bright people could work out that this was a combination of Rangers and Celtic, and they played at juvenile level. He had a few games for them. But he also played for Kilmarnock Amateurs. He was very impressed by the set-up at Rugby Park and he thus came into contact with Willie Waddell. Waddell had of course been a highly successful winger for Rangers in the late 1940s and 1950s, but after his retirement from the playing side of football, became the Manager of Kilmarnock in 1957. Gallagher and Waddell soon developed a mutual admiration for each other, even though both were aware that there was only really the one senior football team that Charlie wanted to play for – and it was the direct antithesis of those whose jersey "the Deedle" (as Waddell was nicknamed) had graced for so long.

What Charlie particularly liked at Rugby Park was the training. For youngsters, this was every Tuesday night. It was very well organised by

Waddell himself, his assistant Malky MacDonald (a Celtic legend from the 1938 Empire Exhibition trophy days) and Walter McCrae who would in time become Scotland's trainer. Everything was arranged so that everyone got a reasonable chance at everything with loads of practice at a variety of things like dribbling, shooting, tackling, passing, taking free-kicks, corner kicks ets. and it was an enjoyable experience which contrasted starkly with the training set-up that Charlie would encounter at Celtic Park in the future. Loads of eager youngsters would turn up and do little other than run round the park.

Kilmarnock would, of course, be a consistently good side in the late 1950s and early 1960s, winning the Scottish League in 1965 and having several near misses, losing two Scottish Cup finals (1957 and 1960) and two Scottish League Cup finals (1960/61 and 1962/63). They did this on a modest budget and with a fairly small fan base – their play certainly deserved more attention – and one of the reasons for their success would certainly be the fact that their players like Frank Beattie, Davie Sneddon and Jackie McInally were always very fit and very well trained.

Willie Waddell remained a great admirer of Charlie Gallagher (something that was apparent ten years later when Waddell was writing for The Scottish Daily Express and continually purred his admiration in match reports for Gallagher's silky play) and on more than one occasion before Gallagher joined Celtic, Waddell offered him professional terms at Rugby Park. Had Gallagher not retained such a great sentimental attraction to Celtic, he might well have joined Kilmarnock there and then. Indeed, he sometimes still wonders what might have been had he done so, but his regrets are minimal, for Celtic had a spell over him, he felt! But in any case, he was still young.

Times were changing in the 1950s. Prosperity was in the air in a way that it hadn't ever been before. It was an era of virtually full employment, and the reforms of the Welfare State and the National Health Service were now gradually beginning to make an impact in the shape of healthier, fitter youngsters. More and more attention was turned to the horrors of the Glasgow slums and the Government, both national and local, were shamed into doing something about them. But it was a slow process.

The Government was Conservative, but a far more benign and enlightened form of Conservative in comparison to what they had been in the 1930s or what they would become again in the 1980s. They accepted Labour's Welfare State, which was the most important thing. Admittedly they made a fool of themselves over Suez in 1956, but Harold McMillan took over after that. He believed in progress and rightly could he claim that "we have never had it so good". It was a benign aristocracy, but many people felt that change wasn't coming quickly enough.

A new large box began to arrive in people's living rooms. This was something called a television. BBC Television had opened in Scotland in 1952 and had slowly expanded as people wanted to see the Coronation of Queen Elizabeth II in 1953, for example. By 1957, the BBC had competition in the form of commercial TV, and advertisements emphasised the point that this was now a consumer society and that people now had enough money to buy nice things.

TV had its effect on football. Already some football had been shown live. The 1954 World Cup, for example, had been beamed from Switzerland. Scottish people wished it hadn't, because one of the games was a 7-0 defeat of Scotland from a virtually unheard of country called Uruguay. Worse still for Celtic fans had been the 1955 Scottish Cup final when Clyde equalised with a corner kick late in the game when the game seemed won. It was the first ever Scottish game to be televised live, and was a Celtic horror show.

Highlights of English games were shown in a programme called Sports Special on Saturday night or sometimes Sunday afternoons, and there was a regular Sportsview programme on a Wednesday night. Horizons were being opened, but the down side was that television was showing that there was another world somewhere other than the narrow one of football. Attendances at football matches had not yet begun to drop as they would a few years later, but people were slowly beginning to realise that there were options to a Saturday spent watching football.

Arguments raged about whether more football should be shown live, but the SFA with men like Bob Kelly and George Graham in charge were totally opposed to it. These men, sworn enemies in some respects, nevertheless were in agreement that television would stop people going to see football matches. So only very occasionally was a match allowed, and normally that was an International game.

But this was still a golden age for Scottish football. Granted, there did seem to be a problem with beating England. At Hampden, 1956 saw Scotland very unlucky with a late Johnny Haynes goal denying victory, but 1958 was a shocking 0-4 defeat, and both 1957 and 1959 had seen narrow but deserved victories for England at Wembley – but the team qualified for the 1958 World Cup in Sweden and tended to beat Wales, Northern Ireland and continental opposition more often than not. The country was not yet the worldwide laughing stock that it would become 50 years later.

Domestically, as we have seen, Celtic were more than a little disappointing, but Rangers at least were challenged by Hearts in the League, the Tynecastle side winning the League in 1958 and 1960. The Scottish Cup was very competitive with Clyde winning it twice in 1955 and 1958, Falkirk in 1957 and St Mirren in 1959. Clyde, indeed had a remarkable four years. Between their two Scottish Cups, they were relegated to the Second Division and then promoted back again to the First! Floodlights began to appear at a few grounds enabling teams to play in the evenings on a winter's night, and allowing games to start at 3.00 pm on a Saturday afternoon even in the darkest of December days.

Celtic had never really challenged for the Scottish League after 1954, although they had been a good second to Aberdeen in 1955. An astonishingly bad team selection and performance on the field cost them the Scottish Cup in 1956 to Hearts, but better times were forthcoming in the Scottish League Cup, this new tournament which had only arrived on the scene after World War II. In Celtic's first League Cup final in October 1956, they were lucky to survive the first game against Partick Thistle, but then delighted their fans with an impressive 3-0 win in the replay. Charlie enjoyed that, but enjoyed the following season's Scottish League Cup even more, for that was the occasion that Celtic walloped Rangers 7-1 – and it should have been a lot more!

But one event dominated football more than anything else in the mid 1950s. Snow was beginning to fall in Glasgow on the afternoon of

Thursday February 6 1958 when stories began to spread about an air crash at Munich affecting the Manchester United team which was returning from a successful European Cup tie in Belgrade. In tune with the grim news which grew worse every hour, the weather got worse and worse so that by Saturday February 8, not a single game was played in Scotland. The games might have been off in any case to mourn the devastation of Manchester United. Matt Busby, the Scottish Manager, survived after a prolonged fight for his life, but men like Duncan Edwards, Roger Byrne and Tommy Taylor were never seen again.

The whole business raised many questions about air travel to European Cup matches, and it was a long time before anyone could fly to a game withouu serious apprehension. However, money would eventually talk rather more loudly than concerns for public safety, and the European Cup was not postponed, being won again by Real Madrid for the third year running.

The snows of February 8 did have one beneficial side-effect for Charlie, however. The Scotland Youth International team were due to play their Ireland counterparts on that day. Charlie was not selected for that game – he would have been the travelling reserve - but by the time that the game was re-scheduled for April 12 1958 at Stair Park, Stranraer, Charlie was in the team!

The legendary Willie Maley of Celtic had died some 10 days previously at the advanced age of 90, and on this very day that Gallagher was playing for Scotland Youth, Hearts were winning the Scottish League for the first time since 1897, by an odd coincidence the year that Maley had become the Manager of Celtic! The Evening Times of that day has a small snippet of information to the effect that Jock Stein "who now looks after youngsters at Parkhead" was going to Stranraer to see the Scotland Youth game – "not talking, just watching" said Jock.

The game finished 2-2, and Press reports say that Ireland were the better team. The Scottish team was Neil, Provan and Lynch; C. Brown, McConnachie and Nicol; H. Brown, McCulloch, Lochhead, Gallagher and Burns. The team was interesting for the future of the game. Apart from Charlie, there was Ian Lochhead, also destined to become a "Kelly Kid" (albeit a very unsuccessful one), Davie Provan at right back who went on to play for Rangers in the early 1960s (not to be confused with Celtic's Davie Provan of the 1980s) and the right half was no less a person than Craig Brown who would become the Manager of Scotland after a less than totally successful playing career with teams like Dundee. The team may have only drawn 2-2 with Ireland, but they did a great deal better than their senior counterparts a week later who managed to go down 0-4 to England at Hampden in one of the worst of their many thrashings from England at that time. A week after that Clyde won the Scottish Cup for the second time in four years by beating Hibs 2-0.

Charlie's father Dan was proud of his son representing Scotland in the Youth International. Dan, like many Irishmen, was no great football fan and seldom went to games, but he did keep a scrapbook of the games that Charlie played in, and he knew enough about the game to know that Charlie was doing well, and continually teased him. If Charlie's team had won 3-0, he would say that it should have been 4-0 and things like that, but it was all good natured.

Round about this time in 1958, the current obsession in Scotland was the trial of a serial killer called Peter Manuel who had committed several murders in North Lanarkshire. He was eventually found guilty and went to the gallows on July 11 1958. The trial at Glasgow High Court was a remarkable one. Manuel, born in America in 1927 but of Scottish parents, was by no means unintelligent, and at one point sacked his lawyers in the middle of the trial and conducted his own defence. It was generally agreed even by Lord Cameron, the Judge, that his defence was nothing short of brilliant with several plausible theories being produced as to how else the murders could have happened. At one point, he questioned a witness who had been brought in on a stretcher and almost convinced the jury that the injured man had murdered his wife and members of his family.

Though clearly a sadistic psychopath, Manuel almost became a Scottish cult hero, for such murder cases were exceptionally well received and read avidly in the Scottish press. But the balance of evidence was too much, and guilty was the verdict. Some people were beginning to feel that the death penalty was not the best way of dealing with such criminals, but Manuel's execution was duly carried out as sales of newspapers soared. He was third last man to be hanged in Scotland.

We next find Charlie Gallagher playing for the Scottish Amateur League against the Airdrie and Coatbridge League at the odd venue of Cowal Park, Dunoon on the equally strange date of June 28 1958. But then again, in the same way that they say that the city of New York never sleeps, the Scottish football season never really stops either. Indeed, the full Scotland team had just returned with their tails between their legs from the World Cup in Sweden after three awful performances against Yugoslavia, Paraguay and France.

The failure to appoint a Manager for Scotland betokened the amateurish approach to all this. Effectively the team was run by senior players like Tommy Younger of Hibs and Bobby Evans of Celtic – fine players both, but something more was required. The good side of the 1958 World Cup however was the fact that it was shown on TV (something that more and more people now aspired to owning) and we were able to see the fabulous Brazilians including the emergence of a superbly talented youngster called Pele, Older Celtic supporters scoffed however and said "You never saw Patsy Gallacher!", but it would have to be admitted that Pele was not a bad player.

But returning to this game "doon the watter" at Dunoon, Charlie Gallagher starred, sending a nice through pass to Ian Lochead to score the first, then he scored himself before contributing to the third goal scored by Robert Burns of Drumchapel. The team won eventually 5-2, and Gallagher's performance was noted, not least by those in important places at Celtic Park.

Charlie was lucky in one regard in his private life. He was just young enough to avoid National Service. Following the end of World War II, the Government (a Labour one, to its shame) decided that young men should be conscripted into the Armed Services for a limited period of time (usually 18 months to 2 years). This involved training in England usually and then often a posting overseas to Aden or Cyprus or Singapore, for example. There were good things about it in that it allowed young men to see a bit of the world, and there are even those today who say that it would be a good thing to instil discipline etc. There were exemptions if you worked in various jobs, and you could always apply for a deferment, a postponement of the inevitable, so that you could finish an apprenticeship for example.

But behind all the guff about "making a man out of you" "defending the realm" and "serving the Queen", the fact remained that it was compulsory and looked upon with dread and horror by those who were taken away from their comfort zone. It played havoc with careers and romances, and frankly, it became harder and harder to justify every year that passed. It would finish altogether in the early 1960s, but in 1957 it was decided that all those born on or after October 1 1939 would not necessarily be called up. The sigh of relief was audible throughout the land, not least from young men like Charlie Gallagher.

In 1958, the Army did not as yet engender the same feelings of hatred in the Glasgow Irish community as it does today, but it is hard to imagine a peaceful man like Charlie Gallagher enjoying life in the Army. On the other hand, the Army did encourage football and would often stretch a point or two to allow a soldier home for the weekend to play in a game, for example. Men like Ronnie Simpson, Steve Chalmers and Jim Kennedy all served their time in the "sodgers" and claimed that it had benefitted them. On the other hand, very few men evinced any desire to stay on after their period of compulsory service had expired.

In August 1958 Charlie signed for Yoker Athletic, a Junior team based at Holm Park, Clydebank. They played in the Central League and various Cup competitions against teams like Johnstone Burgh, Vale of Leven, Petershill, Port Glasgow and Ashfield, and Charlie distinguished himself, so much so that a month after the start of the season, he was signed for Celtic on a provisional basis in October 1958, something that allowed him to continue to play for Yoker. He played in several positions during the 1958/59 season - at outside right, inside right and inside left.

He was already a Celtic provisional by the time that he played his best game for Yoker, and that was in the Dunbartonshire Charity Cup final at Holm Park against Vale of Leven. Vale of Leven is of course a name embroidered on the very fabric of Scottish football, for they were very much involved in the early years of the game. A good quiz question would be "What have Vale of Leven done with the Scottish Cup that Celtic haven't?" And the answer of course is that they won the trophy three years in a row – 1877, 1878 and 1879 – something that Celtic have yet to achieve. Celtic have come close. In the early 1970s they won it 4 years out of 5, and in 1909 only the Hampden Riot prevented them, but they have yet to win the Scottish Cup three years in a row.

All this was in the dim and distant past as far as Vale of Leven were concerned in 1958, when they were ripped apart by Charlie Gallagher in a 5-2 defeat. The Scottish Sunday Express is quite emphatic in its admiration "Star of the Dunbartonshire Charity Cup final was Yoker's teenage right winger, Charlie Gallacher (sic – wrong spelling!). Lucky Celtic – they have him already signed. Gallacher scored two snappy goals in the first half and was always a menace to the Vale of Leven defence. He formed a tip-top right wing with Bobby Dougan, playing his first game for Yoker."

He also starred as Yoker beat Rob Roy 5-0; "a powerful shot from 18 yards" helped Yoker beat Ashfield (who were without their bright star that day – one Stephen Chalmers); equalized with a "rocket shot" against Renfrew, and "headed an equalizer" against Johnstone Burgh – all this was enough to convince the Glasgow journalists that there was future in this boy. Less creditably, he picked up what he claimed to be his first and only "booking" in his career at Junior or Senior level when he deliberately tripped up a Petershill player.

Playing a season in Scottish Junior football is character building for anyone. The term itself is misleading. A "junior" need not necessarily mean a young man. Some gnarled old veterans plied their trade in the junior ranks. Often the players were young men, as Charlie Gallagher was in season 1958/59, but sometimes "juniors" were men who had not made it to the senior ranks, or sometimes men who had been seniors and had returned after perhaps an injury or simply not managing to fulfil their potential.

It is generally agreed that Scottish Junior football is tough. Pitches are not always great with a marked lack of grass on occasion, crowds are small but rabid with every team having its own band of enthusiastic supporters. Tackles are hard and winning is as important as it is to the full-time professional, maybe even more so, for there is not the consolation of the money – at least not a great deal of money. Paying players is generally frowned upon, but it does happen!

There is also the factor of weather. Seldom in a Scottish winter does one get an ideal day for a game of football. Either the pitch is bone-hard, or the opposite is the case, where the pitch resembles a quagmire – but tough players are happy to play on any surface. There was also in Glasgow in the 1950s in particular, an additional problem which has now diminished - that of fog or "smog". Fogs and mists do still happen today of course, but before governments got concerned about clean air, an Atlantic mist could join forces with the polluted air of Glasgow's industrial waste and cause a fog that could last for days, bringing untold misery and loads of health problems.

A thick skin is necessary in Junior football, for players hear every word hurled at them. In a large crowd, individual comments can be drowned in a wall of sound. In a crowd of a couple of hundred, every insult direct by some cretin at your father, your girlfriend, your religion is heard! And it is often claimed that the bravest men in the world are those courageous enough to referee such games. A crowd at a Glasgow Junior game is far more intimidating than Celtic v Rangers, for there a referee has a couple of linesmen to help and a huge amount of policemen. At a Junior game, anything can happen – and the referee is on his own.

That, incidentally, was the opinion of Jack Mowat, arguably Scotland's best ever referee. He was in charge of many Cup finals in the 1950s, including famously the European Cup final at Hampden in 1960 between Real Madrid and Eintracht Frankfurt to which, it was claimed, that he walked from his house in Rutherglen! Jack would always say that once you have done the Glasgow Juniors, you are afraid of nothing!

Charlie Gallagher thrived in this atmosphere. He did not look the toughest of characters, and boasts of his virtually unblemished record as far as referees and discipline went. He was able to ignore provocation and nasty tackles from the likes of Bobby Shearer of Rangers, and he learned this in his year with Yoker Athletic. Above all else, he continued to enjoy his football. He was interested in very little else and lived for his next game. He was happy enough to play wherever he was put. Modest and unassuming he may have been, but he knew that he had a certain amount of talent, and he always enjoyed the chance to put it to the test.

He had been recommended to Jimmy McGrory by one of his teachers at Holyrood, a man called John Murphy who was also the Public Address announcer at Celtic Park. Significantly, all this was done without any input from Jock Stein, then working with the youngsters. According to Charlie, Jock Stein did not know Charlie when he was signed in September 1958 on a provisional basis – and possibly Jock took a subliminal dislike to him for that reason – but presumably Stein was very much involved in the process when he became a full signing in March 1959.

There is still however a minor mystery about Jock Stein's role in all this. Jock's subsequent career, in which he famously knew almost everything that there was to know about players in the juniors and in the opposition – he was often challenged to name Motherwell's team against Falkirk ten days ago, for example, and was able to do it! – makes one wonder if he did know about Gallagher. Charlie himself claims that Stein didn't know him. One wonders, however. There was very little that Stein didn't know.

Charlie was naturally delighted to be signing for Celtic along with another Yoker player called Jimmy Hughes. They were referred to as "the Celtic right wing" of Yoker, with Hughes on the right wing and Gallagher now at inside right. Much debate went on even in the early stages of Gallagher's career about what his best position would be. He seemed to lack the required pace to be a traditional right winger whose skills were those of getting to the dead ball line and cutting the ball back, and an inside position seemed better suited to his undeniable passing ability. He also had a ferocious shot – one report talks of him "ripping the defence apart and bulging the net with a terrific drive", and the general consensus of opinion was that he was ready for full time football. Both Manchester United and Everton had expressed some kind of interest as well, but Charlie did not really consider anyone other than Celtic.

Gallagher and Hughes were part of the much vaunted youth policy of Chairman Bob Kelly. The team which had beaten Rangers 7-1 on October 19 1957 in the Scottish League Cup final was (incredibly) almost immediately dismantled – to be fair, some of them were ageing in any case – and replaced by callow youths. In some ways this was admirable – the "Kelly Kids" seemed to have been a conscious imitation of the very successful "Busby Babes" of Manchester United who would surely have been the best in Europe for many years but for the air crash in the snows of Munich – but the problem with the "Kelly Kids" was Kelly himself.

Frankly, Mr Kelly knew very little about the actual footballing side of the club. He was steeped in the traditions of the club, for his father, James Kelly had been brought into the club from Renton at the very beginning in 1888 and had captained Celtic and Scotland, and in time became Chairman. Bob's withered arm had precluded him from actually playing football, but he involved himself in the administrative side of the game. He had been Chairman of Celtic since 1947 (and would continue to act in that capacity until his death in 1971), and he deserves credit to a certain extent, at least, for the way in which he ran the club. His strong points were that he was strict on discipline and considered the good name of Celtic to be a very important thing. He had in 1952 successfully taken on George Graham of the SFA on the business of whether Celtic should be allowed to fly the Irish flag or not, and he had a laudable belief in a British dimension to football, frequently saying that he wished to see a British Cup, for example.

His weak point was the basic one that he himself insisted on picking the team when there were others who could have done the job better. Already by the time that Charlie came to Celtic Park, two Scottish Cups had been lost because of crazy team selections where Kelly's heart had been allowed to rule his head. In 1955, Bobby Collins had been dropped after the first game of the Scottish Cup final, apparently because of a somewhat undignified and indeed ludicrous (Collins was a very small man!) shoulder charging incident on the Clyde goalkeeper. Celtic then lost the replay. And in 1956, his answer to an injury problem had been to bring in full back Mike Haughney at inside right, and bring in a youngster called Billy Craig who had played only a handful of games for the club. Other, more believable, options existed but Mr Kelly had made up his mind. Hearts beat Celtic easily 3-1.

The frustrating thing was that Celtic probably, man for man, were better than anyone else. In-fact in both 1956/57 and 1957/58, as we have seen, Celtic won the Scottish League Cup, the second of these being the famous 7-1 against Rangers which kept the fans happy – but hid the basic problem. The 7-1 team with great names like Evans, Fernie, Collins, Peacock and

Tully disappeared within two or three years of this (some of them were getting old, but others weren't) and the emphasis was now on youth. In retrospect, we can now, of course, see that it would have been better to blend the youth policy with a few more experienced players, even one or two men bought from another club, if necessary. This however did not happen, and as a result Celtic collapsed miserably in the 1957/58 season after the League Cup win in October. 1958/59, while Charlie was at Yoker, had been one of the worst in the history of Celtic since 1888. There had been some good moments, like putting Rangers out of the Scottish Cup, for example, 2-1 at the end of February 1959, but the general picture was one of potential, promise but under-achievement and no honours won. And there was, of course, more horror to come in future years.

But before then, we had a truly bizarre day on April 18 1959 – something which absolutely bewildered the support of Celtic (and those of Rangers too for that matter), showing the world just how good Celtic could be, and at the same time inflicting a certain amount of distress on their fans. It was the day on which Celtic actually won the Scottish League – for Rangers! Celtic beat Hearts at Parkhead with a good goal from Bertie Auld and an even better one from Eric Smith. Normally this would have been a cause of great rejoicing, but the snag was that it gave Rangers the Championship. A veteran supporter switched off his radio in disgust saying "After playing p*** all season, they have to go and f***in win the day!"

Across the city at Ibrox, Rangers lost to Aberdeen. Aberdeen needed to win that game to dispel any remaining fears of relegation, and duly did so to the delight of their small band of supporters. Rangers trooped off the field disconsolately to the boos and jeers of their crowd who were convinced that Hearts had beaten Celtic at Parkhead, for they had been winning 1-0 at half-time and Celtic, frankly, were generally regarded as a very poor team indeed in 1959. When everyone heard the scores from the other grounds, neither Celtic nor Rangers supporters knew whether to laugh or cry! Hearts supporters knew what to do – they cried, whereas Aberdeen fans heaved a sigh of relief, but no more so than those of Dunfermline who also rescued themselves from relegation by beating Partick Thistle 10-1, a result that, shall we say, raised more than a few eyebrows.

This pantomime on the last day of the Scottish League season underlined just how crazy Scottish football was in those days, and just how annoying it was for Celtic fans that they could not do better. Rangers, described categorically by the eminent and respected journalist Cyril Horne in The Glasgow Herald as "the worst Rangers team that he had ever seen", were the champions! Perhaps just as amazingly, Aberdeen who had escaped relegation with an absolutely dreadful team reached the final of the Scottish Cup! Admittedly they were defeated there by St Mirren, 4-0 conquerors of Celtic in the semi-final, but it showed that there was no really good team in Scotland. Celtic should have done a lot better for the times were ripe for collecting trophies. But they had burned their boats by deploying the youth policy called the "Kelly Kids."

But when Gallagher came to the club, the youth policy was still being praised as a good idea. Time would tell just exactly how good (or bad) it was going to be. It was, of course, certainly a good idea, but in spite of Jock Stein still being around, it was not implemented properly. Youth policies have to be well blended with experience and common sense. Alan Hansen once famously said "You'll get nowhere with kids". In this particular context, Alan was proved wrong, but he did have a point, and perhaps he should have added "until they mature". Celtic's youth policy was a long time in the maturing – but it did eventually come good and some could claim that it eventually won the European Cup - and the early few years of Charlie's career at Celtic Park were an excellent example of how not to do it, as we shall find out.

CHAPTER THREE

DEBUT AND DEBACLES

It was at a particularly dark hour of Celtic's history that Charlie made his debut for the first team. The start of the 1959/60 season could hardly have been worse. By August 22, they were already out of two Cups. Drawn in a League Cup section of Raith Rovers, Partick Thistle and Airdrie, one might have expected Celtic to emerge victorious, but they had already lost their first three games and were in the humiliating position of being the only one of the four unable to qualify! They had also lost 2-1 to Rangers in the Glasgow Cup – a result that was at least respectable, if massively disappointing – and their only win of the season had been a 2-0 win over Kilmarnock, ironically Kilmarnock being the best ranked of all the teams they had played so far!

"Parkhead is more like Purgatory those days" said Gair Henderson in The Evening Times and even in the wake of the win over Kilmarnock, Celtic were badly hit by injuries to Bobby Carroll, Neil Mochan, John Divers and Mike Jackson, and a debut was given to Charlie Gallagher "the boy from Yoker". It was of course part of the "youth policy" that the "Kelly Kids" were gradually to be weaned into the first eleven.

The opponents Raith Rovers who were off to a good start to the season and were enjoying one of the better periods of their history. They had reached three Scottish Cup semi-finals in the decade of the 1950s and were consistently highly placed in the Scottish League. The strength lay in their half back line of Young, McNaught and Leigh, commonly known as the "burglar proof" half back line. They were ageing now, but were still generally regarded as being one of the best in the business. Centre half Willie McNaught had played for Scotland 5 times, and right half

Andy Young ought to have been capped. He had played a couple of games for Celtic at the end of World War II but had been allowed to go, and Andy Leigh was also considered unlucky not to have been given some International recognition. Nevertheless, it is not often that Raith Rovers come to Celtic Park as favourites. This however was one such occasion.

The weather was hot, - indeed The Evening Times talks with a touch of hyperbole about "the Turkish bath atmosphere" at Parkhead for the 20,000 crowd – and this was maybe significant in the way that play was to unfold. A glance at the teams will show that Celtic were mainly young men, certainly in the forward line. Only three men – Mochan, Evans and Peacock – could be described as experienced, (they were also the only ones who had won any trophy) whereas Raith Rovers, including their venerable half-back line, was now approaching the veteran stage.

Of the eight youngsters, Haffey, McNeill, McKay, Gallagher and Auld could be said to have gone on and made some progress, even though Haffey and McKay are sadly always to be identified with Celtic failure, whereas Matt McVittie played 33 times for Celtic and had but one moment of glory in the Scottish Cup defeat of Rangers a few months previously in 1959, Jim Conway played 32 times and was always described as a "promising" youngster even when he had stopped promising and was no longer young. Poor Dan O'Hara with 7 appearances was one of the many players of that era who never made it and simply disappeared. As one says "Many are called, but few are chosen".

Celtic : Haffey, McNeill and Mochan; McKay, Evans and Peacock; McVittie, O'Hara, Conway, Gallagher and Auld

Raith Rovers: Drummond, Polland and McFarlane; Young, McNaught and Leigh; Kerray, Conn, White, McKinven and Urquhart

Referee : Mr T Alexander, Edinburgh

Celtic surprised the Press and delighted their fans by playing fast attacking football with inside forwards Dan O'Hara and Charlie Gallagher being singled out for their good work. Ironically the only goal of the game was an own goal caused by a misunderstanding between McFarlane and Drummond in the Raith goal. Charlie had played a part in the build-up to this goal, teaming up with the great Bertie Peacock to release the speedy O'Hara. Press reports combine to praise Gallagher's contribution, and it is interesting that the two things he is commended for are his passing ability and his "thunderbolt" shot - two things that he would become famous for in later years.

The game finished with a 1-0 victory which should in truth have been a lot more if Celtic had taken all their chances and if goalkeeper Drummond had not been in such fine form in the Raith Rovers goal. Cyril Horne in The Glasgow Herald, a respected journalist and not normally given to exaggeration, even compares Charlie's performance with some games of his late namesake Patsy Gallacher, generally reckoned to have been one of the best players who ever lived. "Not for many a day have I seen a player, young or old, make so many accurate long passes as did the new Gallagher against Raith Rovers. There is no more shrewd centre half than McNaught, yet he was clearly perplexed by the frequency with which Gallagher changed the direction of Celtic's attacks by sweeping the ball right, left and centre".

Following such an encomium of praise, it is perhaps surprising to find that Charlie never played another game for the first team until April of the following spring by which time everything had been lost. Yet it can readily be understood in the chaos that existed at Celtic Park as far as team selection went. Jock Stein was still at Celtic Park but worked more with the reserves than the first team, the nominal Manager was Jimmy McGrory, an immortal centre forward in his day but far too nice a man to be Manager, and the power lay in the autocratic and sometimes arrogant hands of Bob Kelly an "inveterate meddler" who seemed to change the team almost on a whim, as if it were some kind of a hobby.

The men who had been injured before the Raith Rovers game all came back, and there was no place for Gallagher in the game against Partick Thistle on Wednesday night, a game played in a slightly surreal atmosphere for Partick Thistle's manager Davie Meiklejohn had died suddenly after their game against Airdrie on Saturday. Meiklejohn, of course had been one of Rangers best ever players in the 1930s, and all of Scottish football have been stunned by this event, for he was only 58. To their credit, apart from one or two idiots, the Celtic supporters treated Meiklejohn's memory with respect. It had been Meiklejohn who had read the lesson at the funeral of John Thomson in 1931.

Charlie possibly did well to miss this game, but it is still hard to explain why, as the form of the team stuttered and started, and never really rose above the mediocre all season, he never was given another game for so long. Inside left was John Divers, son of the John Divers who had graced the Empire Exhibition Trophy winning side of 1938, but even when Divers was out of the side, his place was given to Neil Mochan. But Gallagher was in the Reserve team which would go on to win the Reserve League and the Reserve League Cup, and he continued to learn his trade there, as a good nucleus of players began to gather. Gallagher himself was quite happy, for he enjoyed playing with the second eleven.

As far as the first XI was concerned, the impression began to be given that, although this was a bad season, long term prospects for success were good. This, at least, was the way that supporters cheered themselves up, but it was Celtic who were clearly the losers in season 1959/60. Out of the Scottish League Cup and Glasgow Cup at an early stage, and nowhere in the Scottish League, won well by Hearts that year, was bad enough for the supporters to put up with, but even worse had been the asset stripping of men like Willie Fernie and Bobby Collins and eventually Bobby Evans at the end of the 1959/60 season. These were men who, as the future would prove, had years of football left in them. Willie Fernie, of course, would come back after a sojourn with Middlesbrough playing alongside Brian Clough and Bobby Collins won a Scottish cap as late as 1965! A great deal of this was to pay, apparently, for the floodlights, quite clearly the best in the land but as great journalists like Cyril Horne, John McKenzie and Gair Henderson and indeed all the fans kept asking, what is the point of having great floodlights if you can't even make it into Europe to use them to their full potential?

The floodlights were switched on for the first time on Monday October 12 1959, impressing everyone as being possibly the best in Britain, an opinion shared by the visiting Wolverhampton Wanderers side. No-one could possibly say however that the Celtic team was anything like the best in Britain, for Wolves, winners of the English League for the past two seasons and who would go on to win the English Cup in 1960, simply swept Celtic aside and quite clearly stopped at 2-0 when they could have really embarrassed Celtic on a night that should have been a great occasion for them.

All this time Gallagher was learning his trade as best as he could in the chaotic circumstance of Celtic Park. Celtic had three teams – the first XI, the reserves who played in the Scottish Reserve League and a third team who played in a Combined Reserve League. Sometimes he would play in one or other of the reserve teams – but Celtic had such a huge squad of youngsters that this could not be guaranteed, and sometimes he was allowed to play for a Junior team.

He did however enjoy the intensive training sessions that the team had at Seamill Hydro. He tells of one occasion when the bus taking them there suddenly stopped at Dalry, a mile or two short of the Seamill Hydro The bus would continue to Seamill with all the equipment, but the players in the interests of fitness were invited to walk the rest of the way. There were a few protests, but then Eric Smith and Bertie Auld, two gallus, cocky, cheeky chappies told the rest of them not to worry, for they knew a short cut. Not for the last time in Charlie's life did he learn the lesson that listening to Eric Smith and Bertie Auld was not necessarily a good idea. A long trek through farm yards, fields with cows in them, crossing rivers, climbing hills followed, and however much Smith and Auld denied it, they were lost – until the bus came looking for them! It would have been greatly embarrassing if the mighty Celtic FC had disappeared in rural Ayrshire!

In March 1960 Jock Stein left Celtic Park. No-one realised the significance of this at the time, indeed it did not make headline news, but this move would have spectacular ramifications. Everyone felt that Jock might make a good Manager and were delighted when Dunfermline Athletic, in one of their seemingly perennial battles against relegation, appointed him Manager. His first game as Manager of the Pars was against Celtic at East End Park on March 19 and they won 3-2! He would eventually rescue the Pars from the drop to Division Two at the end of the season.

The departure of Jock Stein made little difference to Charlie Gallagher who felt that he suffered perhaps through not being a Stein signing.

Charlie was still plying his trade in the reserves who were playing excellent football and had defeated Dunfermline Athletic reserves 5-1, for example, at Parkhead on the Friday night before the first team lost at East End Park. The Celtic Park floodlights, of course, allowed the reserves to play at a sensible time on Friday night, and the team were rewarded by reasonable crowds turning up to watch them. The catalyst for Charlie's return to the first team was another of Celtic's many horror stories that were so prevalent at this dark hour of our history.

Celtic had needed three matches to dispose of St Mirren, but had eventually done so en route to the Scottish Cup semi-final on April 2 to play Rangers. Rangers themselves were not enjoying the best of seasons, clearly being second best to Hearts in the League, and it was felt that the inconsistent Celtic did at least have a chance. The first game against Rangers had been a respectable 1-1 draw with a fine header by young Steve Chalmers to put Celtic in the lead. The replay kicked off at 4.30 pm (Hampden still had no floodlights) on Wednesday April 6, and this time Celtic just collapsed in the second half after seeming to have done the hard bit by coming off at half-time having faced the wind and the strong spring sun at 1-1. In retrospect (always easy!) it might have been better if Celtic had given a game to Charlie Gallagher that night, for left winger Alec Byrne was injured as indeed was Bertie Auld. Celtic put John Divers on to the left wing and brought in at inside left Mike Jackson, a naturally right sided player.

The irony was that this was no great Rangers side. They were virtually out of the League race and were about to undergo a spectacular thrashing from Eintracht Frankfurt in the semi-final European Cup, yet they were clearly so much better than Celtic. Celtic's season had now collapsed and the management belatedly, perhaps, decided that more changes were needed, and that the impressive young Charlie Gallagher should be given a run in the team.

It was thus when Celtic were once again on their knees that Gallagher played his second game for the club. Indeed, he would play in the four remaining, little-at-stake games of the season before low crowds with those fans who were there not slow to vent their annoyance and frustration at what was going on. Only 5,000 for example appeared at Parkhead on

Tuesday April 12 to see Celtic go down 2-4 to Partick Thistle. The defeat was actually even worse than it seemed, for Thistle were 4-0 up at one point, and only a handful of spectators were left to see Celtic's two late goals. They did not even have the strength to stay and boo, and poor Charlie Gallagher on the left wing had the indignity of not having his name mentioned at all in the next day's newspapers, which were in any case full of Rangers' game in Germany against Eintracht Frankfurt.

Nevertheless, Charlie was given another run against Dundee at Dens Park on the Saturday. It was a desolate experience with once again Celtic marginalised in the newspapers, for Hearts hogged the attention with their winning of the League that day in a 4-4 draw against St Mirren at Love Street. At Dens Park, Dundee won 2-0 with a goal from a talented youngster called Alan Gilzean and another from Hugh Robertson before half time with the minuscule Celtic support either drifting away to enjoy the local hostelries or just sitting on the terracing drinking beer and even a few of them horrifying the war veterans with a chorus of "Deutschland Uber Alles" in honour of Eintracht Frankfurt's 6-1 hammering of Rangers on Wednesday night – "Aye, and it should have been 26", said a toothless, unshaven, smelly individual beside me.

But this was not Celtic in any way, shape or form. Young Gallagher did now and again earn a round of applause for a good run or a telling pass, and because of his youth was generally exempt from the barracking that was directed at men like Eric Smith and John Divers. Veterans like Bobby Evans and Bertie Peacock, great players in their day, really did look old that day. Celtic fans often misbehaved in Dundee in those days. Not today however. There were not enough of them, and those who were there were simply too disheartened to throw bottles. They ended up talking to the Dundee supporters and agreeing with them that both teams had seen better days.

But one of the fascinating things about teams in transition is their unpredictability. Celtic then went to Airdrie on the Monday afternoon – it was the local holiday and Easter Monday into the bargain – and thrashed Airdrie 5-2 with Steve Chalmers getting a second half hat-trick and Charlie's cousin Pat Crerand getting a game and playing brilliantly. Charlie himself played well, although perspicacious Celtic supporters perhaps wondered whether left wing was the best place for him because he did not seem to be the speediest of players, and his passing ability seemed to indicate that the centre of the field might be a better option. Still, it was a great feeling to trot off in the spring sunshine with a win to the team's credit for once.

One League game remained. It was against St Mirren and the attendance was described as "sparse". Gallagher was played at inside left. Celtic scored three goals in the first half, then conceded three in the second in what was described as "an entertaining game" as the season limped to its conclusion. There remained the Glasgow Charity Cup games but by then Gallagher had dropped out of the side. He would be kept for next year, though.

Thus ended Gallagher's first season. It was also the beginning of the momentous 1960s. Yet even as summer came, it was difficult not to get a little depressed about Celtic. Evans would soon be on his way to Chelsea leaving only Bertie Peacock and Neil Mochan of the 7-1 side which had been dismantled with astonishing speed since their great day of October 1957. Even they would soon be gone as a new team began to emerge. It would take time, we were all aware, but it was as well that we did not know what the next two or three years would bring.

Ironically it was probably a good era for football in general. Rangers were emphatically not getting their own way. This was because, frankly, they were not really all that good. They were quite lucky to win the Scottish Cup beating Kilmarnock in the final. Hearts had won the League and the League Cup, and in recent years, teams like St Mirren, Falkirk and Clyde had won the Scottish Cup. The national side were respectable at least, and attendances remained high, although there were definite signs that the "affluent society" as it would soon become to be called was showing working men that there were other ways of spending a Saturday afternoon than at a rundown stadium, sometimes with no cover or shelter from the grim Scottish rain, and with inadequate health-hazard toilets. It also seemed that clubs did not realise that such women as attended games might need the toilet as well occasionally! Scottish football was slow to spot these signs and to be pro-active. It would be punished when the fans began to stay away.

Celtic Park, for example, was far from a "dear old Paradise" in 1960. The stand had been built in 1929 and was adequate, but on the far side of the park was the "Jungle" – a hideous barn-shaped monstrosity first opened in 1907 with holes in the roof and toilets which gave off a foul stench of urine and beer. Behind the railway end was a black shelter with windows at the back which were always broken and no-one had ever thought of mending them. It did not have holes in the roof, but it only came halfway down the terracing! It was built recently, but quite clearly on the cheap. At the other end, there was nothing at all in the way of cover. The floodlights were indeed impressive but they shone down on mediocre football and inadequate facilities. But we still loved the Celtic! Life would have to get better, but Gallagher was retained. This was very much part of the youth policy, and we kept hearing words like "promising", "developing" and "maturing". The future, Mr Kelly kept assuring us, was going to be a rosy one, once the fruits of the youth policy became apparent.

Listening to older supporters was at once illuminating but yet disheartening. There were still a good few left who had seen Young, Loney and Hay of the Edwardian era, and everyone's father seemed to go on for ever about Patsy Gallacher and Jimmy McGrory. It was all great to listen to, but the contrast between these great men and what was happening at the moment was stark and depressing. Yet there was the classical story of Pandora's Box which released all the ills of the world – but also Hope.

And there was on May 18 1960 an example on our very doorstep of the way that football should be played. This was the European Cup final at Hampden between Real Madrid and Eintracht Frankfurt, often described as the best game of football ever played at Hampden Park. The game was televised as well, and Real Madrid won 7-3 with Puskas, Ghento and di Stefano at their glorious best. Even the inveterate lovers of Patsy Gallacher and Jimmy McGrory had to admit that Real were at least as good as these two demigods!

Season 1960/61 saw Charlie Gallagher break into the team in the second half of the season, but the season was dominated by one tragic event – the loss of the Cup final to Jock Stein's Dunfermline on that terrible night of April 26. There had also been a false dawn at the start of the season in the Scottish League Cup, but the Scottish Cup final defeat was particularly hard to take because the team had shown definite signs of improvement in the approach to the final. As far as Charlie was concerned, his form mirrored that of the team. He had broken through in January on the right wing, which was by no means the ideal position for him, but he had played well until the final itself, after which he was side lined and would stay out of the team for some considerable time.

That he was struggling to find a place at the beginning of the season 1960/61 became apparent when he was in the "whites" (ie the Possibles) rather than the "green and whites" (the Probables) for the public trail before the start of the season. He was not chosen for the first few games, and thus he cannot be held responsible for this particular one of the Celtic horror stories. The Scottish League Cup was an all-Glasgow section of Rangers, Third Lanark and Partick Thistle. Celtic, for whom a superstar called John Hughes seemed to be emerging, were off to a bright start beating Third Lanark (twice) and Rangers before succumbing to the almost inevitable by blowing up in the last two games, including a tragic game at Parkhead to Rangers. We thus did not qualify for the League Cup quarter final, and then, as frequently happened after a reverse, went down 1-5 to Rangers at Parkhead in a particularly shocking performance in the first Old Firm Scottish League game.

But there was still the Glasgow Cup and Charlie Gallagher was very much involved in that. In their whirlwind start to the season Celtic had defeated Rangers without Gallagher's help, but he did play in the two semi-finals against Third Lanark. The first game at a gloomy Cathkin (where the floodlights were decidedly sub-standard) Gallagher mirrored the floodlights. He "started well but faded badly" in a 0-0 draw that was dull in more senses than one, but then in the replay at Parkhead, he was brought in to change the forward line after the League Cup collapse to Rangers, and attracted a good Press, scoring a goal in the 3-1 win over the experienced Third Lanark side.

One might have thought that that performance would have been enough to guarantee him a run in the team, but he did not play in the Scottish League game against Rangers on the Saturday after, nor the Glasgow Cup final against Partick Thistle. Perhaps tellingly, Celtic lost both these games. The only game in which he played at that time was a goalless draw against Aberdeen at Celtic Park, a desperately awful game in front of a small and disillusioned crowd of little more than 10,000. The poor display was on the Saturday immediately before the Glasgow Cup final, and probably militated against his selection.

It was however a dreadful atmosphere in which a youngster had to learn his trade. There was nothing vaguely approaching a team selection policy, and everything seemed to have been done on the whim of the Chairman. The story is well known about the young reserve goalkeeper standing at a bus stop to go and support the team at Airdrie, being given a lift by the team bus and ending up playing for the team that day! Similar things would happen with the forward line as well with the team being changed between arrival at the ground and the exchange of the team lines. It would be laughable if it were not so serious, and things would give no indication of any improvement for the rest of 1960, as any possible League challenge evaporated in the general inconsistency of Celtic's play in November.

Training was "not very good" as Charlie himself delicately puts it. Stories are told of player being given old, sub-standard, unhygienic training gear and told to do nothing other than run round the track. The "wily old pros" got wise to this, and were known to nip into the Jungle, (no-body was there to oversee their exercises) and hide, even smoking cigarettes! There was little in the way of development, and it was a very rare occasion that the players were given a ball to practice with. The thinking behind this strange concept was the bogus one that players would be all the more determined to kick a ball on a Saturday in a game if they had been deprived of one in midweek! It was unbelievable, and the end result was that Celtic, although full of potentially very fit youngsters, were often outpaced and overrun by the opposition.

One good thing that happened, however, was that Willie Fernie was brought back from Middlesbrough. Why he was allowed to go in the first place remains a mystery, but there was little doubt that some maturity and stability was needed in the forward line. (It is surely significant, incidentally, that although Willie Fernie was at Middlesbrough for less than two years, he is still hailed on Teeside as a "legend" with his photograph on the walls of pubs alongside his team mate Brian Clough! The word "halcyon" is frequently used to describe the Fernie era in North

Yorkshire.) The chopping and changing of the youngsters was something that did few favours to anyone, not least a fringe player like Charlie.

Fernie and Gallagher immediately struck up a rapport. Both good ball players and both detecting in each other a kindred spirit, they became friends with Fernie taking the young Gallagher under his wing and nursing him with words of advice and encouragement – something that that not necessarily been forthcoming from other areas of Celtic Park. Gallagher would begin to flourish with Fernie around.

The last day of 1960 saw Charlie, at last, get a game in the first team. A complicated combination of injuries in the forward line saw Charlie invited to play at inside left for the visit of the strong going Kilmarnock to Celtic Park. A good crowd of 30,000 thus saw Charlie play brilliantly and score the winning goal in the 3-2 victory, even though Kilmarnock had opened the scoring before most of the crowd got in. It was one of Celtic's better performances, and Gallagher played superbly as Steve Chalmers scored twice, before Charlie himself picked up a ball halfway inside the Celtic half, then ran on and scored to give himself and the Celtic fans a happier New Year than they had had for some time. The only fly in the ointment was that this result had actually helped Rangers, for Kilmarnock were one of the very few realistic challengers for the title in season 1960/61! Celtic "challenge" had never even started!

Charlie might have expected, in these circumstances, to be given a game in the January 2 game against Rangers at Ibrox. Sadly he would be disappointed. It was a game, in some ways typical of Old Firm games at that time, in which Celtic were the better team... but Rangers won 2-1. The question was asked however why young Gallagher who had done so well against Kilmarnock was not given a game. The answer was that it was all to "protect" him from the rigours of an Old Firm game!

But opportunity knocked by the end of the week. Third Lanark came to Celtic Park in a snow storm and played a game of sorts before a miserable crowd of 10,000. Charlie found himself on the right wing with Steve Chalmers now at inside left. Thirds won 3-2, but it was difficult to judge or condemn anyone in such conditions, and he was given another chance. He would seize this chance, and would retain the outside right position until the end of the season. It was hardly accidental that the form of the team improved from now on.

One of the great things about a Scottish season is that, for the big clubs at least, the Scottish Cup does not usually start until January. This gives them a fresh start, as it were, and a chance to redeem themselves after failures in the early part of the season. Added spice comes from the fact that there has never been any attempt to "seed" the draw of the Scottish Cup or to "doctor" things for a Celtic v Rangers final, for example. Celtic had won the Scottish Cup 17 times in 1961, twice more than Rangers, and it had always been looked upon as Celtic's special tournament with epic finals recalled from as early as 1892 and including those of 1914, 1925, 1931 and 1937 passed down to the younger generations who were seeking to emulate these feats.

But seven years had now passed since the last victory in 1954, the same amount of years as had passed between 1892 and 1899, as well as the more recent years 1937 – 1951 when, (if one ignores the war years when the Scottish Cup was not contested), another seven seasons had passed without the Scottish Cup being decked with green and white ribbons. So the "Seven Year Itch", a famous 1955 film starring Marilyn Monroe, meant something quite significant to the eager Celtic fans of 1961.

In truth, although no-one could really say that Celtic's record since 1954 in the Scottish Cup had been a failure, the intervening six years had brought more than their fair share of heartbreak. There had been two defeats in the final, both brought about by a faulty team selection and one of them in 1955 after a crazy last minute goalkeeping error in the last minute of the first game before a narrow defeat in the replay. There had been three other appearances in semi-finals. Two of them had seen total collapses to St Mirren in 1959 and Rangers in 1960, and the other in 1957 a replay against Kilmarnock in which serious questions were asked about Celtic's defence, the serious questions, shall we say, being directed at their integrity as well as their competence!

So it was a love-hate relationship with the Scottish Cup and Celtic found themselves paired, at the end of January, with Falkirk at Brockville. This was a ground that was looked upon as something of a bogey ground for

Celtic, even though it had been the scene of Charlie Tully's twice taken corner kick goal in 1953. But before Celtic went to Falkirk, Charlie played in two League games, both of which might have gone badly wrong but which in fact showed that this fast improving team was winning well and playing some nice football. A Scottish Cup run was already being predicted by the optimistic.

The distant field of Pittodrie, for example, in mid-January, saw a 3-1 victory with 3 fine goals from Gallagher, Chalmers and Divers. A forward line of Gallagher, Divers, Hughes, Chalmers and Auld combined well on the bone hard surface, so that the 3-1 scoreline in no way flattered the visitors whose large travelling support were in ecstasy at it all while the home support (Aberdeen were not doing well at this time in their history) had turned on their own team and were reluctantly applauding some of the good Celtic play. It was noticeable and much commented upon that this forward line in particular was playing as a unit, passing to one another and reading each other's intentions rather than the more rustic, "hope for the best" stuff that had been seen earlier in the season.

Even better came the following week at home to Airdrie as Celtic triumphed 4-0, the third goal in particular earning widespread praise, it coming from a defence splitting 30 yards pass from Gallagher to Chalmers who hammered the ball home first time. This was Celtic at their best, and now producing the football that had not been seen at Celtic Park for some time. It was crowd of well over 20,000 and although it was a dull and dark day, the Parkhead lights were on for most of the game and the sight was something to behold with the four pylons creating four shadows for each player on the field, and as they were moving so fast, it was a remarkable spectacle. Words like "eager-beaver" and "trigger-happy" were freely used, and the optimistic were now beginning the hope that glory days were on their way back.

But this Gallagher-inspired Celtic revival would count for little if the team did not win at Brockville on January 28. Anxiety centred on two areas – Brockville had been far from a happy hunting ground for Celtic in recent years, and the Celtic crowd had not always been on its best behaviour at that ground in particular. Celtic succeeded in one of their objectives. They won the game, but once again some of their less enlightened fans let them down with bottles, glasses and cans being thrown onto the field. For this they were duly and rightly castigated in the Press and on TV, although there was a certain obfuscation of "banner waving" and "bottle throwing", which was confusing. Waving a banner is possibly provocative but basically harmless, throwing a bottle is not – and even Celtic goalkeeper Frank Haffey had to run away from a bottle or two coming from his own so-called fans behind the goal. In later years this might be known as "friendly fire"!

Things had not been helped by Falkirk stating first of all that the game would not be all-ticket, then changing their mind under pressure from the police, and then when there were some tickets still unsold on the morning of the match, allowing fans to pay cash after all! The result of this was that there seemed to be more people in the ground than there should have been, and at several points, the terracing was distinctly over crowded with the occasional spilling of fans on to the track. Such muddled organisation was sadly typical of Falkirk in the 1950s, and one wonder how on earth they managed to win the Scottish Cup in 1957.

The game itself was an absolute cracker and it was a shame that the idiotic behaviour of some of our fans deflected attention from what was really a great Celtic performance in which Gallagher played a superb part. By no means a game which lent itself to Charlie's elegant style of play, nevertheless, he had a fine match on the right wing. Celtic won 3-1 in front of the packed crowd, and of the 4 goals scored by both teams, 3 were penalty kicks, all correctly awarded by referee Bobby Davidson. The exception was a clever goal scored by Bertie Auld from a narrow angle, and Bertie Peacock sunk Celtic's two penalties. Gallagher might have won the Man of the Match award, if there were such things in these days, but Willie Fernie had a great game as well.

It was a happy Celtic party that left Brockville that night, and they were rewarded with a home tie in the next round against Montrose. Before that however, the team suffered a rare reverse as they went down 1-2 to St Mirren in the Scottish League at Love Street. The result was of no great importance for only the most absurd of optimists would have said that Celtic had a chance in the Scottish League, and it is one of those things that can happen when there are so many youngsters in the team. The game was lucky to survive the snow – other games in Scotland that day were less fortunate – and it was a last minute goal that settled the issue for the Saints.

In the Scottish Cup however against Montrose, there was little bother from the men from Angus who were so overawed that they managed to score an own goal in the first minute. Celtic ended up winning 6-0 which might on other occasions been the score of the day, but the honour had to go on this occasion to Hibs who beat Peebles Rovers 15-1. The same Hibs however came to Parkhead the following week for a League game and lost 2-0 in front of a 35,000 crowd who appreciated the fine play of Charlie Gallagher who laid on two good goals for Steve Chalmers. Gallagher was singled out as the star man in the Evening Times, as waves of optimism now began to sweep the Celtic support.

All roads on February 25 led to Kirkcaldy to see if Celtic, now in inspired if occasionally inconsistent form, could continue their Scottish Cup run against Raith Rovers. Raith had lost their last five games in a row and were now clearly beginning to struggle with the demands of First Division football, so much so that they didn't feel it necessary to make the game all-ticket. With Celtic fans clearly outnumbering the home support, their team did not let them down and they won comfortably 4-1. Charlie's direct opponent that day was, once again, the great Willie McNaught who had been moved to left back (where he had started his illustrious career which earned him 5 caps for Scotland) and frankly, the young Gallagher was, once again, (like on his debut 18 months ago) just too tricky on the ball for the ageing veteran, a point which the great man was happy to admit in later years.

Willie Fernie was the star of the game, scoring one tremendous goal and playing well throughout. Chalmers was on the score sheet once more, Rovers' Andy Leigh got in the way of a Gallagher pass to Chalmers and conceded an own goal, and with the game more or less dead and buried, John Hughes scored a fourth right at the end. Celtic were now in the quarter final of the Scottish Cup, and the feeling that this might just be Celtic's year began to grow when Motherwell put Rangers out of the Cup in a midweek replay. Celtic had in the meantime been drawn to play Hibs at Parkhead, and having defeated the Edinburgh men a couple of weeks previously, it did not seem too impossible a task to beat them again.

Two days after the victory at Kirkcaldy, Celtic played one of their postponed games against Clyde, a team who had fallen on bad times and were definitely relegation candidates. Any hope that Celtic might hold back against their neighbours in distress vanished as Celtic simply swept them aside and beat them 6-1. Gallagher scored a brilliant goal early in the second half and the comment of Cyril Horne, the veteran and esteemed journalist of The Glasgow Herald is significant "a magnificent shot... after this clever player had for once refrained from passing to an apparently better placed colleague".

This tells us several things, or implies them, about Gallagher's play. One was that Horne thinks highly of him, another is that he had on occasion in the past, apparently, lacked the confidence to shoot and the other was that some of his colleagues had, he felt, let him down on previous occasions after he had done all the hard work. He did however score in this game, admittedly against a poor side but one which now contained a failed Kelly Kid in John Colrain! And poor Clyde were indeed relegated, even though Celtic gave then a hand by beating their rivals Ayr the following Saturday.

March 11 saw happy days at Parkhead again with 56,000 there to see the Scottish Cup quarter final against Hibs. Celtic were the overwhelming favourites and the wonder was that they were not several goals ahead before half time. Young Billy McNeill at centre half was well in charge of the prolific Joe Baker, and with a bit of luck, Celtic could have been 3 up. But Hibs goalkeeper was a veteran called Ronnie Simpson who had two English Cup medals with Newcastle United to his credit, and he was playing a blinder. Gallagher and Crerand were creating enough, but Hibs defence were doing well.

Then early in the second half, the huge Celtic crowd was hushed when Bobby Kinloch put the Edinburgh men ahead following some tricky play down the right wing. The Celtic crowd stayed hushed as well for some time after that, for although they had the pressure, attacks tended to falter on the twin rocks of Ronnie Simpson and ex-Rangers player Sammy Baird who was now in the twilight of his career with Hibs. Attacks grew increasingly desperate but with ten minutes left, cracks in the edifice became obvious as gaps appeared on the terracing. Some of the weaker brethren began to depart, convinced, amidst a barrage of foul mouthed curses that this was still not, after all, going to be Celtic's year. Those of little faith missed a great Celtic moment.

5 minutes remained when Bertie Peacock slipped a ball to Billy McNeill who sent a long "route 1" ball up to find the hitherto inconsistent Alec Byrne. Alec made space for himself then slipped the ball to Steve Chalmers, criminally left unguarded by the Hibs defence, and he swept the ball home, to one of the largest sighs of relief heard at Celtic Park for many a long day. BBC TV that night, most unusually for the time, swept its cameras to behind the goal to see the rejoicing supporters, clapping, cheering, waving scarves and jumping on each other's backs in sheer euphoria, as the players all embraced and hugged each other. For the moment, the team and the season had been saved.

It was not one of Charlie's best games of the season, and the Press possibly had a point when they said that Celtic in general had an off day in comparison with some of their performances earlier in the year. On the other hand, Hibs were undeniably a quality side with many fine players, not least Joe Baker. For the replay on Wednesday night at Easter Road in front of a heaving crowd that was given as 40,000 but must have been many more than that, Celtic had to play without their captain Bertie Peacock who was injured. His experience would be missed but Celtic brought in 20 year-old John Clark who had played only a handful of games up to this point, and Celtic fans feared the worst.

The game was fast and furious once again, but with defences on top. Gallagher had a slightly better game than on Saturday, but the rest of the forward line were far from their best, and once again Ronnie Simpson was in inspired form in the Hibs goal. The 90 minutes came and went, and extra time was called for. This was before the days of the penalty shoot-out at the end of a replay, and a third game on neutral ground, or perhaps after the toss of a coin for venue, would have been the order of the day.

But Celtic had the advantage of being a younger team and were therefore that wee bit better equipped to play extra time at the frenetic place that this Cup tie demanded. Hibs were aware that they had not won the Scottish Cup since 1902, although they had been in the final as recently as 1958 and 1947, and the game meant a great deal to them as well. But Celtic now had the advantage of an extra yard in pace. Crucially they were playing down the famous Easter Road slope in the first period of extra time and it was possibly the least likely player of the 22 who scored the vital goal towards the end of that first period. This was John Clark, never even in his later days as a member of the Lisbon Lions known as a goal scorer, but on this occasion when he won the ball after a cleverly worked short corner with Alec Byrne, he shot straight at goal through a welter of legs of both sides, and at last got the better of Ronnie Simpson.

Hereafter, it was simply a question of defending valiantly against a team who had now visibly tired, and even Joe Baker who had made no impact on McNeill throughout the game, could not turn it round for Hibs. In the second period of extra time, the tired Hibs midfield kept kicking the ball down the slope and beyond the reach of their forwards, as the grateful Celtic defence simply let the ball run out of play. Referee Hugh Phillips' final whistle blew at about ten minutes to ten to indicate that the young Celtic side were now in the semi-final of the Scottish Cup to play Airdrieonians at Hampden on April 1. The other semi-final would be between Dunfermline Athletic and St Mirren at Tynecastle.

Chances looked good, and one felt, once again after the two games with Hibs, that optimism was rising in both the support and the players. Indeed, it had already reached dangerous levels and there was the ever-present danger of complacency. The only team left in the Scottish Cup with any sort of Scottish Cup pedigree was St Mirren, winners in 1926 and 1959, and of course memories were still fresh and raw of the 1959 Scottish Cup semi-final when the young Celtic team simply collapsed against the Buddies. But, the support told themselves, this was a different Celtic team now, playing with the confidence and indeed the expectation of success. St Mirren's opponents were Dunfermline Athletic, a team with no history at all other than a defeat in the League Cup final in the late 1940s, and although it was clear that Jock Stein was doing a good job with them, it was equally clear that they had a long way to go.

The immediate concern however was Airdrie who had to go back to the days of Hughie Gallacher and Bob McPhail in 1924 for their only previous success. On paper they seemed to present few problems, although they always put up a fight against Celtic. Celtic had thrashed them 4-0 in January, however, and there seemed no reason to believe that the same thing couldn't happen again especially now that the team was doing so well. Willie Fernie had clearly steadied the forwards, and the team now seemed to be blessed with two good wingers. Alec Byrne on the left was far more spectacular, scoring good goals, but Charlie Gallagher was equally impressive with his passing ability and accurate delivery of free kicks and corner kicks. Fernie and Gallagher on the right wing in particular enjoyed a good relationship. Both naturally able men with tremendous passing ability, Fernie had the additional benefit of experience, and he was able to look after and to bring out the best in the talented young Gallagher. The understanding between the two men was now clearly visible from the terracings.

Three mundane and, frankly, uninteresting League games lay between Celtic and the semi-final. There was a 2-1 win at Partick Thistle, a game in which there was a little crowd trouble involving a few pitiful specimens of humanity being hauled out of the ground as an elderly fan shook his head and regretted the fact that society had not really advanced even though "we had beaten the Germans twice"; there was a dreadful 1-1 draw against Raith Rovers on a night in which fears were expressed about whether the now famous Parkhead pylons could survive the blast of the vernal equinox. Not surprisingly the football was not all that great, but a better game was seen on the Saturday when fellow Scottish Cup semi-finalists Dunfermline Athletic came to town. Jock Stein was given a polite round of applause and a cheer, and Celtic fought back well to win 2-1 after losing an odd goal which hit one post, then another before entering the net.

It was actually not a bad game, but as far as Celtic were concerned, these were merely the preliminaries to the Scottish Cup semi-final on April 1. The Press stressed that this was one of the youngest Celtic teams ever to contest a semi-final, for only Willie Fernie possessed a Scottish Cup winners medal as Bertie Peacock, now in the twilight of his career, was still out with injury. The only questions really were whether the Celtic forwards could retain their composure in front of the large and expectant Celtic crowd and whether they could get the better of Laurie Leslie in the Airdrie goal, a man whom many (including a few of the more honest Celtic fans) believed was a better candidate for the Scotland job than Celtic's Frank Haffey.

72,612 saw a superb Celtic performance as Airdrie were beaten 4-0. There was one superb save by Frank Haffey in the first half, but by then Celtic were two up with goals from John Hughes, and playing towards their own supporters at the King's Park end of the ground, went in at half-time 4-0 up. Not since the 7-1 game in 1957, had Celtic supporters seen such a dazzling performance from their team. Pat Crerand was simply superb, and every member of the forward line of Gallagher, Fernie, Hughes, Chalmers and Byrne was absolutely on song, interchanging at will, finding each other with an almost telepathic understanding. Every man, woman and child stood up and clapped in the Main Stand as the team left the field at half-time with even the Airdrie supporters compelled to concede that this was a great Celtic team.

No further goals were scored in the second half – although Hughes had one disallowed for an offside decision not agreed with by many people in the ground – and the game became a bit of a bore, as Celtic fans cheered, clapped and sang their way through their repertoire of songs, interrupted occasionally by the odd outburst of hysterical shouting when someone passed them the news (in this case, true) that Rangers were losing 0-2 at Kilmarnock. More relevant, perhaps was the news that Dunfermline and St Mirren had drawn 0-0 at Tynecastle.

It didn't seem to matter who won that semi-final for there seemed no stopping this Celtic team. Already however the seeds of destruction had been sown, for the players, young and impressionable, began to read what the newspapers said about them, and predictably, began to believe it. Worse than that were the supporters. Celtic fans, and the 72,000 crowd told the world how many of them there were, are dreadfully fickle – more so, perhaps, than the supporters of other teams - and prone to generalise. A defeat, even a narrow one, or even a draw will be greeted with cries of "Terrible!" "I'm no' coming back" "That manager has no idea" "The worst I've ever seen!" and so on.

Sadly, it can cut the other way too. A good run, particularly when there haven't been too many good runs of late, is greeted with hyperbolic ecstasy with cries of "Brilliant" and "World beaters". There is nothing wrong with euphoria, of course, but it must always be treated with caution, and there must be someone in the dressing room who can keep everyone's feet on the ground. One imagines that Fernie and Peacock (even though Bertie was still out injured and indeed more or less at the end of his Celtic career) did their best, but it was difficult to keep a lid on things especially when on the Wednesday night, Dunfermline Athletic, who had never been to a Scottish Cup final before, won the replayed semi-final through an own goal! They did seem to be the weaker team to have to meet in the final. Optimism was cranked up a further notch.

That same night, a pitiful crowd failed to get excited in a 1-1 draw against St Johnstone played at Parkhead in heavy rain which highlighted the holes in the roof of the Jungle, and then over the weekend Celtic were twice in Dundee. Both games were played before half-filled stadia, Celtic's 1-0 win over Dundee at Dens Park being so dull that it took second place to the news that Aberdeen were beating Rangers 6-1 at Pittodrie that day, and the game at Tannadice did not even have that distraction as it petered out to a 1-1 draw that holiday Monday afternoon in front of a half-built curiously shaped Orwellian type stand which did not as yet have dressing rooms! It also turned a corner and did not stretch the length of the field! It was like that of Raith Rovers, which at least had the excuse of having to fit the shape of the street. This one was bizarre, and not even, as yet, complete. But it was no worse than the football which was truly terrible.

But no-one seemed to bother. The Scottish Cup final was 12 days away, and in between was the England v Scotland International at Wembley. If Charlie was nervous for his big Hampden date, he was in good company, but in the meantime, Jock Stein was giving the first indications of his managerial ability to win the propaganda war. Dunfermline Athletic more or less took over The Dunfermline Press and appeared in the other newspapers, even the Glasgow based ones, at least as often as Celtic did, as the affable and genial Stein gave interviews and stories about his players. Jock even managed to book his players into Seamill Hydro, the normal haunt of Celtic for many decades. The Dunfermline players were compelled to visit ill supporters in the local hospital, were given smart blazers with the club badge and membership of various local golf courses and made to feel special, whereas such treatment from the far wealthier Celtic was conspicuously absent towards their players.

The character of Jock Stein was, as always, axiomatic to the outcome. Stein would say in later years that Celtic, although not his first love, were his strongest and longest-lasting, but he had a point to prove here. He would always express great and genuine affection for Bob Kelly and Jimmy McGrory, but here he had special reasons for doing them down. He would, in a TV interview many years later, give the impression that he was not given the Celtic Manager's job in 1960 for reasons that were connected with his religion, although this did not prevent him from aspiring to the throne at a later stage. In that he was remarkably prescient, for Celtic would, in desperation, turn to him in 1965. Part of the desperation was brought about by the events of April 1961. Had Celtic won the 1961 Scottish Cup, things would have been a great deal different.

The International at Wembley was a dark day for Scotland as they went down to a 9-3 defeat. Celtic players Frank Haffey and Billy McNeill were in the side, and although McNeill played competently, Haffey is still to this day, in some quarters, held (unfairly) responsible for all 9 goals. The memory remains of the Rangers fans in the Scottish support who cheered the English goals going in past a Celtic goalkeeper! Aye, there are some things that a "fella cannot understand", as Sam Weller might have said in the Pickwick Papers. No-body seems to have told these boneheads that the concession of 9 goals did not really say very much for the two Rangers full backs, Shearer and Caldow!

Charlie had already crossed swords with Bobby Shearer. Shearer was called "Captain Cutlass" because of his robust approach, and on one occasion he informed Gallagher that if Gallagher ever got past him, he (Shearer) would break his leg. Such badinage is by no means uncommon, but Charlie had the right reply. He said quietly and confidently "I don't think that is going to happen". When the angry Shearer asked "Why not?" Charlie replied quite simply "Look at the size of you" in a reference to Shearer's girth! No-one broke anyone's leg that day!

But as far as McNeill and Haffey were concerned, it is difficult to see how this 9-3 result could have in any way helped their confidence for the Scottish Cup final. For the rest of this young Celtic side, the game was eagerly looked forward to, but maybe an extra notch of tension was added when Rangers, having recovered from their bad run of form, beat Wolverhampton Wanderers in the European Cup Winners' Cup semi-final on the Wednesday night. Rangers were on the point of winning the Scottish League as well – they had already won the League Cup – and this put an extra onus on Celtic to deliver the goods here.

For young Gallagher, this week was difficult, yet exciting. Every Celtic fan will be able to identify the feeling of enthusiasm yet apprehension as a big game approaches, and this one was bigger than most., This was in some ways what Charlie's life had been all about so far, for he was now in the team which had the job of returning the Scottish Cup to Celtic Park after its longest absence this century. Great joy would accompany this event, if it happened, yet the consequences of failure would be felt keenly and bitterly by everyone in the Celtic community. Celtic did have the better players; it was generally agreed. McNeill and Crerand were superb players and some of the forward line, Gallagher included, were now beginning to make things tick. Confidence among the supporters remained high, and they were given a further boost with the unfortunate news that Dunfermline's Tommy McDonald had to be rushed into the West Fife Hospital with appendicitis.

It was with a spring in their step that Celtic supporters donned their scarves and made their way to Hampden that spring day of April 22 1961. Other items in the news like the Adolf Eichmann case in Israel or the silly half-hearted American invasion of Cuba in what became known as the Bay of Pigs fiasco or France similarly making an international fool of itself in Algeria all took second place to the very real possibility that for the first time since October 19 1957 Celtic might be the holders of a major Scottish trophy. 17 times Celtic had lifted the trophy since 1892, as distinct from Rangers' 15 and Queen's Park's 10. The Scottish Cup was traditionally looked upon as Celtic's trophy.

Celtic would not divulge their team beforehand because there was a doubt about the veteran Bertie Peacock. Indeed, it was more than a doubt for he had not played since March 11 but there was a possibility that he might yet be included for his experience. There was a capable deputy in the shape of young John Clark, however, and in the event it was Clark who ran out. He did not disgrace himself. Gallagher knew that his direct opponent would be Northern Ireland internationalist Willie Cunningham. He considered this to be a great compliment to his ability as clearly, Stein knew what Gallagher was capable of.

On paper, Celtic deserved to be the favourites and should have won. Haffey may have had the horrors at Wembley, but he had also saved a penalty kick for Scotland against England the previous year at Hampden, and he had not been made Scotland's goalkeeper without cause. Full backs Dunky MacKay and Jim Kennedy had now settled down – MacKay having already played 11 times for Scotland, and Kennedy a hard working, hard tackling, no-nonsense left back. Crerand was already being predicted for greatness with his passing ability and work rate, McNeill was a classy centre half, Clark had impressed in his short career. In the forward line, Charlie's partner Willie Fernie, arguably a shade past his best admittedly, was still one of the best players of that era.

Centre forward John Hughes had burst on the Celtic scene at the start of the season. He had scored goals and attracted all sort of rave notices in the Press, but then he had stuttered for a while as the goals dried up. But now they were coming back. He was big, powerful, athletic and questions were asked about whether he could be the personality goal scoring centre forward that Celtic craved. Steve Chalmers at inside left was speedy. He could also score goals, and had already played all over the forward line. A little weak in the tackle, perhaps, and perhaps without the mighty shoulder muscles that forwards needed, he was nevertheless a fine asset to the team with the crucial ability to score goals just when they were required, as for example in the quarter final against Hibs.

The left wing caused a few disputes among the support. There was little wrong with Alec Byrne – speedy, productive and an accurate crosser of a ball most of the time – but reluctant to go full time and an honest journey man rather than a star. He had been with Celtic since 1954 but it had only been recently that he had been given a run in the team. Many felt that Bertie Auld might have been better. Bertie was the stereotypical gallus Glaswegian from Maryhill, full of patter, aggression on occasion and general cheek – qualities that endeared him to the support, but had exactly the opposite effect on Chairman Bob Kelly. Frankly, Kelly did not like him and even as the Cup final was being played, Kelly had already set wheels in motion to transfer him to England.

The teams were:

Celtic: Haffey; MacKay and Kennedy; Crerand, McNeill and Clark; Gallagher, Fernie, Hughes, Chalmers and Byrne

Dunfermline: Connachan; Fraser and Cunningham; Mailer, Williamson and Miller; Peebles, Smith, Dickson, McAlindon and Melrose

Referee: H Phillips, Wishaw

It is often taken as read that a 0-0 draw is a bore, but the 113,618 who attended Hampden that day would not have agreed. There was disappointment, of course, from both sets of fans and the customary and perhaps predictable claims that it was all a fix for another big gate in the replay on Wednesday, but the general opinion was that the crowd were entertained. Both teams might have scored – Gallagher had his moment in the second half when he shot straight at Connachan – but a draw was a fair result. Cyril Horne in The Glasgow Herald singles out Celtic's wingers Gallagher and Byrne as being "as reluctant to challenge as Dunfermline were eager", and it was generally agreed that, although in Pat Crerand, Celtic had the best man on the field, some of the forwards were a little below form, having found the occasion a bit too much to handle, perhaps. Particularly disappointing was the failure of the Celtic forwards to take advantage of the situation when the Pars centre half Jacky Williamson was stretchered off with 10 minutes to go.

Dunfermline were given a deserved amount of praise, but it was generally agreed that that had now been their apogee, and that Celtic would get the better of them in the replay. Only in 1955 had Celtic lost a Scottish Cup replay, and older supporters recalled the events of 50 years ago when Celtic played out a boring 0-0 draw with Hamilton Academical in the 1911 Scottish Cup final, but won the replay fairly comfortably.

But then fate which had dealt Dunfermline a blow with Tommy

McDonald's appendicitis did the same (and, curiously enough, with the same illness) to Celtic. Left back Jim Kennedy was rushed to a Paisley hospital on the Tuesday night, and Celtic were forced to call upon a young debutant called Willie O'Neill to take over the left back position. In this context must be considered Celtic's odd decision to allow Bertie Peacock, considered unfit for Saturday's Scottish Cup final, to fly to Italy to play in a Friendly International for Northern Ireland on the Tuesday night.

By the time that Kennedy took ill, the Irish game was actually being played on the Tuesday night, and although Peacock might have been rushed back to play, it would have made no sense at all to fly him back and give him his Celtic jersey an hour or two after landing at Abbotsinch Airport. For one thing, he had just recovered from injury and would have been exhausted, and for another, it was the wrong position. However, had Peacock not been allowed to go in the first place, it might have been a different matter. As it turned out, young O'Neill played at left back, thus further diluting the balance between youth and experience in the Celtic side. Peacock's experience might have been vital, given the relative youth of John Clark and the loss of the slightly more experienced Jim Kennedy.

That said, O'Neill had a good game, and the reasons for Celtic's painful defeat lie elsewhere. It is hard however not to feel that Peacock, fully fit and reported as "outstanding" in Italy for Northern Ireland would not have made a difference. Peacock at left half or even inside left (where he used to play a decade ago alongside Charlie Tully) would surely have pepped up the Celtic forward line which tried so hard but simply lacked a little sparkle. Apart from O'Neill for Kennedy, the Celtic team was unchanged, but Jock Stein brought in Sweeney and Thomson for Williamson and McAlindon.

Oh, what a catalogue of pain must now be recorded that dull, miserable night at Hampden on Wednesday April 26! The darkness reflected the mood of the Celtic supporters. Hampden Park had, as yet, no floodlights, and even at 6.15 pm when the game kicked off, the gloom betokened Celtic heartbreak, and by the time that the game finished at about 8.00 pm, it did not seem possible that extra time could have been played, even if Celtic had managed to equalize and taken the game to the extra 30 minutes. 87,866 were there to see this debacle.

There were several components to Celtic's 2-0 defeat. One was feckless finishing, another was inspired goalkeeping by Dunfermline's Eddie Connachan in sharp contrast to Frank Haffey in the Celtic goal who was rightly castigated for losing the second goal, and yet another other factor was sheer bad luck. Yet "luck", however real it may be, cannot really be used as any kind of an excuse. Jock Stein's professional Dunfermline created their own luck; Celtic's amateurish approach – as seen in the allowing of Peacock to go to Italy and the transfer of Bertie Auld to Birmingham City, the negotiations for which were actually going on at this time – brought its own reward. "The two Berties would have won it" was the cry of many supporters. They may have been right, but credit must also be given to Dunfermline Athletic and Jock Stein. The more perceptive of the Celtic support said that "Jock would have won it for us".

It was frankly one of the worst nights in Celtic's long list of historical disasters. Pat Crerand at right half showed that he was world class as he sprayed passes all over the field, but the forwards failed to capitalise. It would be the first time (but not the last) that Pat began to ask himself what he was doing playing for this team that he loved but which was going nowhere. The crowd had been noisy at the start of the game but had, noticeably, gone quiet after half-time when no goals came. When the Pars scored in the 67th minute their own fans celebrated noisily while the Celtic legions lapsed into dangerous introversion.

Full time came with the Pars now two ahead, and some youngsters on the running track trying to avoid the hail of bottles and stones hurled by the idiots further up on the terracing. Apologists have tried to justify or at least to explain this conduct by talking about "frustration", but it simply will not do. The Hampden gloom was symbolically lit up by the white coat of Dunfermline's Manager Jock Stein as he congratulated his players. That of course would be Celtic's future, but the present was almost too awful to endure. Some Celtic supporters even felt a little betrayed by Jock Stein "Fancy big Jock doing that to us!"

Charlie Gallagher, sporting as ever, shook hands with the Dunfermline players – indeed the whole Celtic team behaved with impeccable dignity – but Charlie must have felt that the world as he knew it was, if not coming to an end, suffering irreparable damage. Slowly he trudged up the steps to receive the loser's medal from, of all people, the wife of the Celtic Chairman! Bob Kelly was, of course, also the Chairman on the SFA at this moment in time, and he put a brave face on things too as he shook hands with Charlie and others, Gallagher having to force himself to remember that one had to shake hands with Kelly's left hand, the Chairman's right hand being withered and paralysed after a childhood illness.

Gallagher had not played well over the two games. He had had his moments – but in all newspaper reports, his name is hardly mentioned. He himself was honest enough to say that against the mighty Willie Cunningham, he "never got a kick". This was not literally true, of course. There was the occasional cross and the occasional shot, but little more than that. Fernie similarly was disappointing in the Replay, and Hughes and Chalmers would both have better days in the future. In the mortuary atmosphere of the Celtic dressing room, phrases like "our day will come" "there's always next year" and even "hard luck" failed to console anyone. The situation was beyond words. The desolation was total and all-pervasive, and would stay with Celtic and Gallagher for some considerable time.

This game also perhaps marked not the beginning of the end but perhaps the end of the beginning as far as Pat Crerand was concerned. It was this game, one feels, that began to show to the brilliant Crerand that the current set-up at Celtic Park was dysfunctional and useless. Crerand had played brilliantly in both games, the replay in particular but the squandering of chances by the prodigal forwards had severely disappointed him, and an ill-concealed animosity between him and John Hughes began to take shape. At this stage, given Crerand's (and Gallagher's) background, throwing a tantrum and asking for a transfer was inconceivable, but he did, one suspects, begin to wonder.

The situation, of course, desperate though it might have been, did not however excuse the attitude of one former member of the Celtic playing staff who had now moved to another club. After the game, the players had gone to Willie Fernie's house to lick their wounds and this man was invited as well. Speaking in a loud voice so that Charlie could not but overhear him, this former Kelly Kid roundly criticised Charlie's performance and wondered why he was even given a game.

Charlie was very upset by this and was probably glad to find himself dropped for the next game against Motherwell. He did not play again for the first team, effectively, for well over a year. If there was any consolation in all this, it was that he was still young. He was only 20 and had a great deal to learn. Yet the fact that Celtic did not give him a free transfer at the end of the season or listen to offers from other teams showed that they still believed that there was something there. Several times, the benign Jimmy McGrory would stress that Gallagher still featured in Celtic's plans for the future.

Other than Rangers 4-1 defeat over two legs in the European Cup Winners' Cup final by the Italian side, Fiorentina, there was little to cheer up Celtic supporters. In the last ever year of the Glasgow Charity Cup, Celtic drew with Clyde 1-1 in the final and they were declared joint winners. The summer was pleasant enough. Richie Benaud's Australians beat England in the Ashes, and they at least wore green caps! But it was a grim time for Celtic and Charlie Gallagher. Would it ever get better?

CHAPTER FOUR
IN AND OUT OF THE SIDE

Season 1961/62 was actually, in many ways, a better season for Celtic with some really good football played but we were still haunted by the plague of inconsistency and unreliability. Charlie missed more or less the whole season, playing only once at the end of the season. Yet he had not been "sacked" by the club. He was kept on, for it was always said that he was "in their plans" for the future. But in the meantime men like Mike Jackson, John Divers and others were preferred to him in the rather crazy and erratic selection procedure which prevailed at the time, if indeed there was anything to justify the use of the word "procedure".

The Scottish Cup was, once again, the main talking point and the best chance of an honour in 1962. Cowdenbeath and Morton presented few problems, and then there was one of the best games ever seen at Tynecastle as Celtic came back from the dead against Hearts to win 4-3. A similar resurrection was seen in the next round when Third Lanark came to Parkhead and were 3-1 up at half time. Celtic then rallied and went 4-3 ahead before conceding a late equalizer. Such was the crowd interest that the replay had to be played at Hampden rather than the inadequate Cathkin, and Celtic won 4-0. But then came the awful day of March 31 when Celtic inexplicably went down 0-3 to St Mirren in the semi-final. The defence was unnerved, apparently, by captain Dunky MacKay's odd decision to play against the wind when he won the toss!

That was sheer immaturity and the behaviour of some players was frankly childish, particularly as Celtic had beaten the same opposition 5-0 at Love Street the Monday before! But what made things a million times worse was the invasion of supporters, apparently trying to get the game abandoned!

It was inexcusable and although there can never be any justification for hooliganism, this unsavoury occurrence showed how high the levels of frustration were among the disillusioned and baffled support.

Dundee won the League this season for the first time – and deservedly so – yet there was enough from Celtic to make one think that Celtic were a possibility for honours. Some great games were played, notably in the month of December, - a 5-1 taking apart of Partick Thistle, an epic 4-3 against Hibs and a comprehensive 4-0 beating of Raith Rovers meant that they were on the crest of a wave at the festive season. Christmas was thus spent in pleasurable anticipation of what was to come in the New Year. But bad weather put paid to the New Year fixture against Rangers at Parkhead and a few others, and this seemed to knock the young team off their stride. Three feckless draws followed in January against Kilmarnock, Third Lanark and Motherwell and effectively, Celtic were reduced to outsiders yet again.

Yet, when they were good, they were very good. Twice they wiped the floor with St Mirren and twice paid Dunfermline back for the Scottish Cup of last year. They beat Dundee in early March, thus seriously impairing Dundee's charge for the Championship, and then on the April Holiday Monday against Rangers earned a point which should have been two, thus putting Dundee back in the race again. The talent was clearly there; it was consistency which wasn't.

A feature was the sad inability to beat smaller teams. They lost at Falkirk in September, triggering the customary outbreak of hooliganism in that town, at Stirling in February and at Airdrie in March, before the worst of them all – an absolutely awful defeat to Raith Rovers at Parkhead on the day that they should have been playing in the Scottish Cup final. It was this game which was the catalyst for the return of Charlie Gallagher, currently playing sporadically in the excellent reserve team.

In one respect however, his life took one step forward. Celtic players were frequently invited to Dinners and other social functions organised by Roman Catholic Churches. On Saturday night, he and left winger Bobby Carroll and goalkeeper Frank Haffey were invited along to St Palladius RC Church in Dalry, Ayrshire. Naturally sociable and pleasant he went around talking to various people, including a young lady of his own age called Mary.

She told him that, although her father was a die hard Celtic supporter, she herself knew little about football and was no great fan of the game or the team. This was in spite of the fact that she had been brought up across the road from Celtic Park, in Janefield Street and told him that, when she was younger, she and her sister Dorothy used to go in at half time, when the exit gates were opened, to collect all the bottle tops with a view to making some money out of them! This was indeed a common phenomenon of football crowds in the 1950s and 1960s, which of course, for a variety of reasons would simply not happen today. She told him that she worked for the Gas Board but had been invited to this function because she did some typing in her spare time for the priest. The two of them talked for a while, made arrangements to see each other some other time, and romance soon blossomed.

On the football front, Charlie was mature and realistic enough to accept that he has to bide his time in the reserves. He was still in his early 20s and realised that he still had several years ahead. He had always been assured that he figured in the plans, and kept working away. He was now aware that perhaps the right wing was not the best place for him, and the Celtic management team began to wonder this as well, playing him in one or other of the inside positions in the reserve team, although he was still deployed on the right wing as well.

Steve Chalmers had started off the season in the right wing position in the first team, but was then moved to inside, something that brought him to the verge of International recognition. Gallagher might at that point have wondered about a re-instatement to the right wing to accommodate Chalmers, but the right wing spot went to the worthy Frank Brogan. Bobby Lennox was also given a game against, of all people, League leaders Dundee, but still no recall for Charlie Gallagher.

April 1962 was difficult for Celtic. The fallout of the St Mirren semi-final on March 31 had been immense with despair the order of the day. Apart from the inexplicably bad performance of the team, the fans had rioted and managed to get the game stopped. No-one yet knows what triggered the invasion. It may indeed have been a deliberate attempt to get the game stopped with St Mirren leading 3-0; it may have been an attempt to dodge the many missiles and bottles coming from higher up the terracing or it may simply have been a few misguided youths having a bit of fun on an otherwise depressing day.

To the credit of Mr Kelly, Celtic immediately conceded the game after referee Alistair McKenzie of Coatbridge led the players off, so that even when the pitch was cleared and Celtic scored an irrelevant goal through Alec Byrne, the whole thing did not matter. Celtic were out of the much cherished Scottish Cup and in serious danger of losing credibility in every respect. The cynics among us speculated that, if Celtic had not had such a huge support and generated so much money, they might even have been banned from the Scottish Cup for a year or two because of the indefensible conduct of the fans. It was a grim time to be a Celtic supporter or player with perhaps the only slight comfort being the performances of Pat Crerand and Billy McNeill in the Scotland team which beat England 2-0 on April 14.

The following week saw Celtic at rock bottom. Rangers won the Scottish Cup beating St Mirren fairly easily 2-0 (a result which says something about how bad Celtic had been in the semi-final), Celtic managed to lose 0-1 to Raith Rovers at a desolate Parkhead with a lot fewer than 10,000 being there, the proceedings "scarcely good enough to raise a cheer" as The Evening Times puts it, while Charlie Gallagher played in front of about 100 diehards at Stark's Park, Kirkcaldy against Raith Rovers Reserves. The team lost that one as well, but Gallagher played at inside left in a forward line of "Newman, Lennox, McBride, Gallagher and Murdoch". The McBride was not Joe who would not join the club for another few years, and who the "Newman" was, we can but speculate, but if someone had said that two of these guys would win a European Cup medal in five years time, and another would be a reserve in the final, that man would have been a candidate for a visit to a psychiatrist.

Yet Charlie had been quietly plying his trade at inside left (sometimes inside right), and good reports had gone back about him – not least because he did not cause trouble and did whatever he was told - so much so that in this dark hour of Celtic's history, he was recalled. Charlie made his re-appearance for Celtic in the last League game of the season on Monday 23 April at Fir Park, Motherwell. About 7,000 bothered to turn up to see what was actually one of Celtic's better performances of the season and finished up with a very convincing 4-0 victory. Gallagher was played at inside right and "fitted in well with the rest of the forward line" according to Peter Hendry of The Evening Times. He should, of course, have been there long before then.

That might have been the end of the season, but there was still the Glasgow Cup. Clearly losing out in importance and prestige from its heyday, this tournament had seen Celtic, earlier in the season, reach the final to play Third Lanark. It was normally played in October, but it was often difficult to find a place for it in the crowded calendar, particularly since the Second World War with the arrival of the Scottish League Cup But the Glasgow Charity Cup, usually played at the end of the season, had now been officially discontinued, and an attempt was now made to play the Glasgow Cup at this time. It was still something, and there was a beautiful old Cup and medals for the winners. For Celtic, now trophyless since October 1957, (if we discount the now defunct Glasgow Charity Cup) it was something to go for and assumed a certain importance in the eyes and minds of Celtic fans and players, among them Charlie Gallagher who had played well enough against Motherwell to be included in the Glasgow Cup side.

The final was played at Hampden on the evening of Friday May 4 1962, attracting a crowd of about 20,000. Celtic had won the trophy 20 times and Third Lanark 3, the last time being in 1908/09 when they beat the great Celtic team of Jimmy Quinn and Jimmy McMenemy in a result which shook Edwardian Scotland to its core. 1962's final was a dreadful game, although Celtic had more of the play in a 1-1 draw. John Hughes scored the goal but Billy McNeill missed a penalty kick. Charlie is mentioned as having played well but on one occasion was "off target with his shooting". The replay was scheduled for Celtic Park the following Friday night.

This was an astonishing game. If it had been a Scottish League game, it is doubtful whether it would have been played because the pitch was flooded in several areas following torrential rain. But there was a certain enthusiasm from both sides to get the game played, and referee Mr Tom

Wharton agreed. Yet at one point in the first half, "Tiny" (as Mr Wharton was called, paradoxically because of his huge bulk) stopped the game to get the ground staff to mop up the pitch. Their efforts seemed to yield little fruit, but the game restarted and almost immediately Celtic scored with a left foot Gallagher drive.

In the second half, the rain had now stopped and conditions marginally improved. A squad of ground staff worked on the pitch at half-time and by the time that the players came out again, there was little trace of the water. But things looked bad for Celtic when Billy McNeill was taken off injured, and late in the game, Celtic were 2-1 down. But spurred on by a small but vocal crowd of about 12,000, Celtic equalized through a Hughes header, then with time running out, won a free kick a few yards outside the penalty box. Charlie Gallagher took it and crashed a brilliant goal past veteran Third Lanark goalkeeper Jocky Robertson.

The full time whistle brought disproportionate scenes of wild celebration with Celtic boys invading the field as if they had won a trophy of far greater importance. But it was something, and stand-in captain Jim Kennedy took the trophy to great cheers and scarf waving. Cyril Horne, the respected writer of The Glasgow Herald singles Gallagher out as "the most skilful player on the field", and most supporters left the ground wondering why Gallagher had not been playing earlier in the season, particularly in the awful semi-final against St Mirren where his silky passing skills might just have provided some illumination of the Celtic gloom.

Gloom it certainly was in 1962, but there was at least some hope on the horizon. One recalled yet again the Greek legend of Pandora's box which released many evils on the world, but also released Hope. The Glasgow Cup had provided some sort of sting in the tail and offered a certain amount of Hope. Gallagher had been part of that. There were also Pat Crerand and Billy McNeill. Celtic supporters, forever hopeful and optimistic, passed summer 1962 hoping that their team would at last "arrive" in 1962/63 and lift at least one major trophy that everyone so craved. Dundee had shown that good management could win Leagues, and that the financial resources of Rangers needn't be an insuperable problem. (That Rangers weren't insuperable was also proved by their dismal failure in Europe against Standard Liege.) But good management was the key thing – and it was something that Celtic did not have.

Summer 1962 saw Gallagher, as he did most summers at that time, spending his holidays in Ireland. Pat Crerand was there as well. There they played some illegal professional football. There was an unofficial competition going on there, and Charlie and Pat were given a game for one of the teams and were duly paid for it, secretly and illegally. Had news of this got back to Scotland, there would have been a great deal of trouble, and it is hard to imagine Mr Kelly defending this! On one occasion Pat and Charlie's team were playing a team from the North, and there were one or two sectarian overtones to this, but it was only when the other team came out that they saw that their captain was none other than their old friend Bertie Peacock! It was, they kept telling each other, a good way of keeping themselves fit for the new season! And there was also some money!

Summer 1962 with a new pop group called the Beatles now beginning to appear was an optimistic one. The World Cup was being played in Chile but as Scotland were not there, and there was no great TV coverage, little interest was paid to it. Now, more and more it was beginning to be felt that this season coming up was to be Celtic's big breakthrough. Crerand was a superb player, and he and McNeill were now serving Scotland with distinction, and it was felt that if Celtic could just get a break, glory would soon follow. Mr Kelly was not slow to tell the Press that his youth policy was now maturing and that his Celtic team had "arrived". As if to prove this point that they were now fit to be ranked with the best, Mr Kelly had arranged a friendly with Real Madrid. Some called that optimism, other would describe it as "temerity".

Alas, 1962/63 was another of Celtic's horror stories where poor management was the order of the day in the shape of the selling of their star man (whom they did not replace) and constant, baffling and unnecessary ringing of the changes, particularly in the forward line with Gallagher frequently the blameless victim of irrational and ill-thought out decisions.

The League Cup sectional draw could hardly have been tougher for Celtic. True, Rangers had been avoided but Celtic had been paired alongside Hearts and the two Dundee teams. Dundee were, of course, the Champions of Scotland in 1962 and Hearts had been Champions in 1960 and 1958. The Edinburgh side had won the League Cup on three occasions in recent history, and Celtic fans still recalled with a chill of horror the Scottish Cup final of 1956 when a curiously lacklustre Celtic team had been paralysed into catatonic inactivity by Bauld, Wardhaugh and company. Dundee United were the new kids on the block. They had been promoted from the Second Division in 1960, they had prospered on the back of the success of their neighbours from across the road and they would always put up a good fight, especially at home in front of a passionate and noticeably young support.

It was this young generation which was lost to Celtic in Dundee. In previous decades the descendants of the Irish immigrants who had come to settle in Dundee, working in the whaling industry and then the jute factories which took over after the end of the American Civil War in 1865, would have naturally drifted to Celtic. Dundee United were a poor Second Division team. But this was all changed by the rise of Dundee United (founded in 1909 specifically as the Irish team in Dundee and known until 1923 as Dundee Hibernians) who had been in the First Division before but now showed a desire to stay there with the building of a new, bizarre looking stand that turned a corner. They were also well financed by a lottery called Taypools. This new arrival on the First Division scene gave the Dundonian youngsters of Irish extraction an option, other than the under-performing Celtic, in the Jute City's boom years of the early 1960s.

It was anybody's section, but Celtic must have fancied their chances with a home tie against Hearts for their first game. Charlie did not think he would be playing, but he was part of the squad, and he suddenly found himself in the team, owing his advancement to some quixotic happenings concerning fellow inside forward John Divers. The forward line for the first game against Hearts on the sunny, but windy, day of August ought to have read Lennox, Divers, Hughes, Murdoch and Byrne. Bobby Lennox had played a few games last season, but it was to be the debut of Bobby Murdoch at inside left.

Divers set out from his home in the west of Glasgow driving his car in loads of time. He suddenly remembered that he had left his boots at home. Normally, of course, they would have stayed at Parkhead but John had taken them to Hampden on Wednesday where he was playing in a

Charity Cup game for Glasgow against Manchester United before an astonishing crowd of 82,000 – such was Glasgow's love for football in 1962. He had scored for Glasgow but Manchester United had won 4-2. Naturally he took his boots back home with him, but now he had left them there. He turned round and went back for them, but by then the traffic had increased. He was caught in traffic jams and failed to reach Celtic Park by the appointed time.

In truth he was not all that late. He certainly could have stripped and played, but Mr Kelly was a stickler for things like that and John found himself replaced by Charlie Gallagher. There was no official suspension or anything like that – merely a statement that lateness would not be tolerated, nor was John's name mentioned in the statement. The 42,000 crowd were of course unaware of all this, but were very impressed by young Murdoch who scored in the 6th minute and Gallagher who scored with a fine drive early in the second half in what was generally a good 3-1 victory over Hearts in typical Glasgow summer weather of hot sunshine punctuated by heavy showers.

This was a good start to the season, but then followed a trip to Dens Park, Dundee to take on the League Champions. Dundee had lost to their local rivals United at Tannadice on the Saturday. Dundee provocatively decided to unfurl the League flag on that occasion and got what they deserved in terms of audience reaction with the laughable spectacle of Dundee's Lord Provost Mr McManus, ironically himself a crypto-Celtic supporter but frequently suspected of some dodgy deals of the kind for which Dundee City Council became infamous, going red in the face trying to make himself heard over "Sure It's A Grand Old Team To Play For". Mr Kelly, as Chairman of the SFA was in the platform party and hung his head in embarrassment – but there always is something hilarious about officialdom making a fool of itself. Clearly Dundee had chosen the wrong game to unfurl their flag.

The game itself was a cracker of the type for which Dundee v Celtic games enjoyed a good reputation. Two good attacking teams, two rivals for the Scotland centre half spot in Billy McNeill and Ian Ure, two Yogi Bears (for Ian Ure shared John Hughes' nickname) entertained the 20,000 crowd but it was Dundee who edged it 1-0. Gallagher had a great game teaming up well with Pat Crerand, and had real hard luck with several shots which hit the bar or went past the post. Dundee's goal was scored by Gordon Smith, a man who had now won three Scottish League medals with three separate clubs – Hibs, Hearts and Dundee – and now in the veteran stage of a great career. He took advantage of a Jim Kennedy slip up to score half way through the second half, and then spent the rest of the game defending desperately against waves and waves of Celtic attacks which lacked only luck, as was the way of things in those days.

This was a disappointment but not a disaster and most Celtic fans left Dens Park optimistic about what the future could bring to Celtic this year, for Celtic had clearly been the better team. The Evening Times the following night singled out Gallagher saying that "Charlie was the darling" of the Celtic support, but admitted that Ian Ure got the better of John Hughes and that Lennox and Murdoch were a little out of their depth. However, as Hearts beat Dundee United at Tynecastle that night, the section was all square and still very open.

In the meantime, Dundee FC made the sort of decision that would guarantee their repeated bankruptcies in future years. The pitch had been invaded by youngsters (mainly Celtic ones) at the end but it was merely enthusiasm and no harm was intended. Rather than simply tightening up their policing and stewarding or erect a fence – these things cost money! - Dundee used this as an excuse to close the Boys Gate which gave admission at half price! This compelled, for example, youngsters who supported Hearts to pay the full price for admission at the next game on the Saturday, and alienated their own boys as well. It fooled no-one either. Dundee were simply trying to cash in on their success, and although public pressure eventually compelled them to rescind their decision, it was typical of Dundee's thinking at the time of going for short-term financial gain without thinking of the long term effect on their supporters. It would become a great deal more obvious in future years with the transferring of their star players, as Dundee FC's prolonged suicide began.

For Celtic, there then followed a strange game at Parkhead against Dundee United. The continued exclusion of Divers was raising a few eyebrows although the club were at pains to stress that he was not suspended. It was just that Gallagher and Murdoch were playing so well in the inside positions that John was going to have to play for his place. Divers was a player who aroused strong emotions. Some thought that he was a crafty inside man with a keen positional sense and an eye for goal. Others thought him slow and even lazy and compared him unfavourably with his father, John Divers senior, who had of course played in the Empire Exhibition team of 1938. In fact John suffered from a rare blood disorder which often made him give the impression that he has not trying as hard as he could. But he was a talented player.

The forward line saw only one change – Chalmers for Lennox – for this game on a pleasantly warm day at Celtic Park before a crowd of around 35,000. The team won 4-0, but there were undeniable sounds of booing, a half-hearted slow hand clap and chants of "Divers! Divers!" in the first half before Celtic scored on the stroke of half time. Much of this was because of a good chance missed by John Hughes, and it was only the goal scored by the same player on the stroke of half time which defused the protests.

In truth there was little for even the most inveterate of Celtic moaners to be unhappy about. In the second half Celtic took command against a Dundee United team who in the past and in the future would tend to freeze at Celtic Park, however well they could play at Tannadice. Pat Crerand scored a penalty, the much maligned John Hughes scored a marvellous goal and then Charlie Gallagher headed home a Byrne corner. Those who had been vocal in their criticism of their team in the first half departed homewards convinced that, Divers or no Divers, this was a great Celtic team. Such was the fickleness of those who wore the green and white colours. But as Hearts had beaten Dundee at Dens that day, it was clear that next Saturday's game at Tynecastle was going to be a very important one indeed.

But before that could happen there was a midweek League match to be played at Brockville, Falkirk. There was a very poor crowd here with Celtic fans staging some kind of half-hearted boycott in protest at the way they had been treated by Falkirk FC and Falkirk Police in the past. Coincidentally, this game saw Gallagher and Murdoch dropped to allow in Jackson and Divers. Possibly this was a sop to the protests on Saturday, possibly it was just a device to give everyone a game at this early stage of the season, but Charlie would have had cause to feel badly treated, even though Celtic won 3-1 against a dreadful Falkirk team who had now lost all four games this season. The crowd cannot have reached 10,000 because Falkirk fans too were staging their own boycott about their team's dreadful start to the season. In the past crushing and hooliganism had been a problem at this fixture. This game passed with hardly a whimper.

Celtic then made a decision that had their fans and the Press scratching their heads. Divers and Jackson who had played well in midweek were dropped for the game at Tynecastle, and Gallagher and Murdoch were re-instated! What made this worse was that a decision was made and announced on the Friday morning, which gave everyone loads of time to speculate about really was going on at Parkhead. "Horses for courses" was one way of putting it, and a less charitable way was "musical chairs" – but the whole thing seemed so arbitrary and whimsical and lead to humorous speculation about whether Divers had lost his boots again, having left them in the Falkirk dressing room. It was strange. It must also have been very unsettling for the players concerned, particularly as it was so obviously the wrong decision as, for this trip to Tynecastle, surely the experience of Divers would have been preferable to young Murdoch. Yet this sort of team selection was typical of the disorganised chaos that reigned at Celtic Park at the time.

The game at Tynecastle saw some strange refereeing by Mr McKenzie of Coatbridge, mainly to the benefit of Hearts who won 3-2. But that was not the whole story either. Hearts were 2-0 up at half time and then were awarded a penalty kick which mystified the Press. It was duly scored but then Celtic came back into the game and were awarded a penalty kick which Pat Crerand unfortunately missed. The game now seemed over and the Celtic fans trudging disconsolately to the exits clearly thought so, but the team rallied again and scored two goals within the last 10 minutes. With a little luck, better penalty-taking and better refereeing, they might have had an equalizer or even gone on to win, but 2-3 it was and a major blow to Celtic's chances of qualification. Gallagher did not have one of his better games, it would have to be said, but he did have several good shots which might just have sneaked in.

But then on the Wednesday, the picture changed dramatically again. Hearts surprisingly blew up at Tannadice at the same time as Celtic showed their fans the football of which they were capable with a 3-0 win over Dundee at Celtic Park. This time it was Charlie Gallagher who put Celtic ahead in the very first minute with a fine shot from a Hughes pass, and the score stayed like this at 1-0 for the next 80 minutes until at last Hughes broke free of the shackles of Ian Ure and scored two fine late goals to make the score 3-0. Gallagher had a good game that night, passing sweetly and not being afraid to shoot when the chance beckoned.

The goals scored were significant because it meant that Celtic now had the advantage over Hearts on goal average, both teams having six points. For their final game, Celtic had to travel to Tannadice Park to meet a Dundee United team who had won both their home games (and lost their away games) whereas Hearts had a home fixture against Dundee who had as yet failed to reproduce the form that had won them the Scottish League last season. Any sort of win was likely to be enough for Celtic, but it was certainly very close.

The crowd at Tannadice that fine afternoon of September 1 1962 clearly exceeded Tannadice's then official capacity of 20,000. They saw (and Celtic fans clearly were in the overwhelming majority) an entertaining game but one of the most frustrating and unlucky in Celtic's 74-year history. The records will show that the game finished 0-0, but that does not tell of the times that Celtic hit the woodwork – at least four times with Gallagher hitting the post in one half and the bar in another, and then one of the biggest outrages in Celtic's history when a ball was a good two feet over the line and was fished out by Dundee United's left back, but the goal was not given!

It happened at the "Shed" end of the ground where were concentrated the Celtic fans. They clearly saw the ball over the line and voiced their displeasure volubly and loudly, but laudably, the Celtic players accepted the decision of the match officials and played on. One says "laudably" but it was one of those decisions or non-decisions which would have changed the course of Celtic history at least for the rest of the season, and possibly for several seasons after that. And it involved Charlie Gallagher intimately.

The game had gone 30 minutes with Gallagher playing superbly. Harry Andrew of The Scottish Sunday Express says "inside right Charlie Gallagher was a superb inside forward combining elegance with more strength that I thought he possessed" and that was in the context of how he thought that this was "sustained high class football" from the whole team. The details of the controversial incident remain vividly in mind some 54 years later. Gallagher shot from about the six-yard line to the right of the goal. Goalkeeper Donald MacKay got a hand to it, and the ball then grazed the thigh of Doug Smith before crossing the line by nearly a yard as left half Stewart Fraser hooked the ball out.

The "Shed" claimed "Goal", but our hearts sank as we saw Referee Hugh Phillips look across to his linesman. This meant that he had been unsighted and could not give the goal. The linesman on the open terrace side of the ground had not pointed to the centre line nor had he run up field. It meant that the goal could not be given. Photographs appeared in the Sunday papers and in the Monday ones (even The Dundee Courier) which showed that the ball was over the line, but what could they do? The lessons were threefold for Gallagher and the young Celtic team – there is injustice in the world, you sometimes don't get the luck that you deserve, and there are times when you simply have to shrug your shoulders and move on. But it was a significant moment in that season.

The rest of the game was almost a rerun of the 1961 Cup final with poor finishing, an inspired and lucky goalkeeper and sheer bad luck, almost as if some divine power has decreed that you are not going to get a goal. It was anguish. Goalkeeper Donald MacKay had just joined United from Forfar Athletic in the summer. It was the best game of his career but - as with Eddie Connachan in April 1961 – there was a considerable amount of luck as well. It recalls how men like Julius Caesar and Napoleon always looked for commanders to work for them who were "lucky".

That massive Celtic crowd – as large as had been seen in the city of Dundee since the boom days of the late 1940s – roared on their team with their vast repertoire of chants and songs including their new one called Sean South of Garryowen and the old one about how they beat the Rangers in the Cup 5-0 in 1925, but eventually when Mr Phillips pointed to the pavilion, the heads went down. But then, just as the teams were leaving the field shaking hands (it had been a very sporting and civilised encounter) a cruel rumour spread that Dundee had beaten Hearts at Tynecastle and that Celtic had qualified after all. For a while cheering, dancing, hugging and slapping each other's backs was the order of the day until the Tannadice PA system, obviously enjoying the discomfiture of both Celtic and Dundee, announced brutally that Hearts had in fact beaten Dundee 2-0.

The blow was severe, and although one cannot travel in time and change history, it is nice occasionally to indulge in "what if" speculation. The reality was that Hearts went on to win that trophy in October beating in the final an outraged Kilmarnock. Kilmarnock thought that they had equalised through Frank Beattie at the very end only to have the goal disallowed by referee Tom Wharton. The controversy about this goal, incidentally, would have been much greater if this game had not coincided with the Cuban Missile Crisis which was reaching its height at that time and threatened the world, apparently, with nuclear war! But nuclear war or no nuclear war, BBC's Sports programme that night featured Andy Stewart singing "The Heart of Midlothian", and oh, how jealous we were of the Hearts! Yet, had we known what the future was bringing to the men from Edinburgh (they did not win another trophy for 36 years, they would transfer Willie Wallace to us, they would go bankrupt, they would be relegated, they would lose Scottish Cup ties to teams like Forfar and of course, there was Albert Kidd in 1986!), then we would have realised that jealousy was a redundant emotion.

But to return to "what if", Celtic could have won the League Cup that year. They would have faced Morton in the quarter finals, then St Johnstone in the semis (Kilmarnock beat Rangers at the equivalent stage) and we would have faced Kilmarnock on the day that John F Kennedy and Nikita Khruschev's itchy fingers were being tempted by the nuclear button. Had we won that game, (and always assuming that no nuclear holocaust happened) we would have faced the rest of the season with our supporters celebrating, the League Cup bedecked in green and white, and the real horrors of 1962/63 would not have happened. Pat Crerand, for example, would almost certainly have stayed with his beloved Celtic.

But in the reality of early September 1962 (Glasgow's tram lines were being dismantled at that time) Celtic simply had to bear the slings and arrows of outrageous fortune, take the blow on the chin and come back fighting. On a personal level, Charlie Gallagher had done more than enough to prove himself worthy of a green and white jersey. His passing had on occasion been a sight to behold, and not for the last time the word "silky" was applied to him. He also had a phenomenal shot. Although he lacked the speed of Lennox or Chalmers, he was no slouch either and had a surprising ability to resist a tackle, something which his slender frame would not have indicated. The club's decision to persevere with him, after the horrors of the 1961 Scottish Cup final seemed justified.

The support, although clearly devastated by the events of Tannadice, were still optimistic, for their team had played some good football, but the John Divers issue would not go away. Someone would say "Divers lost a lot of money by forgetting his boots" and another would say "Aye, but Celtic lost a lot more" as if Divers might have made a difference to Celtic qualifying for the League Cup quarter finals. He might have, of course, for every game would have been different, but it is hard to imagine that he would have been a lot better than Gallagher. The problem did not lie in creating goal scoring opportunities – the traditional role of an inside forward – it lay, as Tannadice had painfully highlighted, in actually scoring them. John Hughes had his moments. There was no doubting his potential or indeed his achievements. It was just that he seemed to find it difficult to do it every week.

The defence was good. Frank Haffey, that great character, would never play for Scotland again after his Wembley fiasco in 1961, but his cheerful extroverted nature hid a very good goalkeeper indeed. And even in our misery at Tannadice that day, he had endeared himself to the support by his clear identification with the cause, talking to supporters and asking how long to go as Celtic mounted attack after attack on the distant Arklay Street goal. Full backs MacKay and Kennedy were experienced and competent, and in Billy McNeill, there was as good a centre half as you would find anywhere in the British Isles. Wing halves Pat Crerand and Billy Price were excellent players with Crerand in particular, apart from his unfortunate tendency to miss important penalties as good a passer of a ball as had been seen since Peter Wilson in the years before the war.

But the team was poorly led. Training was still haphazard and disorganised with emphasis on running round the track to the expense of ball control. This was no real problem to Gallagher with his innate ability to pass a ball, but he still could have done with some coaching, not least so that the other forwards could read his intentions. Charlie himself was always a great "reader" of a particular game and could take into account ground conditions, the fitness of his team mates, the abilities of the opposition defenders and even the way that referees and linesmen would react to certain given situations. He was a very thoughtful player. But, like everyone else, he needed encouragement.

The Manager of course was the great Jimmy McGrory. Benign, pipe-smoking, modest, charming and of course in 1962 the greatest football player still alive, McGrory, however, was no real Manager. Frankly, he was too nice a person. He lacked the ability to bawl someone out, to turn nasty or to even pretend to be angry, and Celtic would suffer for those deficiencies. But McGrory was only a front man for Chairman Bob Kelly, who was a different kind of person altogether.

Bob Kelly was the son of James Kelly, the man who was brought from Renton in 1888 to launch this new venture called the Celtic or the Keltic. Bob Kelly could not therefore have been more anchored into the concept of Celtic. He had never played football himself – his withered arm put paid to that – but he had nevertheless dedicated his life to the club. His problem was that he seemed to take everything personally. There were several players – Neil Mochan, Bobby Collins, Bertie Auld, for example - that he simply did not like and this had nothing to do with their undoubted footballing ability in all three cases. He therefore wasted no opportunity to keep them out of the team even when, for footballing reasons, they should have been included. And of course, he picked the team. As someone put it rather accurately, the club was firmly led, but not necessarily in the right direction. He was virtually a dictator

However, that may be, Kelly decided that the same team that failed so narrowly and so heartbreakingly at Tannadice should play in the first Old Firm game of the season when Rangers came to Parkhead on Saturday 8 September. A couple of days after that, on the Monday, Celtic had their friendly against the prestigious Real Madrid, for it had been one of Mr Kelly's brighter ideas to invite them back to Glasgow, a city which still talked in glowing terms about their performance against Eintracht Frankfurt in the European Cup final of 1960 at Hampden.

But Rangers came first. They had qualified for the League Cup quarter finals, but not without a struggle and not without a few performances that were tactfully described as "indifferent". But an Old Firm game has a momentum of its own, and a 70,000 crowd assembled on a warm sunny day to see the two Glasgow rivals. Charlie Gallagher's direct opponent that day was no less a person than Jim Baxter, and it would be fair to say that honours were equal in that particular competition with neither Baxter nor Gallagher being able to impose himself on the play. But for Celtic it was another heartbreak.

The game hinged on a penalty awarded to Celtic on the half hour mark. Pat Crerand had been fouled and it was Pat who decided to take the kick. He allowed himself to get involved in some badinage about where the ball should be placed with Baxter and some other Rangers defenders. Crerand even at one point invited the Rangers players to place the ball on the spot for him. He then had the mortification to see goalkeeper Billy Ritchie save his kick. It had been the second crucial penalty kick that Pat had missed in two weeks.

But even at that, Celtic were still fractionally the better team until very late in the game when Willie Henderson shot for goal and Jim Kennedy in trying to clear simply knocked it into the net. It was another galling way in which to lose a game, and particularly after last week, it was simply too much to take, especially when Celtic supporters knew that the talent was there. Some call it professionalism, others call it luck. Whatever it was Celtic did not have it. Rangers on the other hand had both.

The Real Madrid game was a happier one, even though Celtic lost 3-1, for it was a fine game of football with Gallagher's passing by no means out of place in such distinguished company. Ferenc Puskas went out of his way to praise the Celtic fans for their enthusiasm and the atmosphere that they produced. It was noticeable that when Celtic were allowed three substitutes at half-time (such things were only permitted by negotiation in Friendlies in 1962), Gallagher was not one of the three men taken off.

September saw Gallagher play in a good game against Clyde at Shawfield but then he was dropped for the game against Aberdeen when the Dons, by no means a great side in 1962, hushed a large Parkhead crowd by winning 2-1. But then he went to Spain to play against Valencia in Celtic's first ever European adventure – a 2-4 defeat, as it turned out, but very much a learning experience.

Charlie has some vivid but not too happy recollections of his time in Spain "For some reason we were staying in what I can only describe as beach huts or cabins down next to the beach. The night before the game, there was quite a bad storm and the entire place was flooded. I don't know why we were staying where we were, but we were effectively evacuated in the middle of the night. We had to change accommodation and to this day I don't know if it was a bit of gamesmanship from the locals or not. Put it this way, the weather conditions must have been forecast so why we were based there I just don't know. I'd say I probably remember all of that more than the game itself…It was a big round stadium, like a bullring actually, and we were the bulls being intimidated by the matadors. It was a really intimidating venue. In fairness, we weren't used to it. It was obviously our first European tie and we really didn't know what to expect. It was like an adventure for us."

As autumn and winter descended in 1962, Celtic fans were increasingly baffled by team selections and team performances which sometimes seemed to lack any kind of logic. A new player called Bobby Craig was signed from Blackburn Rovers and he more or less got off the train at Glasgow Central, was taken in a taxi to Celtic Park and then played in the second leg of the European tie against Valencia a few hours later! Hardly surprisingly, this was less than a total success and that night saw Celtic's first exit from a European Cup competition, the quaintly named Inter Cities Fairs Cup. Valencia went on to win the trophy that year.

Yet Celtic then turned it on – beating Airdrie 6-1 and St Mirren 7-0 with new boy Bobby Craig playing at inside right and Charlie Gallagher at inside left and playing splendidly. The corner seemed to have been turned, but then Celtic blew up again by losing to, of all people, an incredulous Queen of the South at Parkhead. Similarly, a very hard working performance in the Glasgow Cup gave Celtic a deserved but rare win over Rangers one foggy Wednesday afternoon at Parkhead, but then the team blotted their copy book against Partick Thistle three days later and lost 0-2 to kill off what little chance there was of a League challenge that year. It was a terrible performance from Celtic in front of a big crowd, and Gallagher seemed to be made the scapegoat. He was moved about the forward line during the game, and was dropped for the next few games. He returned to play against Third Lanark on December 15 at Cathkin. Celtic lost 0-2 in what would be the last time that they would ever lose a League match at Cathkin.

1962 thus came to an end with the Scottish Cup the only realistic prospect of a major honour in 1963. 1962 had been no better than 1961, or 1960 for that matter. What was as disturbing as anything was the constant chopping and changing of the team at the whim, apparently, of Chairman Bob Kelly, with no discernible policy in view. If the fans were concerned at all that, it must have been a great deal worse for the players, not least a man like Charlie Gallagher who was as much a victim of this inconsistency in team selection (and therefore inconsistency in results) as anyone else. Valid questions might have been asked about his future at Celtic Park.

But the team also depended rather too much on Pat Crerand, Charlie's cousin. Crerand was a brilliant player "the best passer of a ball since Peter Wilson" in the words of one veteran supporter, but it was becoming increasingly obvious that Pat was unhappy and disillusioned at Parkhead. He had cause to feel this way, of course, for the team was going nowhere, and maybe he had been feeling this way since the Scottish Cup final of 1961.

More importantly, it was also becoming increasingly obvious that he was none too popular with Bob Kelly. Maybe Kelly disapproved of his friendship with Jim Baxter (they both wrote a ghosted column in The Evening Citizen every Saturday night and had obviously met on International duty) or maybe Kelly simply did not like his attitude. Pat, for his part, was beginning to entertain previously heretical thoughts that perhaps his career might be advanced at somewhere other than at Celtic Park. He was certainly aware that quite a few English teams had their eye on him, following his performances for Scotland and the Scottish League. Yet he was Celtic through and through.

Celtic had limped to the end of 1962 with a couple of narrow and unsatisfactory wins over Dunfermline Athletic and Queen of the South, but the crisis came on New Year's Day at Ibrox. It might have been better if the game had been called off. Indeed, the pitch was hard, for a severe frost had hit Scotland on Hogmanay and would not really lift until early March. But the pitch passed the morning inspection, but the conditions were hardly ideal for Gallagher.

The game was a total Celtic disaster. Some historians rate the year 1963 as the worst in all Celtic's history – certainly it was their 75th anniversary of their first game, and no-one made any great effort to celebrate it – and if this is so, it certainly began appropriately, for Celtic went down 0-4 to Rangers on a very cold day. But within a few days everyone, in the gossipy city that was Glasgow, knew that Pat Crerand had fallen out badly with Sean Fallon, the Assistant Manager. Where was Jimmy McGrory, it might have been asked?

Celtic were down 1-0 at half-time. The game was by no means lost, especially on the hard pitch where anything could have happened. But when Sean Fallon suggested that Pat might try a little harder and that Celtic should make an immediate onslaught on the Rangers goal, Pat demurred suggesting instead that Celtic should try more containment to limit the damage, then try to hit them on the break. Voices were raised and before anyone could stop them, a full blown argument was going on. No blows were struck, but Pat, allegedly, invited Sean to do something unlikely with his Celtic jersey.

Eventually they calmed down and Pat was persuaded to go out for the second half. Had substitutes been allowed, Pat would probably not have taken the field. (One recalls a similar incident involving Mark Viduka in 2000 in the infamous defeat to Inverness Caledonian Thistle). As it was, Pat hardly kicked a ball in the second half, and made no impact on the game as Celtic collapsed to a 0-4 defeat. Gallagher had a poor game but so too did everyone else. Crerand, on whom so much depended, would never play for Celtic again.

The broken green and white brigade made their way home through the ice and the frost for their consolation New Year drinks, but they could not figure out what was going on. It was well that the game against Clyde on January 2 was indeed called off, and the only thing that saved the next game on January 5 was the fact that it was at distant Pittodrie where the proximity to the east coast made the temperature a degree or two milder. Those who made the journey north were not many in number, nor were they in good heart as they set out but they returned home delighted with a fine performance from their favourites. Crerand was dropped as he had to be after his half-time behaviour, and the forward line was totally rejigged with Gallagher back in his 1961 position of the right wing. At full back in came Ian Young and Tommy Gemmell. Tommy was so unfamiliar to the writer of The Evening Times that he was called "Peter". He was making his debut although Ian Young had played a game or two before then. The two of them with the enthusiasm and the fearlessness of youth, tackled like tanks that day.

Celtic turned it on and beat Aberdeen 5-1, John Hughes scoring a hat trick and Bobby Craig getting two. It was an astonishing reversal of form from New Year's Day and the small band of diehards made the most of it with an accordion helping supporters with their songs. Charlie played well that day, having a part in most of the goals, and it would have been nice to see how the team would have performed in the next few games with this formation. Sadly, however, it was only a temporary respite in the bad weather and the only other game to be played in January was the victory in the Scottish Cup at Brockville.

On other occasions this might have been a real banana skin for an unwary Celtic, but on this Monday night of January 28 before a small crowd on a heavily sanded pitch, Celtic won comfortably over a poor Falkirk side. The game was threatened with ice, snow and then fog, but at 5.00 pm the referee Mr Barclay of Kirkcaldy declared the pitch playable. Once again there was no Pat Crerand but his replacement John McNamee played splendidly and Celtic ran out 2-0 winners, the second goal coming late in the game from a Gallagher shot after a fine move involving several Celtic players.

This victory put Celtic into the next round with a game against Hearts at Parkhead. It was a potential thriller but the big freeze meant that it could not be played until March. By this time, things had changed totally with the transfer of Pat Crerand to Manchester United, a move which caused tremendous distress to all concerned, not least one feels to Pat himself. It happened on February 6. There had been some speculation for some time, particularly when Crerand was not in the team for the Falkirk Scottish Cup tie. Sources disagree about who approached who first, but on Wednesday February 6 Pat flew to Manchester, met Matt Busby at 10.00 am and was a Manchester United player by 10.30 am.

This meant that Pat's last game had been the tragic New Year Day game at Ibrox. Gallagher was sad about all this, because even if Celtic had won two games since then without Crerand, only a fool would argue that the team did not suffer because of the transfer of a player of Crerand's undoubted ability. As well as being cousins through marriage, Pat and Charlie, both Gorbals boys, were good friends, and it hurt Charlie that Pat would no longer be around.

The support was totally devastated. Pat Crerand had been the hero. Pictures of him, usually one from The Evening Citizen in black and white, but with green stripes painted on amateurishly so that the newspaper could claim that this was a "colour" photograph, adorned the walls of all supporters. These were now torn down with ferocity and anger by tearful fans to the bafflement and disquiet of their mothers. His name was now not to be mentioned – and yet it was, with the picture in The Scottish Daily Express of Pat leaving Celtic Park, head bowed with a holdall in his hand, trying to tell everyone how sad he was to leave. It was presumably staged for the benefit of the camera, but it remains an iconic image of this particularly desolating time of Celtic's history.

And yet, a more detached look at things might have presented a more favourable picture of Pat. He was no "Judas" in the sense that Maurice Johnstone would be. He was more like Kenny Dalglish or Charlie Nicholas who, quite simply, wanted to sample life in England. The difference however was that both Dalglish and Nicholas had experienced success with Celtic, in Dalglish's case a considerable amount of success, whereas Crerand had won nothing. He was fed up of being the star man in a good team.

He also saw that Celtic were heading absolutely nowhere under Bob Kelly. There was a death wish about the club with no great or obvious ability or even (at Director level) desire to overtake Rangers Had Crerand stayed around until Jock Stein came back in 1965, it would of course have been a totally different story, but as it was, Pat went on to win trophies for Manchester United, playing for Matt Busby. Both Busby and Crerand on a Saturday after a game would ask each other "How did Celtic do today?" as all Celtic supporters did!

None of this excuses in any way Crerand's behaviour on New Year's Day. Clearly some disciplinary measures needed to be taken against him, but as far as Celtic were concerned, accepting £55,000 for their star player (and not replacing him with the money) betokened a miserable lack of ambition at the club. The bitter harvest of this move would be reaped on the lonely, empty, desolate East Terracing of Hampden on the night of May 15. All that was missing that night was the tumbleweed of the ghost towns that we saw on the American cowboy movies!

Celtic were able to play a few games in February in Ireland where the weather was not so bad, but they only started playing serious football again when the thaw came with devastating speed causing landslides and flooding throughout Scotland in early March. Gallagher was not listed either at outside right nor inside left when football restarted with a game against Airdrie on March 2. Presumably this was because of a belief that the ground would be too heavy for Charlie's delicate touch, but his next game was against, of all teams, Gala Fairydean in the Scottish Cup at Parkhead on Wednesday March 13 after Celtic had beaten Hearts in the same competition the previous Wednesday.

Gallagher played on the right wing as they won 6-0, was then dropped, played again, dropped again and was then picked for the infamous game at Kilmarnock where a makeshift team lost 0-6, one of the club's biggest ever hammerings. There were allegedly six injuries and Celtic were fairly obviously keeping all their injured or recovering men for the Scottish Cup game at St Mirren on the Saturday, the Scottish League challenge having long been abandoned.

Admittedly after such a long lay-off, there were bound to be a lot of knocks and injuries as everyone was playing two games per week, but the Celtic team selection policy (if there were such a thing), frankly defied analysis. It baffled supporters then and continues to do so now well over 50 years later. It cannot have helped the confidence of these youngsters and it is no surprise that results were haywire. Gallagher did not play in the Glasgow Cup final on April 8 when an inept Celtic team were beaten 2-1 by Third Lanark, but he was brought back for the Scottish Cup semi-final against Raith Rovers at Ibrox on April 13

Raith Rovers were heading inexorably for relegation after many honourable years in the top tier, and this semi-final, played on a dry but windy day at Ibrox, was probably one of the worst ever seen. The standard of play was dreadful but Celtic did win 5-2 to earn a place in the first Old Firm Scottish Cup final since 1928, Rangers having beaten Dundee United by the same score 5-2 at Hampden. Gallagher played at inside left and was no worse than any other player that day. He might have, in view of Celtic's victory, hoped to hold on to his place for a few games, but this was the last game that he played this season. Frankly, it defied analysis.

In some ways he was lucky. The last four games of the season saw Celtic in the Scottish Cup final, then they went to Dundee United, then Motherwell at home before the Scottish Cup final replay. They took the field with four separate teams, and Gallagher was not in any of them! The first Scottish Cup final game against Rangers was respectable at least with wingers Jimmy Johnstone and Frank Brogan playing well, and with a bit of luck, they might just have pulled it off. The Dundee United game was extraordinary in its fecklessness, the Motherwell game was a spectacular 6-0 win, but then the Scottish Cup replay was one of the darkest hours of Celtic's 75 years. It might easily have ended up a revenge 7-1; as it happened, Rangers decided to fool around, for Celtic presented no threat whatsoever, and kept it at 3-0. Little wonder 50,000 Celtic fans turned their backs on their team and walked out midway through the second half. Had this not been the final game of the season, there would have been serious supporter unrest at the next game. As it was, the support cursed Bob Kelly and Pat Crerand, and then tried to forget all about football.

It simply was not good enough. For Gallagher there were two ways of looking at this. One was that he was glad to be out of it. He could not be blamed for it all. Indeed, many supporters recalled his fine play earlier in the season and wondered why he was not there. The other way was to reckon if he could not even make that Celtic team, there was little hope for him!

But he was only 22. He still had youth on his side, and Celtic kept him on. For his part, he was committed to the club. He had played well in the Reserve team and there was clearly still something that they saw in him. He himself evinced no desire to move on. Celtic were his club, and he felt that he ought to stick with them. His day might come, but for Celtic supporters everywhere (and that, of course, included Charlie Gallagher) summer 1963 was one of total misery.

It was not just that there had been a poor season and the miserable transfer of the star player without any real attempt to replace him. (Pat Crerand had, incidentally, won an English Cup medal for Manchester United some ten days after the Hampden fiasco!) It was the feeling of complacency that permeated the whole organisation and the increasing contempt felt by the disillusioned and betrayed support for Chairman Bob Kelly who seemed to be treating them with disdain and assuming that they would always turn up regardless of the quality of the Celtic side. Rangers may well have been a good side in 1963 in Scotland, but they were not all that good for they consistently failed to function against good teams in Europe. And in any case nothing could excuse what seemed to be the shrugging of shoulders and "Yes, but what can we do about it?" attitude of the Celtic Board.

The older supporters had seen better days, and knew that the club could come again. Even on the day after the horrendous Scottish Cup final replay, when we were on our knees, there was some comfort in the memories of Jimmy McGrory and Jimmy Quinn. "They'll come again" was the cry. Indeed, even those in their 20s and 30s had happy memories of better teams than this. Granted such success as there had been in the 1950s had not lasted long, and only once since World War II had Celtic been the champions of Scotland. It was frankly intolerable. It must have been a thoroughly depressing time to be a young Celtic player, - it was certainly a bad time to be a young Celtic supporter - but Gallagher decided to plod on. When you are at the bottom, the only way you can look is up. Once again, there was Hope.

CHAPTER FIVE

ON THE FRINGES

Charlie may well have detected a further threat to his place in the Celtic team when Paddy Turner was signed in the summer of 1963. He need not have worried on that score for Turner was a total misfit. He possibly had more cause for being upset in the general approach to the season – total chaos with training once again a shambles and no-one seeming prepared to take a grip of things.

Paddy Turner was unusual in that Celtic had bought him. Celtic seldom did such things in 1963, and when they did, the player was usually a misfit like Bobby Craig of last season. Craig did at least have a few good games. That could not have been said about Paddy Turner, yet he had looked good for Morton and indeed in summer 1963 he actually played in the Ireland team which beat Scotland in Dublin. Sadly, he was very much involved in Celtic's calamitous start to the season, and never really recovered.

Having finished the season with a dreadful 3-0 defeat from Rangers in the Scottish Cup final, what Celtic and their fans did not need was a League Cup draw which put Celtic in the same section as Rangers, along with Queen of the South and Kilmarnock. Celtic approached the new season like a man approaching the dentist's, full of apprehension and knowing full well that, whatever anyone said, things would soon become painful. Indeed, they did, so much so that comparisons were made to the Russian Revolution. The overthrow of the Romanovs happened because of repeated defeats in war; repeated defeats to Rangers almost overthrew the Kelly regime. It might have been better if they had succeeded.

1963 was a great summer with loads of fine weather. The West Indies cricket team made a real impact on British society, and the Beatles were permanently heard on the new phenomenon of the age – the transistor radio, now small enough to fit into someone's pocket. And of course more or less everyone possessed a television (now available to hire for a very cheap rate) and could enjoy what was going on.

Sadly, Pope John XIII, a kindly man and much loved, not only by Roman Catholics, passed away in early June. Charlie was sad about that but had been happy for his cousin Pat Crerand who had won an English Cup winners medal as Manchester United beat Leicester City, but feelings for Crerand in the support were mixed. There were those who were delighted that he had had a chance to prove how good he really was away from the stifling atmosphere of Bob Kelly's Celtic. Others could not bring themselves to forgive him. The pain was still too great – and it was ongoing. He seemed to have upset a few people in the Scotland set up as well, for he lost his place there when he would surely have made an impact on them.

Away from football, a certain amount of light relief was brought about by the travails of the Conservative Government. It emerged that John Profumo, the Minister for War, (an odd title considering that the Second World War had finished 18 years previously) had been associating with a young lady of dubious repute who had also been friendly with a Soviet attache. There was a serious security risk here, but such is human nature that the sexual side of all this took precedence in public attention. Jokes abounded, and eventually not only did Mr Profumo have to resign, but so too did Prime Minister Harold McMillan in the autumn.

Back at Parkhead Gallagher, on returning for training in late July, realised that he would have to fight if he were to have any kind of a chance of regaining his place. That he was not first choice (or anything like it) became apparent when he found himself playing for the Whites rather than the Greens in the Trial Match on August 3. The Greens were recognised as the first team or the Probables rather than the Possibles, and the Greens won 3-0. Paddy Turner was impressive however!

Charlie was thus mercifully absent from the opening game of the season on August 10. It was a dreadful experience. The rain was relentless as

Celtic went down 0-3 to Rangers. For a spell things looked good, but John Hughes kept trying to bore a hole through Ron McKinnon in the Rangers defence rather than use some guile, then Billy McNeill was short with a pass back and young Jim Forrest nipped in to put Rangers ahead. In the second half, Celtic once again obeyed the rule that they must collapse to Rangers, and the roof fell in. Two miserable draws followed at Kilmarnock (a sterile 0-0 affair) and in a home game against Queen of the South, where Celtic scored their first goal of the season.

The Queen of the South game was remarkable for the slow-handclapping, shrill whistles and prolonged booing. After the game, supporters going home saw the remarkable and virtually unprecedented sight of mounted police galloping up London Road to disperse an angry mob which had gathered outside the Main Entrance. More frightening was the appearance of some supporters with bricks and sticks in their hands. Gallagher did well to miss, all this for he was playing for the Reserves at Dumfries.

It was nightmarish stuff, and the wonder remains that Kelly did not resign. What saved him, at least temporarily was a 4-0 win against Queen of the South in the League at Celtic Park which settled the restive 14,000 crowd. But it was clear that so much was wrong, and that the players were all suffering a collective inferiority complex. There was even a problem with the much vaunted floodlights which had a major fault and compelled the club to kick off their home games at an earlier time! It did not help dispel the general belief in Glasgow that Celtic were "finished".

In these horrendous circumstances, Gallagher was brought back into the team and put on the right wing in place of the talented Frank Brogan who had done little wrong but was simply being played in the wrong place on the wrong wing. Perhaps too he was in the wrong club! Charlie was far from convinced that the right wing was his position either, but he was grateful to get a game even in the most difficult of circumstances in which Celtic found themselves with several public figures like Glasgow Baillies stating publicly that major changes had to come at Parkhead, and various supporters clubs saying that they were thinking of staging boycotts. Many supporters were already staging their own unofficial boycotts by simply not turning up. Others agreed with the Rangers fans and joined in the general ridicule of the club.

Celtic travelled to Ibrox on Saturday August 24, already, to all intents and purposes, out of the Scottish League Cup and expecting another hammering. In such dispiriting circumstances, it was hard to see anything else happening. Gallagher had not a bad game against left back Davie Provan (not the most difficult of opponents, it would have to be admitted, and a man that Charlie had played again many times before at Schoolboy and Amateur level) but the team were defeated, yet again, 3-0, and the half empty Celtic end threw bottles in protest, leading to many arrests. The weather was fine and in total contrast to the bleak, grim unrelenting horror that was unfolding in front of us. The team had held their own (even though they had chosen, eccentrically, to play against the wind) until nearly half-time but then lost a goal at the wrong time just when half-time beckoned. They then conceded a penalty early in the second half and folded piteously.

It all meant, as the Press were not slow to point out that in the space of little more than three months, Celtic had now lost 3-0 to Rangers at each of the three Glasgow grounds. Of the forward line that day at Ibrox, Gallagher, Turner, Divers, Chalmers and Jeffrey, Charlie was by some distance the best but that did not spare him from the abuse and scorn hurled at the team from the unhappy supporters who, by the end, had dwindled to a few hundreds. 34 had been removed by the police, more had gone home to avoid being hit by bottles and still more left in disgust to enjoy, if that were the right word in such circumstances, the summer sunshine.

The players had no such option. They had to stay and endure the taunts of the gloating ignorant at one end with their chant of "Easy! Easy!", and the abuse of their own supporters at the other end. It hurt men like Gallagher all the more because he was a Celtic supporter and was hurting inside in any case. The Rangers players, to their credit, eased off a little for they certainly could have hit Celtic for a lot more than they did, but the full time whistle came to feelings of blessed relief. Life could not be so terrible! Maybe it could. Celtic had to come back to Ibrox for a League fixture in a fortnight's time!

The Celtic Supporters Handbook for 1964 in reviewing this awful time talks about "rumours going round Glasgow that Celtic were finished, and that thousands were flocking to the banner of a more militant organisation".

Filmstar looks, 1965

Celtic FC 'Possibles' before public trial. 9th August, 1960

Youth International. Stair Park, Stranraer. Scotland v Ireland.
12th April 1958

Glasgow Schools Team v Edinburgh Schools Team. A 6-2 win for Glasgow.
(Charlie - Top row, 2nd player from left).

Jim Forrest (Rangers), Charlie and Alex Willoughby in the mid-1960s.

Glasgow Cup Final 1962

Celtic in Dublin with President of Ireland, Éamon de Valera (between Jock Stein and Sir Robert Kelly).

Charlie, Willie Fernie, John Hughes, Stevie Chalmers and Alec Byrne get in some sprint work on the track at Celtic Park in preparation for the Scottish Cu final against Dundermline in April 1965.

Squad photo. Season 1963-64

CELTIC

Official Programme

Charlie Gallagher

SCOTTISH LEAGUE—DIVISION 1

CELTIC v. KILMARNOCK

Saturday, 27th November, 1965

Kick-off 3.00 p.m.

No. 9. PRICE · THREEPENCE

The Celtic 'bench' look on in the Stadion Juliska in Prague, April 1967, as the Scottish Champions earn the 0-0 draw which takes them through to the European Cup Final in Lisbon

Celtic Team 1965

By this they mean one of the many sporadic and uncoordinated groups trying to oust Kelly from power. In this they would be a lot less successful that the "Celts For Change" of thirty years later, for in 1963, Kelly remained the dictator.

Two League Cup games of little interest remained – Kilmarnock at Parkhead on Wednesday and then Queen of the South at Palmerston the following Saturday. The Kilmarnock game kicked off at 6.30 pm rather than 7.30 so that it could finish in daylight because of the fault in the floodlights which had not yet been repaired – barely credible, but then we are talking about Celtic in 1963! – and it attracted a paltry, unhappy crowd of little more than 10,000. In fact, they saw a performance by Celtic which was just about worthy of the name. It was a 2-0 win, and Gallagher scored the second with a marvellous drive when he met a cross from Paddy Turner from the left. That at least brought a smile to some faces. More goals should have been scored, but it was at least a win.

The final game of the section at Dumfries saw another win. The crowd was once again meagre with a noticeable paucity of green and white favours in the crowd, but Gallagher converted a penalty kick and the team won 3-2 to bring to the end a League Cup campaign which had revealed once again that the Rangers complex was still in full swing. Yet as journalists like Gair Henderson would never tire of pointing out, Rangers were not all that good. Real Madrid would soon prove that very point.

The bruised and battered Celtic team could have done with someone else for their next week's League fixture. It was Rangers at Ibrox! But Gallagher was dropped from the right wing position in favour of Bobby Lennox, the naturally left sided Bobby Lennox! It was a miserable day of rain, but Gallagher had his moment of glory at Parkhead when, playing in the inside left position, he scored the only goal of the game in the Reserve Match, while the first XI went down yet again to Rangers. Admittedly, it was a more respectable (and even unlucky) 1-2 defeat at Ibrox, but it was another day of misery for the dwindling support with much talk about the "thinly populated Celtic end" while at Celtic Park for the Reserve game, Charlie's goal was greeted with a louder cheer than one would expect at a Reserve game. The crowd was given as 10,000, clearly many Celtic fans having decided to spare themselves the agonies of Ibrox.

For Gallagher, reserve team football would become the norm once again for several weeks. The first team had a dreadful September, but rallied a little in October with a win in the European Cup Winners' Cup over Basle, a boost being given by Real Madrid's tanking of Rangers in the other European competition. It was ironic, incidentally, that Celtic's awful Scottish Cup final of last May had gained them entry to Europe!

In the meantime, the Celtic Supporters Association had managed to have a meeting with Mr Kelly. Mr Kelly had listened politely, taken on board some of the points well made by the supporters and had basically promised to improve the performance. It may have been coincidence, but things seemed to settle down after that. By the time that Gallagher came back into the first team, Celtic had had two successive 3-0 victories over Aberdeen and Dundee United. They were picking up, and Charlie would not have got into the team on October 26 had it not been for Jimmy Johnstone picking up a dose of flu. He was therefore back on the right wing!

It was an odd match to come back to as well. Although Celtic may have had a couple of good results and may have survived their first round in Europe while Rangers had blown up spectacularly in Madrid, nevertheless Celtic's game against Airdrie attracted a crowd of 13,000 while a mile up the road at Hampden Park a six figure crowd were watching Rangers win the Scottish League Cup over Second Division Morton. The fact that Morton were a Second Division team, incidentally, spoke volumes about the standard of football in the First Division, the lack of any resistance to Rangers, and how much the game in Scotland was crying out for a good Celtic team to offer some kind of a challenge to Rangers.

But the meagre crowd at Parkhead that day enjoyed a treat, for Celtic beat Airdrie 9-0. Gallagher scored the first goal and a spectacular one it was as well, a 20-yard volley. He then played superbly throughout but so too did the rest of the team, playing with confidence and panache as the two Johns, Divers and Hughes each helped themselves to hat-tricks. Late in the game Celtic were awarded a penalty and in response to cries from the crowd, Billy McNeill asked goalkeeper Frank Haffey to take it. This would have made double figures, but Frank, out of respect for a fellow goalkeeper, perhaps, duly missed it!

Charlie also played in the next game, another strange one. It was at the unusual venue of Firs Park, the home of East Stirlingshire who were in the First Division that year. Celtic won 5-1 without a great deal of trouble but Billy McNeill was sent off by referee Mr Rodgers of Stenhousemuir for reasons that no-one seemed to understand. This happened when McNeill was playing on the left wing because he had been injured! Charlie however had played well and had earned a few ripples of applause from the Celtic fans in the covered enclosure.

Jimmy Johnstone was restored after the East Stirlingshire game, and Charlie, without having done anything wrong, now found himself back in the Reserves. A couple of weeks after his time in the first team he was in the dressing room at Kilmarnock before a Reserve game one Friday night (Reserve games were often played then and attracted reasonably large crowds) when someone came in with the news that someone had shot the President of the United States. At half time the story was that he was now dead, and at full time, after the Reserves had lost 4-2, the story was confirmed that John F Kennedy had been shot in Dallas. It was an event that took over everything, and the following day there was an impressive tribute paid to the President in a minute's silence. Celtic then went on to win 5-0 over Kilmarnock in one of their best performances of the season.

Charlie however played only one other game for the firsts before the New Year, and that was in a 1-1 draw at Dens Park, when Johnstone was suspended. Once again he played well enough, but he was not Jimmy Johnstone and could not complain at having to give way, for Johnstone was in sparkling form and already well on his way to becoming a hero with the Celtic support. The team finished 1963 strongly and their good form included a fine win in Europe over Dinamo Zagreb, but everyone knew that it could only really be called a revival if they could beat Rangers who were due to appear at Celtic Park on New Year's Day.

The team duly lost on New Year's Day, unluckily and frustratingly for the fans, not least Charlie Gallagher who must have felt that he could make a difference to that feckless forward line who did everything but score. A penalty kick should have been awarded when Chalmers was brought down - but it wasn't, and when Rangers scored in the second half against the run of play, the inferiority complex took over and Rangers won again.

So much of this game was psychological. Coming into this game, Celtic's form had been quite impressive – certainly far better than the start of the season – but crucially, they had not been playing Rangers! Whenever the blue jerseys appeared on the horizon, Celtic seemed to believe that the fun was over, and it was time to lose again!

In those days at New Year, footballers played another game on January 2, and for this one Gallagher was drafted in to take over from the injured Bobby Murdoch for the game against Third Lanark at Cathkin Park. The game had all the atmosphere of a public library, for Celtic fans were so visibly disappointed at yesterday's failure, and only 14,000 appeared. The weather was dull as well, the ground was hard and Celtic, who were also without Billy McNeill and John Clark, were lucky to get a draw. There was little doubt, however, that it was Rangers who were in absentia preventing them from scoring, for such are the ingrained feelings in Glasgow about the Old Firm. How the other member of the divide is doing inevitably plays a vital part. A few shattered Celtic supporters turned on their team with boos and slow handclaps, and Gallagher although he had had no part in yesterday's defeat, was not spared.

A 7-0 thrashing of Falkirk may have dissipated a few woes and cleared a few New Year hangovers, but Charlie wasn't playing that day. He played in a Glasgow Cup game against Third Lanark (an appalling 1-1 draw) and then in the replay which was a much better performance, Celtic winning 3-0. He also played on the day that Eyemouth of the East of Scotland League paid an unprecedented visit to Celtic Park on Scottish Cup business. He scored a good goal with his head in the 3-0 win after the Borderers had stunned all of Scotland by holding out until half-time. When the half-time scoreboards at the other grounds showed that the score after 45 minutes was Celtic 0 Eyemouth 0, there was a certain amount of disbelief. Booing and whistling were heard at Parkhead, a particular cause of frustration being Celtic's tendency to be caught offside. The second half was a different matter altogether, however.

The defeat of Eyemouth put Celtic into the next round of the Scottish Cup and the draw threw up the game that had all Scotland talking, the newspapers printing hysterical rubbish, and the real feeling that there might here be a genuine upset. Celtic were drawn against Greenock

Morton at Cappielow. Morton were in the Second Division but were absolutely paralysing the opposition. They had played 23 games and had won them all. Granted, the opposition was occasionally a little less than top notch, but a record like that demanded respect. They had also of course reached the final of the Scottish League Cup before losing 5-0 to Rangers.

They were well managed by Hal Stewart and had some fine forwards like Allan McGraw and Jimmy Wilson. Clearly they could inflict damage on Celtic, and this was now a vulnerable Celtic who had impressed in November and December but had let everyone down on New Year's Day. There were additional factors as well – the tight little ground, the traditional feelings of animosity towards Celtic in Greenock generated by trouble in the past and the feeling that the Scottish Cup might just provide a great upset. The Press continually played this up and the good people of Greenock might have been forgiven for thinking that they had already won.

Charlie was given a game when John Divers called off with an ankle injury. The forward line was the fairly settled one of Johnstone, Murdoch, Chalmers, Divers and Hughes but Charlie had covered for Divers when he had flu earlier in month, and now he was called in again. It was probably as well for Celtic that he was. It had been a fairly last minute decision, however, and Charlie had travelled to Greenock with the team on January 25, unaware if he would be playing or not.

The precaution was taken of starting the game at 2.30 pm so that the game could finish in daylight. Before an excited, chanting, all-ticket crowd of 22,000 (tickets had been changing hands for phenomenal prices on the black market outside the ground), Celtic started off playing towards the higher terracing at Cappielow and the game was played at a rapid pace with loads of fierce tackles on both sides. But the game was well controlled by Tom "Tiny" Wharton. It was a typical Scottish Cup tie, not really very suited for Charlie's more leisurely, controlled, elegant passing type of football.

Morton drew first blood through Allan McGraw, but then John Hughes scored one of his classic goals where he beat several men, then crashed home a thunderbolt from about 20 yards. Jimmy McGrory would later describe it as "one of the greatest goals I have ever seen." And then came the moment when Celtic fans feared that it had all been thrown away, and that was when Bobby Murdoch, by at least a couple of yards, missed a penalty, awarded when John Hughes was brought down. Half time came with the teams locked at 1-1 and only a brave man would have predicted the winners of the tie. But Celtic started more strongly in the second half and in the 52nd minute came the moment that swung the tie in Celtic's favour.

They had forced a corner on the left, on the other side of the packed ground from the main stand, and Charlie Gallagher trotted across to take the kick. He decided to use his right foot, try an inswinger and hope to find the head of Chalmers or Hughes perhaps. He did so, putting a curl on the ball which deceived the right back in the first instance, deceived his own forwards as well, eluded the despairing dive of goalkeeper Miller and ended up in the back of the net!

Scoring a goal direct from a corner kick is an unusual way of scoring. Charlie Tully had famously done it twice at Falkirk in 1953, as had Alec Cheyne for Scotland against England at Hampden in 1929, but it was not common. Some spectators even wondered whether it was legal, but it certainly was. There was a brief split second until everyone realised what had happened before mayhem broke out. The Celtic fans on that small packed terracing went crazy, hugging each other and jumping up and down in a green and white sea of noise and ecstasy, while the Celtic players all rushed across to congratulate Charlie. A few spectators invaded the field as well, but they were soon calmed down and ushered off by the Greenock police.

Gallagher had put Celtic ahead, and now there was no stopping Celtic. About five minutes later Jimmy Johnstone hit another goal after some fine work from John Hughes, and Celtic finished the game well on top. There was even a moment of light comedy when goalkeeper John Fallon was given a reprimand by a promotion hunting policeman for holding his arms up in triumph to the Celtic crowd! Celtic got another two corners in that second half, and although the crowd shouted "Again! Again!" Charlie was unable to reproduce his first corner. It was however a great day for Celtic. Often a victory over a Second Division team is looked upon as an empty victory but Morton in 1964 were no ordinary Second Division side. And Charlie had played his part. Indeed, Rodger Aitken in The Sunday Mirror went as far as to say that "Charlie Was Their Darlin'"

He played in another game – a miserable 0-1 defeat at Dunfermline – at inside left before giving way to John Divers, then he played a game against Airdrie on the right wing. This was a comic sort of match, beginning in a blizzard which continued until nearly half-time. Celtic, out of the Scottish League race and with European commitments pending, played a weakened team with people like Samuel Henderson, Frank Brogan, Paddy Turner and Charlie Gallagher all getting a game. Less than 10,000 folk huddled under Broomfield's inadequate shelters to see a 2-0 victory with the football surprisingly good in the awful circumstances.

But effectively Gallagher was now out of the team for a spell. Because of his versatility and willingness to play all over the forward line, he was normally the reserve who travelled with the team. It is a pity that substitutes were not allowed in 1964, for Charlie would surely have been given more of a chance. Celtic duly beat Slovan Bratislava to reach the semi-final of the European Cup Winners' Cup, although it did not look that way when the game at Parkhead finished with Celtic only 1-0 ahead, and that was through a Bobby Murdoch penalty. A fine performance abroad however meant that Celtic won through.

The trip to Bratislava was a good one, and the team were welcomed back by an enthusiastic bunch of supporters desperate for success, but it was not forthcoming at Ibrox on the following Saturday in the Scottish Cup. Sadly, once again Celtic collapsed to Rangers losing a goal on either side of half time, and never really after that looking like they were likely to get back into the game. The team selection was a funny one that day as well with Frank Brogan on the right wing and Jimmy Johnstone at inside right with Bobby Murdoch pulled back to right half because of an injury to John Clark. Gallagher, in these circumstances might have hoped for a call up, but all he could do was sit and watch that day which effectively killed off Celtic' season, at least as far as Scotland was concerned.

He may have now begun to worry, yet again (it was becoming an annual occurrence) about his future. He was no longer a Kelly Kid who would one day mature, develop and "arrive" as the saying went. He was now 23 and he should have been commanding a place in the team in the opinion of many of the supporters who appreciated his ball play, his superb passing ability and his thunderball shot which was deceptive in that he did not look as if he possessed the ability to hit a ball with such ferocity. But 1964 was not finished with him yet. Indeed, as had happened in 1962, he was brought in after the damage had been done. Once again the stable door was locked after the horse had been stolen!

Celtic had won the Glasgow Cup on Wednesday March 25 but in a somewhat pedestrian and uninspired performance before a crowd of about 14,000, winning 2-0 over Second Division Clyde. John Divers had scored the second goal but had not played particularly well (indeed his form had been indifferent for some time). This triumph (such as it was) masked a general malaise at the club. On the Saturday before, they had gone to Rugby Park to lose 4-0 to the strong going Kilmarnock and the forwards had not really got going. On the other hand, the Reserves, well marshalled by Gallagher had sparkled to beat their Kilmarnock equivalents 4-1. The time seemed ripe to make a change. Indeed, on the day after the Glasgow Cup win, The Evening Times says categorically that the forwards were a flop, and that this was not European form.

Accordingly, when the few supporters turned up at Motherwell on Saturday March 28 for a meaningless League game, they discovered that Charlie was at inside left. This was a rare outbreak of common sense. Charlie Gallagher, the best ball player on their books, was given a start and in a position in which he could do himself justice. They were rewarded by a far better team performance, a 4-0 win for Celtic who played good attacking football from the start.

It was indeed one of Celtic's better performances of the season and it was a shame that it attracted so little attention. Only 8,000 were there, with the attention of the media focussed on the Scottish Cup semi-finals of that day in which Rangers edged it 1-0 over Dunfermline at Hampden while at Ibrox Dundee impressively beat Kilmarnock 4-0, the same Kilmarnock who had over-run the Gallagher-less Celtic at Rugby Park the previous week!

And Gallagher, with silent but grim determination, now seized his chance. Dundee, arguably the best footballing team in Scotland at the moment, came to Celtic Park on Wednesday April 1 to play a postponed game. The 17,000 crowd saw Alan Gilzean put them one ahead in the first half. But Celtic then started to play some fine football, inspired by Gallagher. Yet they could not score, with Chalmers in particular having an off night and being unable to convert a barrow load of chances. Then with 15 minutes to go, Gallagher equalized in a way that made everyone wonder what the problem had been hitherto. He picked up a ball in the middle of the Dundee half, made a yard or two, then simply lashed the ball home from about 35 yards. It was another of these memorable moments when there is a split second of pause so that everyone takes it all in, and then an explosion of acclamation and joy and an invasion of youngsters, who had had little cause to express themselves in this way before.

They were duly shooed back into the terracing and everyone then began to ask just why Gallagher had not been in the first team earlier, for shooting like that would have been exactly what we needed at Ibrox in our Scottish Cup demise. But there was still a game to be won, and Celtic now pressed and pressed until with almost the last kick of the ball, the luckless Steve Chalmers eventually scored with a tap in to give Celtic a victory which actually put them second in the League! Yes, things could have been a lot different in 1964!

The next game at Muirton Park, Perth was a lot less happy for Gallagher and Celtic. Rangers finally won the League Championship that day and Celtic could only draw 1-1 with St Johnstone. Indeed, but for a last minute save of a penalty kick by John Fallon, St Johnstone would have won. But Gallagher had no reason to reproach himself. Indeed, he probably strengthened his position in the team, because his main rival, John Divers, was also given a game that day and played very badly, even being (unfairly) described as "lazy" by some supporters. Jock Stein, in the meantime, had moved from Dunfermline to Hibs and took charge of them for the first time that day. Some supporters felt that Celtic might have gone for him…

But the big match appearing on the horizon for Celtic was the European Cup Winners' Cup semi-final against the Hungarian side MTK Budapest.

It was the last chance for an honour, but it would have meant a great deal to the club and to Scotland as well if they could only win that trophy. When MTK arrived, Scottish football was on a high, for Scotland had beaten England 1-0 at Hampden the previous Saturday, the goal being scored by Dundee's Alan Gilzean while Celtic's Billy McNeill and Jim Kennedy had played admirably.

51,000 were at Celtic Park on Wednesday April 15 to see Celtic play some marvellous football and in fact the Hungarians were lucky to get off with a 3-0 defeat. And these men were Hungarians who still had some sort of mythical status! People still associated them with their great teams of Puskas and Hidegkuti of the early 1950s before their country was crushed by the Russians! The first half was mundane until Jimmy Johnstone squeezed a goal home, and then in the second half, with Celtic attacking the Rangers end of the ground, came two goals from Steve Chalmers, one a speculative shot which took everyone by surprise, the other a header. It was very impressive stuff, and the euphoria was justified. Gallagher's role at inside left in all this had been less spectacular than some, but none the less effective for all that. The BBC highlights programme that night showed something like a Celtic performance which had been missing for so long.

Celtic and their supporters were now on a high, a dangerous high. Everyone started talking about going to the Final. It would be in Brussels on May 13, and might just be within the price range of supporters in the economic boom time of 1964. The players themselves were not immune to such optimism. 3-0 would surely be enough, and the precedent was noted of the game against Dinamo Zagreb last December where Celtic won 3-0 at Parkhead and then held on to win the tie in Zagreb. And in Bratislava, against Slovan they had actually won the game away from home! Such was the talk among the supporters as they assembled to see the last two home games of the season, a 1-1 draw with Hearts and a similar score in a friendly against Chelsea which was stopped prematurely because of heavy rain.

Celtic however fell into a trap. The fault was sheer naivety. The great performance at Parkhead went to their heads, and Bob Kelly announced that Celtic would attack in Budapest, conned by the MTK Chairman's admiration for Jimmy Johnstone and his statement that people in Budapest would love the little redhead and the great Celtic forward line. The Scottish Press played its part in all this as well, and Celtic marched gaily to their doom.

A few sensible people urged caution and pointed to the precedent of Manchester United in the same tournament. They too had had a similar lead and had lost it. Scotland's International teams had always been impressive at Hampden, but had found foreign travel not quite so easy. It might be a better idea to put out a slightly more defensive team, or at least to deploy the players in a more defensive set up but such wiser counsel did not prevail. Hungary may well have been noted for its great football team in the early 1950s, but it was still on the wrong side of the Iron Curtain. Indeed, it was very much under the control of the grim tyranny of the Soviet Union, for only eight years previously in 1956, a rebellion against the Soviets had been put down with brutal and murderous severity.

It was as well that there were no Celtic supporters (or certainly very few) there, for it was one of the worst Celtic performances of all time. They lost 4-0. They complained about the referee, but the fault lay in Celtic expecting anything other than a "homer" of a referee. In-fact they were out-thought and out-played and the sense of disappointment was total. They took the field with the same personnel and exactly the same formation as they had deployed at Parkhead. The Hungarian press singled out Jimmy Johnstone and mentioned Charlie Gallagher as having a few nice touches and passes, but they were as amazed as anyone that Celtic had collapsed so totally. It was, effectively, the last game of the season, and there were no repercussions at managerial level, but quite a few people supporters and players, like Gallagher, now began to despair of Celtic.

But Gallagher had little to reproach himself for. He had been out of the side for most of the season, but when the chance presented itself towards the end he had seized it. He could realistically hope to be a first team regular next season, but this particular summer, he had other things on his mind. He had a life outside of football as well.

On June 13 1964, he married Mary Rose MacKay on June 13 1964 at St Anne's RC Church in Whitevale Street just off Duke Street and not very far from Celtic Park. It would be a very successful marriage with three children – Paul born in 1967, Kieran in 1971 and Claire in 1972. They now have 8 grandchildren. Their reception was in Rutherglen, and they then went off on honeymoon to the Channel Islands. By an amazing coincidence, when they were there, they met Bobby and Kathleen Murdoch who had been married the week before!

Bobby and Kathleen became great friends of the Gallaghers, - Bobby and Mary were great swimmers, while Charlie and Kathleen were less so - and indeed the men had so much in common. Both were supremely talented, both loved Celtic, but neither were getting a fair deal at the club. Yet their moments of glory were not far away.

Back home in Glasgow, the Gallaghers settled in Wellshot Road to the east of Celtic Park. They lived happily in this flat, blissfully unaware (until later) that a previous inhabitant had committed suicide there! Mary would become in time, a very successful Estate Agent. On the footballing front, Hope sprang eternal yet again, and the 1964/65 season actually began quite well for the team and outstandingly well for Gallagher. Admittedly the opening game against Partick Thistle was a dreadful 0-0 draw, but after that, the team rallied and, playing some bright attractive football, reached the quarter finals of the Scottish League Cup for the first time since season 1958/59. Gallagher was well to the fore in all this and now seemed to be the permanent inside left at the expense of John Divers. The League Cup section was by no means an easy one of Partick Thistle, Kilmarnock and Hearts but Celtic emerged triumphant.

Gallagher was the driving force behind all this. In the game against Kilmarnock, a 4-1 victory at Celtic Park, for example, he broke down the stubborn Killie defence by his ability to release Jimmy Johnstone and Steve Chalmers on numerous occasions, and he even headed two goals himself. (He also missed a penalty, but no-one blamed him for that in the context of the fine 4-1 win). The Sunday Post sings his praises "Two goal Gallagher was the outstanding forward afield. He collected full marks for opportunism, position play and behind-the-full-back passes that were a delight…"

He was hugely instrumental in a 5-1 victory in a game against Partick

Thsitle at Firhill where Celtic were described as "sizzling". Charlie scored a pile-driver which The Evening Times labelled "unsaveable", and Jack Harkness of The Sunday Post describes it thus. "He (Gallagher) took the ball on the drop and it had high in the net before anyone knew anything about it". Against Hearts at Parkhead, in the game which saw Celtic qualify, he scored twice in the 6-1 rout of the Tynecastle men, one of them a brilliant piece of inter-passing with Stevie Chalmers followed by a dash for goal then another "unsaveable" shot.

This particular goal triggered off a pitch invasion by enthusiastic but misguided youngsters whom James Sanderson in the Scottish Daily Mail describes as "frenzied". He goes on to say "They rushed on to the field past a cordon of policemen as Gallagher hit one of the finest goals seen at Parkhead for years. Chalmers and Gallagher combined in a move reminiscent of the twin-spearhead attack by the great di Stefano and Puskas …a move that saw Gallagher run 40 yards, beat four men and slam the ball past Hearts goalkeeper Cruickshanks. I have seen many goals all over the world but this one ranks with the best".

Hearts goal that night was scored by Willie Wallace. He was also involved that night in an incident with Gallagher. Willie, of course, was not without his aggressive side when he later joined Celtic, and on this occasion, Charlie claims that he was on the wrong end of Wallace's boot. Not only that, but words "papist" and "fenian" were used. Several years later when Wallace joined Celtic, Charlie, playfully, raised the subject with him. Wallace said that he was told by his Manager to do and say such things on the grounds that it might upset and unsettle the Celtic players. If Tommy Walker (Hearts Manager) did say that, it was an astonishingly unsuccessful piece of advice!

The trigger to this Celtic form which had all the scribes using words like "brilliant" and "phenomenal" seemed to be a bizarre and, in the end, embarrassing attempt to sign Alfredo di Stefano from Real Madrid! It was never likely to happen, but it did provide interesting headlines in the newspapers and it sent out the message that Celtic did, apparently, mean business. It was also, of course, a threat to the position of some players, but the players responded brilliantly, Gallagher in particular relishing in being given a steady place at inside left in the team. His "play anywhere" role now seemed to be in the past.

There was a down side to all this, and it tended to centre on Kilmarnock. In the first game at Parkhead, Gallagher "picked up a knock to his ankle" (as the papers tactfully put it – it was more like a deliberate attempt to crock him) causing him to miss the League game at Motherwell, but that was nothing compared to the game at Rugby Park. The section was over by that time, but Killie were out for revenge. McNeill and Murdoch were carried off, and at one point the referee called the Killie captain and Celtic's acting captain Jim Kennedy together, and told them that he was considering the extreme step of abandoning the game if everyone did not settle down. The game duly finished, Kilmarnock won 2-0, but of course Celtic had won the section in any case.

This meant that Celtic would have to face their first big game of the season against Rangers on September 5 without McNeill and Murdoch. John Clark was also missing, and Celtic had to throw together a side by bringing in John Cushley, Jim Brogan and playing John Divers at inside right while Charlie Gallagher was at inside left. In some ways this was the acid test for Celtic, for five defeats last season meant that there was a credibility problem as far as Rangers were concerned. All the good work so far this season would count for very little if Celtic could not beat Rangers. But how well did Gallagher and Celtic rise to the test!

The game was played in incessant, Biblical rain, but it was Celtic's finest performance against Rangers since the 7-1. Yet in the early stages with Celtic attacking the goal at the Rangers end of the ground, it looked as if the fates were once again conspiring against us. John Hughes ran the length of the Rangers half to score a brilliant goal which had the Celtic End in raptures until referee Hugh Phillips called him back for some obscure infringement on the half way line. Then Celtic were awarded a penalty kick when Jimmy Johnstone was brought down.

Up stepped Charlie Gallagher to take it, knowing that the rest of Celtic's season possibly depended on it. Were Celtic once again to wilt against Rangers when they had the game for the winning? Charlie looked confident as goalkeeper Billy Ritchie crouched low ready to dive. In the event Ritchie guessed correctly and dived to his right but was nowhere near the ball. But to the chagrin of the distant Celtic End and the soaked inhabitants of the Jungle, the ball hit the post and bounced out of play on the main stand side of the ground.

This was heart breaking stuff but it was to the eternal credit of Gallagher and his team mates that Celtic rallied, shook off their disappointment and ran out 3-1 winners with Chalmers and Hughes scoring the goals, as the Celtic End went delirious with joy. In the second half, Celtic were well on top and Gallagher and Divers sprayed passes at will to Jimmy Johnstone and John Hughes. Rangers scored a late consolation goal, but it was great to see men like Willie Henderson and Jim Baxter having to realise that there was now a team that could stand up to them. It was even better to see the Rangers End crumbling like a cake as the second half wore on. The key thing about this performance was that Celtic overcame early disasters and came back to win. This required character. It also required good football players, and this Celtic now at last seemed to have grasped with the deployment of Charlie Gallagher.

Much was the talk of a League and Cup double now at Celtic Park, but such talk was sadly premature. The danger signs were up when the team lost 0-2 to East Fife at Bayview in the League Cup quarter final first leg. Fortunately, that game was just a first leg and the damage was more than adequately repaired at Celtic Park, but there were also a couple of dismal draws against Clyde and Dundee United followed by a 4-2 defeat by Hearts at Tynecastle.

With the benefit of hindsight, it is easy to spot the reason. It was lack of leadership. One of the most difficult tasks that a Manager has is to deal with success. He must prevent heads from getting too big, and to keep the feet firmly on the floor. The win over Rangers should have been a springboard for success. Sadly it wasn't and that was because of the lack of an effective Manager. Jock Stein would have made a huge difference, but he was still with Hibs.

In addition, there was a loss of leadership on the field in Billy McNeill who would be out of action until the middle of November. John Cushley, his deputy, was adequate but he lacked the inspirational ability of McNeill, and the team was allowed to flounder. Yet it was not all bad news either, for the team did not suddenly become a bad team, and progress was made in the Inter Cities Fairs Cup against a tough Portuguese side called Leixoes, and also on September 29 Gallagher scored the crucial goal which put Celtic into the Scottish League Cup final.

He had just recovered from a stomach bug, picked up probably in Portugal in the 1-1 draw the previous week and which had caused him to miss the 4-2 defeat at Tynecastle. It was a good feeling for the club to have reached the Scottish League Cup final for the first time since the 7-1 game. They had defeated Morton 2-0 at Ibrox with Gallagher, in spite of being badly fouled in the first half by ex-Celt Eric Smith, scoring the second goal late in the game with an "unsaveable" shot after it had begun to seem as if the Greenock men were beginning to make a comeback. The opponents on October 24 1964 were to be Rangers who had just pipped the luckless Dundee United for a place. There was thus to be a new test for Celtic. Having beaten Rangers at Parkhead in the rain in September, could they now consolidate and win something tangible? Or was the old Celtic defeatist attitude and inferiority complex going to kick in once again?

But bad luck struck Celtic when Leixoes came to Celtic Park for the second leg. The first leg on September 23 had already seen Celtic in the wars (some players came back complaining that they had been suffering from mosquito bites, and Gallagher and Clark claimed they had bite marks inflicted on them by Leixoes players!) and of course Steve Chalmers and Ian Young were sent off, for reasons obvious only to the French referee. Young's ordering off was for retaliation, while Chalmers' "offence" remains a mystery. The mild-mannered Jimmy McGrory described it all as a "damned disgrace" while Bob Kelly said that he would pay for the French referee to come to Scotland to explain his decisions!

All this was bad enough and highlighted the problems of travelling to Europe in those days to face brutal teams and incompetent referees, but the second leg at Parkhead on October 7 was a great deal worse, certainly for Gallagher when he was taken off with a bad injury to his leg. Whether it was a deliberate attempt to injure him or simply a mistimed tackle, no-one knows but one inclines to the former. It certainly would have been in tune with the rest of the game, made notorious by the repeated manhandling of the English referee by the Portuguese after a couple of penalties were awarded to Celtic. Ten man Celtic won 3-0, but it was an empty victory over a side with little idea of how to play football. The English referee, Ernie Crawford from Doncaster, might have sent some of the Portuguese players off, but he was at least competent enough to prevent mayhem from taking over completely.

Gallagher's injury was a bad blow to both him and Celtic, for it effectively prevented him playing in the Scottish League Cup final. By October 24, the day of the final, he was actually fit, but he was not quite MATCH fit and in a narrow decision, Jimmy McGrory and Sean Fallon (or was it Bob Kelly?) gave Divers the nod, rather than Gallagher. It would have to be admitted that Divers had played well in the intervening three games against Aberdeen at Pittodrie, and against Morton and St Mirren at home, scoring in both home games. Indeed, Celtic seemed to have recovered from their bad spell, and several newspapers had tipped Celtic to win the League Cup.

Some 9 days earlier in the British General Election, Harold Wilson's Labour Government had been returned after 13 years of Conservative rule. The parallels were strikingly obvious. Celtic too had been in the doldrums for too long. Was their run of misfortune about to come to an end as well?

Gallagher was included in the 13 to be taken to Hampden. It must have been after 2.00 pm (the kick-off was 3.00 pm) when he and Bobby Lennox were given the heart breaking news that the forward line was to be Johnstone, Murdoch, Chalmers, Divers and Hughes. It was disappointing, for Cup finals do not come around very often, but he was able to see the reason why he was not chosen. Had he passed a fitness test and played in last week's game against St Mirren, he would have been chosen, but in the circumstances, a League Cup final against Rangers was hardly the place to take a chance on a man who had been out for three games and was not yet guaranteed to be totally fit.

And yet Alec Young in the Scottish Daily Mail asks the question whether Divers was actually match fit. Divers was a languid looking player and often gave the impression of not being totally active. There were medical reasons for this in John's case, and he was certainly always on the slow side. It was in truth a difficult and cruel decision for the Celtic management team to have to take, and it was cruel for Gallagher who had done so much to get Celtic to the League Cup final. Nevertheless, he accepted the decision philosophically and phlegmatically.

Charlie thus had to take his seat in the stand (there were no substitutes in 1964, of course, otherwise things might have been different) to watch yet another of Celtic's horror stories. Neutral sources and history books say that this was one of the better League Cup finals in the standard of play by both sides, but Celtic fans look back on it with nothing other than unhappiness. Celtic started off playing towards their own expectant supporters (who probably outnumbered those of Rangers) at the King's Park End of the ground. They played well, but missed several chances – one by Jimmy Johnstone in particular, another by Bobby Murdoch and a stonewall penalty claim was turned down by referee Hugh Phillips when Jimmy Johnstone was blatantly brought down by Davie Provan.

Celtic were clearly the better team but the self-destruct button had already been pressed when Jim Forrest scored two goals in quick succession, and the heads dropped. Chalmers claimed that he had the ball over the line, but photographic evidence did not support that contention, and Rangers began to take control. It was at this point that a man beside me on the King's Part terracing made the perceptive point "This is whaur ye miss Charlie Gallagher. He can read a game. He can control things. He can slow it down and look for someone to pass to".

Yet Celtic gave themselves a lifeline late in the game through Jimmy Johnstone, Hard though they tried however, an equalizer did not come, much as it would have been deserved in the opinion of all neutrals. As the full time whistle came, depression settled on the Celtic End, and it would be a long time before any of us felt better. The win in September in the Parkhead rain had been a flash in the pan, if one could use such a metaphor about that weather! Gallagher, though absolved from any blame in the League Cup final, was as shattered as everyone – but there was worse to come.

Celtic now hit the freefall button, as often happens in the wake of a defeat by Rangers. Gallagher was brought back for the trip to Kilmarnock on the Wednesday night, but he must have wished that he wasn't, for the team, with a collective death wish about them, collapsed pitifully and lost 5-2. Even that distressing score line gave a better impression of the game than was justified, for Celtic's two goals came late in the game after they had been almost totally outplayed. Frankly, this was a Celtic team which lacked any sense of direction, purpose or even heart. Gallagher scored the second of the two goals but by that time, there were hardly enough Celtic fans left to raise a cheer, most of them having departed to the pub or now sitting disconsolately in their buses waiting the trip back home. Kilmarnock would, of course, go on to win the League that year and it was an excellent example of what they could do when they cut out the rough stuff, but for Celtic, it was an abysmal performance.

The next game on Hallowe'en was a victory but hardly a convincing one. Before a crowd of less than 10,000 at a desolate Parkhead, Celtic beat bottom club Airdrie 2-1. Gallagher was injured in the first half and had to be played on the left wing where his value was limited. Steve Chalmers scored two goals, but when Airdrie pulled one back, it was only some good saves from goalkeeper John Fallon that kept the Lanarkshire men from earning a draw. The silence as the crowd drifted away was quite eerie. Normally there was some sort of cheering or animation after a win, but not today. The feeling was that Celtic were definitely on the slide. Words like "finished" were again being used – and it was still October!

Gallagher's injury meant that he missed the next three games. It was no accident that without his craft, the three games were lost, a 0-3 defeat to an incredulous St Johnstone at Muirton, a 0-2 defeat to Dundee at home on a day of tremendous rain and thunderstorms, and then a 1-3 defeat in Barcelona on a game where the team at least were not disgraced and in which the defence was tightened by the return of Billy McNeill. Veteran Ronnie Simpson also came in for his Celtic debut – against Barcelona!

Charlie returned for the game against Falkirk at Parkhead on November 21, and on this occasion the team played a lot better. They got off to the best possible start when Hugh Maxwell, a new signing from Falkirk, (ironically enough), scored within the first minute against his old team mates, but this was in any case a far more settled performance with Bobby Murdoch at right half (which many supporters thought was his best position) and Charlie Gallagher at inside right. John Hughes scored another two goals, and Celtic were deserved 3-0 winners and got a deserved round of applause from the poor crowd of 15,000.

Another 3-0 win followed this time at Cathkin Park, home of Third Lanark. No-one realised it at the time but this would be Celtic's last ever visit to the home of the grand old Glasgow club. They would be relegated in 1965 and would fold after two awful seasons in the Second Division. Already they were clearly struggling with their stadium (once the venue for Scotland Internationals) visibly falling apart and rumours abounding about problems at the bank on payday. On this damp Glasgow day, Celtic simply took them apart with Gallagher playing well, laying off passes for the other forwards and earning plaudits from various journalists.

This mini-revival even gave some of us hope that we might overturn the deficit against Barcelona on the Wednesday December 2. That proved to be a little over-optimistic but 43,000 turned up at Parkhead to see a tolerably respectable 0-0 draw. The next game against Hibs at Parkhead was fogged off, but the week after that Celtic went to Firhill and in a good game of football won 4-2 against Partick Thistle. Charlie was deployed at outside left that day – such was the Celtic penchant for chopping and changing – but he excelled there as well, scoring a brilliant goal from 40 yards which caught everyone by surprise to equalise for Celtic, and having real bad luck with several other efforts. The crowd was a small one on a cold December day but the old cliché of "Firhill for thrills" certainly applied that day.

The odd thing was that in spite of Celtic's appalling form in September and November, they were not considered to be totally out of the League race. Rangers were also showing some dreadful and inconsistent form, and there were about seven teams "in the mix" – both Edinburgh teams, Dunfermline, Kilmarnock and Dundee as well as Celtic and Rangers. In such circumstances with all teams beating each other, no one team emerged as clear leaders or likely winners. The common perception however was that Rangers would turn it on in the spring and the other teams would continue to cut each other's throats or generally "blow up", as often happened with provincial teams. That particular prediction would prove to be wide of the mark, and it would be a genuinely very exciting League race that year, involving neither Celtic nor Rangers!

But for Celtic the mini-revival hit the buffers when Dunfermline came to town on December 19. This was the game that really got the Press using words like "crisis" in the context of Celtic Park and highlighted the fact that the club really were in a mess, and that changes really had to come.

The game against the Pars was actually a good game and Celtic could, in other circumstances, have considered themselves unlucky, but the paltry crowd who were lighting bonfires on the terracings to keep themselves warm, were less charitable. They used the abundant litter that permeated the ground before the police stopped them even doing that! On the park, Celtic were simply not getting the breaks.

For one thing, Tommy Gemmell, an increasingly influential if occasionally still accident prone player, was injured in the first half and had to play on the left wing. For another, Dunfermline were a good side and able to fight for their 2-1 victory with a late goal from Alex Ferguson. Celtic's goal came just before half-time when Gallagher scored with a low header from a Johnstone cross, deservedly praised in the Press. But the atmosphere at the end was sour and now even more were heard the "we're no comin' back" cries of the disgruntled. The fact that it was midwinter, cold and bleak made life all the more depressing.

For some reason, either injury or another odd selection decision, Gallagher missed the Boxing Day game at Celtic Park against Motherwell – a competent enough 2-0 win with John Hughes playing in sandshoes and scoring two goals – but he returned for the first Celtic horror show of early 1965. The New Year's Day game at Ibrox saw Jimmy Johnstone sent off before half-time and Bobby Murdoch missed a late penalty which would have given 10-man Celtic a deserved draw, then the predictable happened when Clyde came to Parkhead on January 2 – a Celtic team, still thinking of yesterday's disaster, could only draw amidst widespread booing and general frustration from the low crowd. The pitch was hard, and Charlie seldom thrived in such conditions. The Scottish Daily Express is particularly severe on him when it says "Gallagher couldn't put a foot right on the slippery surface and couldn't control the ball properly". Sadly, this comprehensive damnation was echoed by the opinions of most supporters who were now openly using yet again, the word "finished" to describe Celtic. Indeed, the current regime had not long to go. They were "finished".

More pain was inflicted by Dundee United at Tannadice on January 9 before a small but defiant travelling support who were determined, like some people on the Titanic, to go down with the team while others had fled. But then in the following midweek, something significant happened. Bertie Auld was brought back from Birmingham. Bertie of course should never have been allowed to go in the first place in 1961, and the fact the Chairman Bob Kelly who did not like Bertie nor his attitude agreed to this, might have alerted us to the thought that someone else was behind all this.

Bertie made his return in a game against Hearts on January 16. It was another day of grim Glasgow rain, and although the team fought with a certain amount of determination, they went down 1-2 to a good Hearts team who were going well in the Scottish League. Gallagher had a few good passes, but newcomer Bertie Auld looked out of place on the left wing and never really contributed. The attendance of 21,000 looked respectable but it was misleading for it was probably the only occasion in history when the Hearts supporters outnumbered the Celtic ones at Parkhead. They even came into the Jungle (for there was loads of room!) trying to find some shelter from the dreadful January rain. Probably they did not realise that the Jungle had holes in the roof, but in any case it was better than nothing!

Charlie was not adjudged to have played well in all this – and indeed he disappeared from the first team after the defeat by Hearts - but neither did anyone else perform in what must have been an appalling atmosphere to play football with little in the way of off the field leadership. Training arrangements continued to be poor and team selections were erratic, quixotic and unpredictable. Some players, notably McNeill and Murdoch, were beginning to talk about moves to England or even emigration to Australia. Charlie himself wondered about moving for the appearance of Bertie Auld might also have been considered to be a threat to his position. But he was not to know (although there were plenty of rumours) that dealings had been going on behind the scenes about changes in management. He did know however that he was now out of the team and would remain so for some considerable time. Yet once again he bit the bullet and did his best for the Reserves.

By the time that he did come back into the first team, things had changed, and changed utterly as WB Yeats said about the Easter Rising of 1916. Indeed, a "terrible beauty" was about to be born.

CHAPTER SIX
HAMPDEN GLORY

Jock Stein apparently said soon after he took over at Celtic Park in March 1965 that he wanted to rid himself of Jimmy Johnstone, John Hughes and Charlie Gallagher. Whether he actually said this or not has never been proved, and it may just be a "story". He certainly never said it in public, and subsequent events would indicate that if he did want to get rid of those three, he certainly did not do so immediately. Indeed Charlie Gallagher was still there five years later, John Hughes a year after that and Jimmy Johnstone lasted until 1975! Nevertheless, any change of Manager can be a threatening experience for a player, especially when they had met before as, of course, had been the case in the late 1950s when Charlie was a young player at Celtic Park and Jock Stein was the Youth Coach. They remembered each other, and not necessarily with any great affection.

In the case of Jimmy Johnstone, Stein's reputed statement does not square with the story of how when he was still Manager of Hibs, and met Jimmy in the toilet after a reserve game in which Jimmy had been playing. Stein said to Jimmy "What are you doing here? You're far too good a player to be playing in the reserves". Clearly he saw some potential there. John Hughes and Jock Stein certainly did not get on (although this may have been more true of the later years rather than the earlier ones) and Yogi has not been slow to share his feelings with the world about Stein, and Gallagher has similar reservations about him, while at the same time admiring his managerial ability and tactical nous, and also agreeing that without Stein, things like the European Cup and the nine League Championships in a row would have remained fantasies.

The news of Stein's appointment was released on Sunday January 31 1965, but rumours had been going round for some time. As if sensing something was happening, Celtic, without Gallagher but with John Hughes playing in sandshoes and scoring 5 goals, beat Aberdeen 8-0 on Saturday January 30 (the day of the funeral of Sir Winston Churchill in London) and the Sunday papers were full of good news of the great victory over the Dons but also hints of big changes at Parkhead. Rodger Baillie of The Sunday Mirror went so far as to say "An old Celtic favourite is involved". We were able from that to put 2 and 2 together and come up with Jock Stein, before the official announcement was made that very Sunday.

Hibs would not let Stein go until March 8, insisting that he serve his notice. All this time, Gallagher was out of the team while the team with a left wing pairing of Lennox and Auld made a partial recovery in February from all the disasters suffered in January and before the New Year. Crucially Celtic stayed in the Scottish Cup, beating St Mirren 3-0, Queen's Park 1-0 and Kilmarnock 3-2. The Kilmarnock game on March 6 was Jimmy McGrory's last game in charge and also the last game that Celtic would ever play in their change strip of white with green sleeves. It was also a fine game of football and put Celtic into the semi-final of the Scottish Cup. But all this time, Gallagher was in the reserves and he must have wondered just what the future had in store for him once the new Manager arrived.

The decision to appoint Stein was nothing short of revolutionary. It was an admission, at long last, that Celtic had been on the wrong track, and that someone with a footballing brain was necessary. He also of course knew the club inside, having been there as a player and as a coach in the fairly recent past. Some newspapers decided to mention his religion. Possibly a few on the lunatic fringe of the support may have thought that it was significant, but the bulk of the huge, dormant, latent and increasingly desperate support scoffed at that being in any way important. One wonders however whether it was ever an issue at Board level.

But the main revolutionary aspect of all this was that Jock, and only Jock, would have total say about team matters – selection, tactics, team formation – and everything else. The days of the haphazard, chaotic, whimsical selection an hour before kick-off had gone. There would now be a definite selection policy – things has been so weird before that the word "policy" could not have been used. Jock would occasionally, out of deference to the wishes of his Chairman, drop a player for disciplinary reasons, perhaps, but that happened very seldom, and in the important decisions, for example, the one involving Bobby Murdoch, Jock would make the call.

In a sense, it was a return to the situation when Willie Maley was in charge. Maley was the Manager, an employee of the Board, who, theoretically, picked the team every week. In fact, such was Maley's footballing brain, that he was given virtually carte blanche to do what he wanted, enjoying a good relationship with the Board and being very tactful in his decisions. This system had made Celtic pre-eminent in the great days before World War 1, and this was now a parallel situation of a brilliant tactical Manager, a supportive Board and a good relationship existing between them. In both cases, the "good relationship" would have its wobbles towards the end, but in both cases, Celtic would become the best team in the world.

Jimmy McGrory would stay in genteel retirement, almost, as a Public Relations Officer. Much respected and much loved, he was the ideal man to meet opposing teams, to deal with fans wanting to see the ground and to be around as the benign and totally acceptable face of Celtic. Stein insisted that the players called McGrory "Boss", while everyone else, even Rangers fans, talked about Mr McGrory. He did not have an enemy in the world, and it was often hard to imagine that this soft-spoken, charming, gentle and modest man had once scored 550 goals!

These changes at the top made Gallagher wonder, particularly as he was now out of the team. He had never been a great favourite of Stein in the past, although he felt flattered in the 1961 Scottish Cup final when Stein told Willie Cunningham to man-mark him out of the game, something that was a total success as far as Dunfermline were concerned. He must have wondered, not for the first time in his life, what the future would be under this tough, abrasive but footballing genius of an ex-miner from the wilds of Lanarkshire.

Every new Manager worth his salt will make a few changes in any case, for he will want his own men. All that Charlie could hope for was a chance to prove himself. He got it and he took it, but it was in strange circumstances. The Scottish League was now insignificant as far as Celtic were concerned, and in the month of March under Stein, Celtic played four games – a win, a draw and 2 shocking defeats, one a particularly bad one to Stein's old team Hibs on the Monday before the Scottish Cup semi-final on March 27.

But in February before the arrival of Stein in that curious interregnum where no-one really knew that was going on, Gallagher continued to play for the Reserves, and was now beginning to impress. He was not to blame for the defeat by Rangers on February 6, and then after that the Reserves began to turn it on beating St Mirren, Third Lanark and Kilmarnock, the game at Rugby Park in particular being a particularly good one for Charlie as he orchestrated the youngsters in the attack and scored twice on a 5-1 won on February 27. The omniscient Stein, although still Manager of Hibs would pay attention and notice all this. In any case Sean Fallon, his lieutenant, would have kept him informed.

The Scottish Cup represented Celtic's only realistic chance of an honour this season. Stein's last game in charge at Easter Road on March 6 had seen Hibs defeat Rangers in the quarter final on the same day that Celtic beat Kilmarnock. This was, of course, a great boost to Celtic. The semi-final draw paired Stein's two old teams, Hibs and Dunfermline, together while giving Celtic the opportunity to play a Motherwell side who, while not being the best side in the Scottish League, were no pushovers either.

Without Gallagher, there had been a shocker of a game against St Johnstone at Parkhead and the game against Hibs at Parkhead on the Monday night before the semi-final had been a particularly poor performance. Hibs, playing some sparkling football and still clearly Stein's side, had won 4-2 and the Celtic forward line of Chalmers, Murdoch, Hughes, Maxwell and Lennox had made no impact whatsoever. Nevertheless, it was still a shock on the Friday before the semi-final to discover that Charlie Gallagher was being recalled to the inside right position for his first game since the defeat to Hearts on January 16.

The reasons were complex. In the first place the defeat by Hibs highlighted the fact that the earnest Hugh Maxwell, signed from Falkirk the previous November, was little more than an honest journeyman who was a little short of Celtic class. But the main reason for Gallagher's elevation was a side effect of Stein's best ever decision, namely the pulling back of Bobby Murdoch from inside right to right half. It was this decision that did more than any other to win the European Cup in two years time. Bobby, hitherto a good enough but not outstanding inside forward became a world class right half virtually overnight.

The idea, much touted long before Stein's arrival by perceptive supporters, notably a very primitive but prescient fanzine called The Shamrock, had been tried the Saturday before at Dens Park in an entertaining 3-3 draw. It was a partial success. Murdoch had indeed played well, relishing his role as a play maker and a ball winner with the ball in front of him rather than further forward where he had to wait for the ball to be passed to him. The gap at inside right, however, on that occasion had been filled by Stevie Chalmers, but Stevie had failed to impress against Dundee in that role. Charlie had been doing well in the reserves, but nevertheless he must have been surprised and even perhaps overwhelmed to be recalled for the Scottish Cup semi-final against Motherwell at Hampden Park, a stadium which would inevitably recall for him the horrors of the 1961 Scottish Cup final, in which he lost to Jock Stein's Dunfermline. He was now to play his first game for Jock Stein in a crucial match in that very stadium!

Peter Hendry in The Evening Times broke the news on the Friday evening saying that the return of Gallagher "is a surprise, but one which many Celtic fans will welcome". He then goes on to add that "Gallagher, on his day, is one of the best of the younger school of skilful inside forwards, and it may be that this new look Celtic forward line will open the door to a Scottish Cup final appearance on April 24."

This was confident stuff but many supporters believed that Stein was still at the experimental stage, and the question was reasonably asked if a Cup semi-final was the appropriate time for an experiment involving a man who had not played first team football for over two months and who was beginning to reasonably suspect that his days at Celtic might be numbered. To a certain extent, the answer was yes, it was experimental. Stein, after all, was naturally thinking of longer term than the 1965 Scottish Cup. But supporters who had not seen green and white ribbons on a trophy for a long time were desperate for the team to lift that Scottish Cup. Would Gallagher rise to the occasion? Many supporters were happy to see him back; others wondered.

Stein himself may have wondered if he was doing the right thing. In fact there is no indication that he viewed this as a permanent move. He cannot have had much to go on other than hearsay, second hand evidence of a few reserve matches, the opinion, admittedly a respected one, of Sean Fallon and of Charlie's attitude in training which was, of course, first class. As for a Scottish Cup semi-final, Stein could only hope that he had made the right decision. There were certainly enough who told him he had made the wrong one.

Be that as it may, the team was Fallon, Young and Gemmell; Murdoch, McNeill and Clark; Johnstone, Gallagher, Hughes, Lennox and Auld. A crowd of a little over 50,000 were there on a blustery unpleasant day to see a vital game in Celtic's history. If what Stein had reportedly said about wanting to rid himself of these three players, Johnstone, Gallagher and Hughes was true, it was more than a little ironic that all three of them were in, filling the number 7, 8 and 9 spots!

Not for the first time, the wind at Hampden spoilt the game as a spectacle, but no-one could have said that Celtic played well. Gallagher was one of the better players, however, but the best man on the field was Bertie Auld. The real culprits were the normally reliable Billy McNeill and John Fallon who twice failed to stop Joe McBride (who would join Celtic a couple of months later) put Motherwell ahead. But the good thing about it from a Celtic point of view was that the team did show some character, twice coming back when the team were behind.

One man revelled in all this and it was Bertie Auld. There may have been some Stein influence in the return of Auld before Stein was officially appointed, and it was clear that the relationship between the two of them was to be a very productive one from the night of Jock's first game when Auld scored five goals against Airdrie! Now here at Hampden the longer the game went on, the more it began to look as if Celtic were mastering the elements better than Motherwell. In Celtic's last desperate push for victory, Bertie Auld, who had equalised with a penalty kick to make it 2-2, seemed to have scored a winner just at the very end of the game, but the goal was chalked off for a marginal offside decision given by referee Mr Webster who hailed from the tiny village of Throsk in Stirlingshire, although he had now moved to Falkirk.

So 2-2 it was, and Celtic's fight back and sheer hard luck in the tricky conditions did not prevent them from being widely and vitriolically criticised for a sub-standard performance. They were considered lucky to get a chance of a replay in some quarters, but Stein decided to retain Gallagher. Gallagher, for his part, felt that he had done well enough and deserved another chance. Stein made one change however and that was on the right wing where Jimmy Johnstone had failed to impress and was replaced by Steve Chalmers whose speed might serve Celtic better than Jimmy's trickery.

This indeed was the key difference, for Wednesday night was as good as Saturday was bad. Gallagher teamed up with Chalmers on the right wing a great deal better than he had done with Johnstone on Saturday, and Celtic won 3-0 with goals from Chalmers, Hughes and Lennox. Gallagher was unspectacular but efficient, winning balls in midfield, distributing to all the other forwards and on one or two occasions having a shot himself. Celtic were 1-0 up at half-time and totally dominated in the second half, and left the field to the cheers of their supporters who, most unusually, had increased in number from Saturday's 52,000 to 58,000! It was a satisfactory night for Gallagher who now began to entertain hopes of his first Scottish Cup winner's medal. The opponents, in a situation replete with irony, were to be Dunfermline Athletic who had beaten Hibs in the other semi-final. They were the opponents in 1961, and their Manager had then been Jock Stein.

In retrospect one can see clearly that the semi-final replay was Gallagher's career changing moment. It did not necessarily look that way at the time, but the way that Celtic played on that Wednesday night made quite a few journalists and certainly all the supporters purr with pleasure. Murdoch in midfield was superb, a hint at great things to come, and that fact the Gallagher was also playing well in the inside right position made Jock

Stein think that he had now possibly hit on the best combination to bring back the much coveted and desired Scottish Cup.

The fact that Charlie had played in the semi-final replay and played well did not, of course, necessarily guarantee him a place in the Cup final line up. Four fairly irrelevant Scottish League games remained to be played before Scottish Cup final day on April 24. They were irrelevant from the point of view of Celtic doing anything in the League but they were vital for Stein to decide what his best line up was to be.

On the Saturday after Celtic reached the Scottish Cup final, they were given an exultant reception by a small but animated Celtic crowd when they ran out to play the Third Lanark team who were now doomed to relegation, and eventually extinction. It would be the last time that Thirds ever appeared at Celtic Park, for even at this stage, some two years before their demise, rumours were circulating about their financial problems. The reception that Celtic got at the start was in direct contrast to what they got at the end, for the boos indicated a truly terrible performance, for although Celtic won 1-0, the only goal of the game was an own goal scored, ironically enough, by ex-Celtic captain Dunky MacKay! Stein was furious and everyone got a deserved round of the guns for letting the fans down like this.

The roasting seems to have worked, for on the Wednesday night, the performance was like chalk and cheese, and this time it was in a game that mattered, at least for the opposition. Hibs, it will be recalled had beaten Celtic 4-2 at Parkhead a couple of weeks previously without Charlie. This time at Easter Road, with Charlie in the team, Celtic thrashed them 4-0, thereby more or less killing what chance Hibs had of winning the Scottish League. Indeed, it could have been a great deal more and some newspapers would use words like "invincible" to describe Celtic's performance that night. Other sources like the Celtic Supporters Handbook for the following season merely say that they were "attuning for the Scottish Cup final".

It would of course be facile to suggest that Gallagher's presence made all the difference, but there was an element of truth in it. More likely would be the role of Bobby Murdoch at right half now, plus the basic fact that the team were beginning to understand each other. After the Parkhead game, when the players had expected Stein to go mad at them, all he had done was to say quite calmly that the way Hibs played that night was the way he wanted Celtic to play. Hibs were, of course, to all intents and purposes still his team. He did not really expect a revolution in only 16 days between the two games between Celtic and Hibs, but he wished Celtic to play the way that Hibs had. There was still a lack of consistency, but basically some of the new Celtic team were beginning to grow together and to understand each other.

It is incidentally quite interesting to reflect on what effect this result had on Hibs. Two weeks previously, they could have won a League and Cup double. Now they were more or less out of both. The League had not yet gone, but the blow to their confidence was a heavy one. They were now destined for the next few years to play good football, but to win nothing, whereas if Jock Stein had stayed with them, it might have been a different story altogether.

Maybe Stein did this deliberately to fool Willie Cunningham of Dunfermline, but Celtic changed the team for the next two games – and they were bad - 2-6 at Falkirk on a Wednesday night to allow for the Scotland v England game at Wembley on the Saturday, and then the week before the Cup final, a horrible 1-2 defeat to Partick Thistle. Perceptive supporters noticed however a propos of the Partick Thistle game in which Gallagher was not playing, that although Celtic were poor, they did not need to win that game, whereas on the other hand, on that same day, Dunfermline would still have had a chance of the Scottish League if they could beat St Johnstone – but failed to do so. They could only draw. Celtic could afford to play around with their team selection, and although a win would have been a confidence boost of sorts, everyone knew that next Saturday, and only next Saturday, was the day that mattered.

In truth, these League games did not matter, and Stein had already made up his mind about who he was to pick for the Cup Final. His only real problem was whether to play Steve Chalmers or Jimmy Johnstone on the right wing. He may have had some reservations about Charlie Gallagher and Bertie Auld playing in the same team when they were such similar players – indeed he said this publicly – but decided to stick with the two of them with Gallagher on the right and Auld on the left in a fairly traditional Scottish team formation of two inside forwards being the "fetch and carry" men who would supply the ammunition for John Hughes, and the two wingers.

He did decide on Chalmers rather than Johnstone on the right wing, possibly preferring Stevie's speed and maybe feeling that Johnstone's emotional insecurity might let him down on the big occasion. In addition he had cause for thinking that Gallagher and Chalmers was a better combination than Gallagher and Johnstone. Stein was not yet Manager of Celtic on New Year's Day 1965, but he was very aware of how Rangers had goaded Jimmy to a violent reaction and an early bath. From his own personal experience, he knew that Dunfermline had a few players who could do just that as well.

The players were told who was in the team as early as the Tuesday before the game, and although the Press and the supporters were not officially told, they were able to guess. Essentially, it was the side which had performed so well in Celtic's two good recent performances – namely against Motherwell in the Scottish Cup semi-final replay, and the defeat of Hibs at Easter Road. Sadly, it was the end of the line for men like Jim Kennedy, Hugh Maxwell and John Divers. Divers would stay around for a while yet but he had now clearly lost out to Charlie Gallagher and Bertie Auld. He had been a good player, but crucially lacked pace and often gave the impression of being none too bothered about what was going on. He also suffered from being compared unfavourably to his father, John Divers senior, who had of course played in the great Empire Exhibition Trophy win of 1938. Jim Kennedy still had a year or two left in him with Greenock Morton, whereas Hugh Maxwell, who had looked a desperate buy in November, moved on to St Johnstone.

So Fallon, Young and Gemmell; Murdoch, McNeill and Clark; Chalmers, Gallagher, Hughes, Lennox and Auld were the men charged with bringing home the silverware on what historians like to called Celtic's Day of Destiny. This was no exaggeration, for 11 long years had passed since Celtic last won the Scottish Cup in 1954, during which time there had been 4 unhappy Cup finals, 3 of which had been made worse by going to replays, and a factor in all of them had been a crazy team selection by

Mr Kelly. Mr Kelly had now however been supplanted by a man who knew his football. In fact, Mr Kelly would claim the credit for what was to come, and to a certain extent he deserves a little praise in that he knew when to step aside. He was "wise in confessing his own ignorance". What a pity he did not do so sooner!

What was not acceptable was Mr Kelly's implication that all this was part of a grand plan, whereby Stein would be, as it were, leased to Dunfermline so that he could learn the trade and return and win the European Cup with the fruits of the "Kelly Kids" policy of the late 1950s and early 1960s. This was in fact what happened, but to claim that it was all done deliberately is a gross distortion of the truth.

For those of a historical inclination, the wilderness years had allowed something terrible to happen to the Scottish Cup. This trophy, so often looked upon as Celtic's own special one – which Celtic youngster had not been told of Jimmy Quinn's hat trick in 1904, Patsy Gallacher's somersault and McGrory's equalizer in 1925, and the comeback from the dead in 1931? - had now seen Rangers overtake Celtic in times of victories. That awful night of 1963 had seen Rangers equal Celtic's total of 17, 1964 when Rangers beat Dundee took them to 18, so Celtic had to win today to level the score.

The Scottish League had similarly not been won since 1954, and if we ignore the Glasgow Cup, Celtic's last major trophy was in fact the Scottish League Cup of blessed memory – the 7-1 defeat of Rangers. Little wonder the fans kept on about "seven, seven, seven". There had been little else to be happy about. It was therefore with a thrill of anticipation but also with a dread of yet another heartbreak that Celtic supporters made their way from all over the British Isles and beyond to Hampden Park to form part of the 108,000 crowd.

The build-up throughout Scotland was intense, made all the more so by the fact that the Scottish League was to be decided that day as well. It had, in fact, been quite a thrilling campaign. Celtic had never really been in the race other than as outsiders since early December, Rangers had similarly disappeared out of contention after Jim Baxter broke his leg, and Hibs and Dunfermline both looked likely candidates until they had both blown up at exactly the wrong time. So it boiled down to the favourites Hearts and outsiders Kilmarnock. By sheer chance they were playing each other that day at Tynecastle. Under the complicated system of goal average, (not the simpler goal difference) Kilmarnock could just pip Hearts if they managed to beat the home side 2-0. It did not look likely, but then again as the late Willie Maley would often say "Only a fool would predict the result of a football match".

Perhaps Gair Henderson of The Evening Times might have done well to listen to Mr Maley, for he predicted victories for Dunfermline and Hearts! The town of Dunfermline was girding itself up for another celebration like they had experienced in 1961, and the Provost, a man with the unlikely name of John Forker, (and we can, I suppose, guess, what they called him!) and the MP Adam Hunter were all set to gain some more political credibility by being part of it. Celtic on the other hand played it low key. They had returned from Seamill Hydro on the Thursday, with all their preparations complete, and had an ordinary, routine day at Parkhead on the Friday with Stein making the bland statement that there was no point in upsetting any routine at this stage of the season.

There was even more of a special atmosphere on Cup final day in Glasgow that day as the trains and the buses rolled in. Green and white favours prevailed, rosettes were on sale at Buchanan Street Station and even some of the ladies in the cafeteria of Lewis's Polytechnic were wearing green. Dunfermline supporters too, always a decent bunch with loads of women and children and a distinct absence of aggressive young men, added to the occasion with their black and white favours and willingness to discuss the game with Celtic fans.

The Evening Citizen which came out at Saturday lunch time before the game – the much bruited and trumpeted "Cellic Soovenir Speshul" as the leather voiced street vendors called it – contained a stark warning to several players saying that changes were to come at Celtic Park, and that no player was to think himself immune from the possibility of being "moved on" even those who thought that they had been "built in with the bricks". Gallagher as one of the longest serving players at Parkhead may have been aimed at here, but the same newspaper also predicts that "even if, by some unkind quirk of fate, the Scottish Cup is not wearing green and white ribbons tonight" the future will be good for Celtic. Echoing this mood, a couple of supporters at Central Station while awaiting their train to Mount Florida or King's Park began to sing a pop song of a group called Herman's Hermits with the lyrics "Something tells me I'm into something good".

Players and supporters, however, were genuinely finding it hard to contain their excitement. Cup finals always are exciting occasions, but this particular one had more riding on it than most. Victory would mean ecstasy, defeat would plunge us yet again into the depths of depression with even less chance now of seeing our way out of it. We had a new charismatic Manager, he had chosen the best team available, we must not fail. We could not face any more of this. Already this season, there had been alarming signs of attendances dropping and Celtic supporters beginning to speak about English football, or horse racing or snooker or golf. Celtic had been dangerously near the edge in midwinter. But now on April 24 1965, glory beckoned.

The game was played on a bright, breezy spring day in front of a crowd given as 108,000 but which was probably a great deal bigger than that, given the amount of children lifted over the turnstile and the amount of young men who were able to climb over the wall. Allowing for Dunfermline supporters and neutrals (in 1965 a remarkable amount of people, genuine football fans, went to every Scottish Cup final, no matter who was playing) it would probably not be an exaggeration to state that Celtic fans made up over 80,000 of that crowd. "We'll forgive everythin, Cellic, everythin, as lang as ye just win the day" seemed to be the motto or war cry of the green and white brigade.

When the teams came out just before 3.00 pm, Charlie would have seen green and white all over the ground with the isolated pocket or two of the black and white of Dunfermline. The huge King's Park terracing was grossly over-populated by Celtic fans with overcrowding particularly bad near the top. If Gallagher had not known already just exactly what Celtic meant to so many people – and how could he not know that? - here was the proof. It was indeed Celtic's Day of Destiny.

The teams were:

Celtic: *Fallon, Young and Gemmell; Murdoch, McNeill and Clark; Chalmers, Gallagher, Hughes, Auld and Lennox.*

Dunfermline: *Herriot, W. Callaghan and Lunn; Thomson, McLean and T. Callaghan; Edwards, Smith, McLaughlin, Melrose and Sinclair*

Referee: *H Phillips, Wishaw*

Celtic started off playing towards the King's Park End – the traditional Celtic End, as distinct from the Mount Florida End where Rangers supporters congregated on Old Firm days - but it was Dunfermline who drew first blood with a well taken goal from that crusty character called Harry Melrose. But Celtic had now settled a little and were better able to cope with the swirling wind. Slowly Gallagher and Murdoch began to make inroads and round about the half hour mark, Charlie Gallagher, with his slightly hunched shoulders which made him so easily recognisable even from the top of the huge terracing picked up a ball about half way inside the Dunfermline half, took a step or two forward, beat a man, changed the ball from his right to his left and crashed a terrific shot which looked destined for the net, but seemed to rise just a fraction in the wind and smacked against the bar.

Believe it or not, the sound of the ball hitting the bar was heard in many parts of the ground in spite of the noise of 108,000 people! But the cries of chagrin from the serried ranks behind that goal changed from exasperation to expectation when it was seen that the ball did not go over the bar, or even bounce back into play but in fact rose straight UP in the air, and not only that, but Bertie Auld was rushing in to head the ball in when it came down! Celtic were level, Bertie sat in the back of the net milking the moment, but congratulations were also due to the ever modest Gallagher for his terrific piece of play. It was not exactly his first great moment but it was the first time that he played a crucial part in the changing of the course of Celtic history. It was also one of the Scottish Cup final's most remarkable goals, and would have been much more talked about, had it not been overtaken by even more momentous events.

1-1, and half-time approached. The interval would give Celtic a chance to regroup and mount an offensive in the second half. But then disaster struck when the Pars were awarded a free kick on the edge of the box. A loudspeaker announcement came just at the wrong time, distracted the Celtic defence, and the ball was passed to John McLaughlin, a man with a fine Celtic name, who beat Fallon with a fine angular drive. Minutes later, referee Hugh Phillips blew the half-time whistle and Celtic trudged off, depressed and disconsolate.

The depression on the terracing was commensurate with that in the dressing room. Celtic had been (marginally) the better team, but Dunfermline had availed themselves of the opportunities presented to them. There did of course remain 45 minutes, but it was hard not to recall an almost parallel situation in this season's League Cup final when Celtic had the better of the game, but half time had seen them pegged at 0-0. Then Rangers got the breaks in the second half. It was even worse now, for Celtic were actually behind.

What exactly Jock Stein said at half-time will never be known for, apart from anything else, it is protected by "dressing room confidentiality" and none of the players seem clearly to remember in any case! Charlie himself has no great recollection. John Hughes, no great lover of Jock Stein, described him as "remarkably laidback" with "a word in our ear" and an "arm over an individual's shoulders" with none of the "acid tongue" that he would use in later years. He probably didn't say any more than "just keep doing what you are doing and the goals will come" sort of platitudes. Indeed, the team had little to reproach themselves for. They were unlucky to be behind.

But this was a real Celtic team who knew how to fight back. Auld and Lennox combined brilliantly to level the scores just after half-time, and then a real battle began with both sides coming close, never more so than when John Fallon saved brilliantly from Alex Edwards, grabbing a ball that seemed to have gone behind him and over his head. Gradually, Celtic's midfield of Gallagher, Murdoch and Auld began to get the ascendancy, but a replay on Wednesday night now began to look more of a possibility. Indeed, many of the crowd would have welcomed that, for they would have enjoyed a relief from the tension. Most people were cynical enough in addition to suspect that the authorities and the clubs themselves would have welcomed an extra game and another big gate!

But Destiny was beckoning for Celtic and for Charlie Gallagher.

Nine minutes remained when Celtic forced a corner on the left on the Main Stand side of the field. Across trotted (newspapers always use the word "trotted" when a player takes a corner kick!) Charlie Gallagher. The move had been rehearsed and Charlie knew that McNeill would come up for the corner. This ploy was new enough, however, for it to carry the element of surprise for the well-drilled and organised Dunfermline defence. Even as he shaped to take the kick with his right foot for an inswinger, he noticed McNeill starting his run. Charlie sent over a perfect corner at exactly the right height with the right pace and the angel of Destiny, Captain Courageous of all the Boys Own yarns, Billy McNeill arrived just at the right time to propel Celtic to a decade of unprecedented glory.

High up on the East Terracing, as far away as you could get from the action without being outside the ground, your back was pummelled, people you had never seen before hugged and kissed you, your feet left the ground as people shouted "Billy McNeill! Billy McNeill! Billy McNeill!". Someone ventured to suggest it might have been Tommy Gemmell with the fair hair. "Was it f***! It was Billy McNeill! Billy McNeill!"

You simply could not make all this up. The next nine minutes were painful for all the fans as the green and white flags gradually began to wave with more and more courage and conviction. Bertie Auld was capering and wasting time making great play with the pile of policeman's coats stacked near the corner flag. Dunfermline got the ball over the half way line, and we all held our breath, but Ian Young booted the ball down the field. We tried not to think of the wilderness years which might have been coming to an end. "Just kick the baw onywhere Cellic". Fortunately, Charlie Gallagher did not obey this advice and passed the ball about sensibly to Bobby Murdoch and Bertie Auld, until referee Mr Phillips signalled full time to unleash an enormous tide of emotion. Gentle reader, you cannot imagine what it was like on that King's Park terracing with tears, hugs, embraces, singing, dancing and general madness. It really had to be experienced to be believed

Tom Campbell and Pat Woods in The Glory And The Dream, still one of the best books ever written about our club, describe the winning goal and its aftermath thus "Another corner, this time on the left, to be taken by Gallagher, hurrying over to place the ball. Across it comes, a high, floating ball and too far out for the keeper, but he has left his goal... somebody is there – McNeill... and his header rages into the net. For two seconds, Hampden's vast bowl was still, stunned by the sudden shock of decision, and then erupted into bedlam; the roar continued minute after minute and its prevailing note changed; it was not merely the burst of joy that a goal produces, rather it was a tumultuous welcome to the future and the instinctive realisation by all Celtic's support that the young men had grown up and that nothing, now nor in the years to come, would withstand their collective spirit. McNeill, the young captain, had emerged from nowhere to score the goal that history demanded. As a member of the team in the past he had delighted in the joy of victory and been despondent in the misery of defeat, but now in full maturity he stood revelling in the moment of triumph"

This is fine literary stuff, and captures the flavour of the moment, although this author cannot in all honest claim that he experienced any "instinctive realisation" that "nothing...would withstand their collective spirit". Rather he was standing at the top of the East Terracing, gripping tenaciously the post that indicated stairway 25, and praying to God to allow Mr Phillips to blow that whistle!

Charlie went out of his way to shake the hands of all the Dunfermline players. He knew how they were feeling, and there were some fine players among them, several of them Celtic supporters in their boyhood, and of course Tommy Callaghan would join Celtic in 1968 in circumstances which we shall discuss. The Scottish Cup was presented – the green and whites collecting the Scottish Cup! - and Charlie was given his medal. It was his greatest day. The team came up to show the trophy to the exultant fans on the East Terracing, quite a few of whom were unashamedly in tears, having feared that this moment would never come. A veteran supporter who had seen Scottish Cup finals since Joe Cassidy in 1923, and who had played his part in the liberation of Italy in 1943, stated quite emphatically, that he had never seen anything like this.

There was a sequel in the dressing room. Jock Stein had, apparently, said at one point that it was difficult to imagine a successful Celtic team with both Bertie Auld and Charlie Gallagher in it, because they were both the same type of player. Bertie came up to Charlie and said "Come on, put on your medal, and come and talk to him". The self-effacing Charlie would never have done this on his own, but the street wise cocky Auld had no such qualms, and he led Charlie to the smiling Stein. "Hey boss, what was that you said about us no' being able to play in the same team?" Normally such insubordination – and sheer impertinence - would have earned a suspension or even a transfer to another club, but these were special circumstances, and Stein, although temporarily discomfited, made a quick riposte and turned to beam on someone else.

The next few hours passed like a dream for Charlie Gallagher with the bus going through thousands of Celtic fans in the heartlands of the Gorbals to the Central Hotel for the celebration meal, and the bus being stopped several times by the sheer pressure of the fans. Charlie, of course, recalled the day when he had been one of the fans running to see the team with the Coronation Cup of 1953. Now he was on the bus waving in triumph to the adoring thousands. And in the front of the bus was the source of all the euphoria, the Scottish Cup, now won by Celtic for the 18th time. Seldom had it been won in such dramatic circumstances by any team, and never had it meant anything like as much to the supporters of Celtic. They had now won it 18 times. Charlie Gallagher remains so proud to have played such a significant part in this proud day of Celtic history.

The team and their wives (who were all friendly with each other) had their meal in the Central Hotel, near Central Station, and then some of them went to Charlie and Mary's new flat in Wellshot Road near Tollcross to celebrate. (Goalkeeper John Fallon didn't, though, for his wife had gone into labour and gave birth the following day!) Charlie tells a story about this occasion. They were all queuing for a fleet of taxis to take them to Charlie's house, when Charlie was approached by a couple of fans from Bishopbriggs whom he knew well. They asked if they could come to the party. The answer was a polite but firm "no", so they asked again, asking as well what the "kitty" was for the drinks. They were told £100, a large amount in 1965, and they promised they would double it if they were allowed to come. True to their word, they did just that, then spent the evening, happily dispensing drinks to the players! As drink was involved, it was a fair bet that Mr Stein was not invited!

The players watched the highlights of the game on TV. Bob Crampsey, of course, one of Charlie's old teachers at Holyrood, was very much involved in STV's coverage and praised the contribution of Charlie. This provoked cries of "teacher's pet" and "that's yer faither, Charlie" and other things about Charlie from the other players! It was believed that Crampsey, basically a Queen's Park supporter but sometimes finding it hard to hide his admiration of Celtic, never said anything bad about Charlie. It was a great night, and although the team were as yet far from world beaters, it was now abundantly clear that something big was happening for Celtic.

Supporters changed overnight. Shy, diffident, insecure youngsters suddenly began to talk about football with confidence, assurance and happiness. Gnarled old veterans who used to hold the floor talking about Patsy Gallacher and James McGrory now smiled and yielded gracefully to their sons and grandsons who sang the praises of Bertie Auld, Billy McNeill and the new Gallagher. The exile in the wilderness was over. Parkhead was Paradise once more. The Celtic people had risen.

Historians, football ones included, love to play "what if". If Celtic had not won that day, Celtic would still, under Jock Stein, have gained some sort of success, one feels, in Scotland at least. He was too good a Manager and the players were all sufficiently good that the perpetual continuation of the wilderness years a la Newcastle United would probably not have happened, although one can never say with certainty. But it is certainly difficult to imagine Celtic winning the European Cup in two years' time. It was just as well that Charlie found Billy's head that afternoon then, wasn't it?

And there was even more to come in 1965. In the midst of all this, everyone seemed to have forgotten about the Glasgow Cup, won by Celtic in 1962 and 1964 and how nice it would be if Celtic could win it again so that the Scottish Cup could have some company in the Parkhead Boardroom! Rangers were coming to Parkhead on the night of Friday April 30.

First Celtic had to play their last irrelevant League fixture. Ironically enough it was at Dunfermline. It might not have been irrelevant for the Pars had they not failed to win their second last game against St Johnstone. As it was, Kilmarnock having won the Scottish League with their epic 2-0 win at Tynecastle on Saturday – Kilmarnock's greatest ever day, perhaps – the game had little at stake. True to Celtic's habit this season of Stein not really bothering with fixtures that did not matter, he gave Gallagher, Young, Auld and Lennox a rest and the team went down 5-1, thus giving the Fifers a little feeling of revenge for what must have been a somewhat devastating experience for them on Saturday. Dunfermline's supporters tend to be a reasonable lot, and we were magnanimous enough to feel a little sorry for them. But Dunfermline's glory days were not yet over.

That was on Wednesday April 28. Two days later at Celtic Park, a 41,000 crowd turned up to see the Old Firm Glasgow Cup tie. It was a more orthodox Celtic side, but frankly it was a dreadful performance with Rangers playing virtually all of the second half with only 9 men thanks to injuries and even at that with outfielder Davie Provan in the Rangers goal. Hardly surprisingly Celtic won, but only 2-1 and even the most ardent of Celtic fans was able to admit that on the night the glory really belonged to the gallant Rangers. Celtic fans were now sufficiently secure in themselves to admit that!

This game, of no lasting importance if you are not interested in the Glasgow Cup, showed however the fundamental shift that was now going on in Scottish football. For the past decade, Rangers had had all the luck, winning games that they should have lost, getting the benefit of dodgy refereeing decisions and seeing Celtic, in particular, freeze whenever they saw them. This had now all changed, and such are the ways of the world, it would now be Celtic that would get the breaks more often than not. No-one can ever explain all this, but there is certainly in football a thing called momentum which ensures that when you start winning games, you keep on winning them. Celtic were now beginning to get lucky – and all because of that great game in the Scottish Cup final. For Rangers, the whirligigs of time had indeed brought their revenge. Nemesis had appeared.

As far as Celtic were concerned, however, there was nothing lucky about the Glasgow Cup semi-final in which Celtic beat Clyde 3-0 with first half goals. Clyde made a fight of things in the second half, but by then it was all too late. 12,500 spectators enjoyed this game on Monday May 3, and on Tuesday May 11, Celtic finished off a great season by beating Queen's Park 5-0 at Hampden to lift the beautiful Glasgow Cup. Gallagher played well that night, and the season thus finished on a high note with a second winner's medal for 1965. 17,851 saw Lennox score twice, then Chalmers, Auld and Murdoch in what was really a rather one-sided game. The story went that the Scottish Cup sitting bedecked in green and white ribbons in the Parkhead Boardroom was so delighted to see the beautiful Glasgow Cup appear as well that she burst into song and sang "Take my hand, I'm a stranger in Paradise"! But then again, so were we all!

Then Celtic played a friendly in Austria against Vienna at the end of May. Already without some players who were with the Scotland squad (as indeed was Jock Stein who was temporary Manager of Scotland), Gallagher was also not chosen for the Austrian game, and Celtic lost 0-1. But it was a meaningless occasion, more of a holiday as a reward for winning the Scottish Cup rather than anything else.

Thus ended the remarkable season of 1964/65. British military historians talk about the Battle of El Alamein in 1942 in the Second World War in terms of "before El Alamein we never had a victory; after it, we never had a defeat". Celtic fans could look upon the Dunfermline Cup final in similar terms, even though the statement would not be quite literally true. Things changed on April 24 1965. It was a "hymn for the dawn of the free" in the words of a rebel song. "Goodly news, goodly news do I bring, youth of Forth; Goodly news shall you hear Bargy Man. For the boys march at morn from the South to the North, led by Kelly, the Boy From Killan". How appropriate these words were!

It is often said that Celtic, like the race that shares their name, have extremes of joy and sorrow in large measure. This was certainly true of that season and for the newly wed Gallagher in particular who had been part of the euphoria at the start of the season, then the pain following the League Cup final disaster, the change of manager when he was out of the team, then being brought back in apparently only to allow Murdoch to play right half, but very soon claiming a place in his own right, and now he had two medals! There was a great deal to look forward to in summer 1965. Things had got better. They could get better yet, although much would depend on Gallagher's rather uncertain relationship with the prickly Jock Stein.

But in the meantime Celtic supporters everywhere thought, ate, drank, talked and slept Celtic. No doubt Charlie Gallagher did the same. The contrast with previous summers could hardly be exaggerated. In the past few summers, Celtic supporters had welcomed the summer with the fine weather and a relief from their sufferings. Now we could hardly wait for August with statements heard like "The fixtures will soon be out, and the season starts seven weeks come Saturday".

CHAPTER SEVEN

THE FRINGES OF IMMORTALITY

The new season 1965/66 simply could not come quick enough. It was a wonderful time to be alive and to be a Celtic supporter. Not only was there the Scottish Cup to play over and over in our memories, but there was also the promise of things to come under this dynamic new Manager whose declared aim was to make Celtic "the best in Britain". Even that would turn out to be an understatement! There was an early sign of his intent, for in early June Stein bought Joe McBride from Motherwell, a man of many clubs but Celtic-daft and now where he wanted to be.

The media, often accused in the past (and not entirely without cause) of being pro-Rangers now swung round. They were manipulated brilliantly by Jock Stein who organised Open Days for the Press, fed them coffee and biscuits, gave them stories to fill the pages in the quiet month of July and allowed them to photograph the players training, which was made far more enjoyable and rewarding than ever before for the players themselves who clearly relished the spotlight – even naturally shy men like Charlie Gallagher.

Training, instead of the turgid repetitive lapping of the track became a pleasure. This had always been a bugbear of Charlie in the past, that training was simply poor. Now it was imaginative and even a little fun. It was hard work certainly but made competitive and enjoyable all under the watching eye of Jock Stein, frequently seen with his tracksuit supervising things. Neil Mochan had been appointed trainer before Stein arrived. This had been another excellent decision of Bob Kelly who had swallowed his pride to appoint Mochan, for Neil had never seemed to be a favourite in his playing days. But Neil had so much to offer. With Sean Fallon and Bob

Rooney at Celtic Park as well, things were certainly on the move.

Three pre-season games had been arranged in summer 1965 against Motherwell on the Isle of Man, against Shamrock Rovers in Dublin and against Sunderland at Roker Park. Sunderland were now replete with two men of undeniable Rangers connections. Ian McColl had "left" (or was he sacked, as he claimed?) the Scotland job and was now the Manager of the Mackems. And of course there was Jim Baxter whom Rangers had been finding a little difficult to handle of late. Baxter had not coped well with the rise of Celtic in Scotland and the consequent lessening of the spotlight on him. He had recovered from his broken leg, but would never really be the same again.

Charlie did not play in the Motherwell game – a 1-1 draw, and played only in the first half in Dublin scoring the first goal before he was taken off at half-time to give Steve Chalmers a game on this light-hearted occasion which ended up 7-0 for Celtic against mediocre opposition. Equally impressive were both Gallagher and Celtic in the 5-0 defeat of the far more competitive Sunderland at Roker Park, but the game was overshadowed by darker events.

This was the spectre of hooliganism, both in the ground and in the surrounding area including pubs and railway stations. There were several factors – the Scotland v England flashpoint, the Rangers influence on Sunderland, the addition to the Celtic ranks of a few Newcastle supporters who had developed a sudden love for the green and white, a hot day, loads of drink available – but basically the whole thing was a disgrace. As always, Celtic apologists would say that Sunderland's fans attacked first, but it always does take two to make a fight, and in the first ever edition of The Celtic View Jock Stein minced no words. This could not be allowed to go on. He would frequently say that the elimination of hooliganism was as important as success on the field. He would eventually succeed in both his objectives.

All this thuggery was a shame because Gallagher's performance on the field got nowhere near the credit and the praise that it deserved. Playing for the injured Bertie Auld, Charlie distributed passes to all and sundry, clearly outclassing Jim Baxter who would never reach any great heights for Sunderland, riding tackles, now and again earning a reluctant ripple of applause from Sunderland season ticket holders and not being afraid to have a shot himself as Celtic simply tore the home side apart. This area, albeit football mad, had been deprived of good football for some time – and indeed still is – but Gallagher's performance that day was one of the best they had seen since the days of Raich Carter or Len Shackleton. Jim Baxter on the other hand failed to perform, and had the indignity of having an orange thrown at him!

And then Celtic returned to Scotland for the real stuff. They were in a difficult League Cup section of Motherwell and the two Dundee teams. Celtic had, we recall, lost last year's League Cup final and indeed the Scottish League Cup was Celtic's least favourite tournament with only two wins in the 19 years of its existence. Amazingly, East Fife had win the trophy on three occasions, before Celtic even appeared in a final! Mind you, one Scottish League Cup won was the immortal 7-1 in October 1957 and the other was the year before that in 1956. But as Celtic were traditional poor starters to the season, the League Cup had been littered with many failures.

But April 1965 had changed a lot of things, not least that Celtic now had a winning mentality. They now expected to win tournaments. Certainly the crowd for the first competitive game of the season – at Tannadice Park on August 14 contained the largest contingent of Celtic supporters seen for many years in the city of Dundee. Gallagher of course had bitter memories of this ground where he had scored the "goal that never was" in the League Cup of 1962. On this occasion, the weather was beautiful and the crowd was colourful and cheerful. They received, however, a severe blow to their dreams when they went down 1-2 to Dundee United, one of the Dundee United goals being scored by ex-Celt and friend of Charlie Gallagher, Bobby Carroll.

One might have been forgiven for thinking that the world had come to an end, such was the talk about balloons bursting and Celtic having built up their support only to shatter their dreams with a defeat. Seeing the result in some sort of perspective did not seem to come into it. For one thing, it was away from home at a difficult venue. For another Celtic were without John Hughes and Joe McBride. In addition, Dundee

United's winning goal was scored when Bertie Auld was off injured receiving attention for overstretching himself scoring Celtic's equalizer. But the main thing was that it was only the first game of the season! At least another fifty games remained!

Jock Stein was not immune to the hysteria. Gallagher had not played well at Tannadice, but it was surely a knee-jerk reaction to drop him and replace him by John Divers, a man who had been in danger of being transferred, ironically enough, to Dundee United that summer. To be fair to Jock, this move seemed to work, for Divers scored the only goal of the game in a curiously lacklustre performance against Motherwell.

That at least was a win, but when the team went down to Dundee at Parkhead on the Saturday, things began to look bad for Celtic. Charlie was still out of the first team, playing for the reserves at Dens Park that day and scoring a brilliant goal. But Celtic had now lost two League Cup sectional games, and really could not afford any further reverses if they were to qualify for the quarter finals. The League Cup bogey seemed about to strike again.

But before that could be addressed, there was the opening League game to be played. The fixtures in those days saw everyone playing once against all the three teams in their League Cup section, and then before they started the reverse round of fixtures, there would be a League game played on the Wednesday night, the first League game of the season. By sheer chance, the fixture list had thrown up another game at Tannadice Park. No-one could blame computers in 1965 – it was simply stupid, as it appeared. Far better surely to have a game against someone not in the same League Cup section?

Well, maybe not, as far as Celtic were concerned. This game would turn out to be a highly significant game in the history of the club for it was the first game of Celtic's nine League Championships in a row. It was also a game in which Jock made the right decision, even though it appeared to be a whimsical one at the last possible moment, of dropping Jimmy Johnstone and Bertie Auld and replacing them with Steve Chalmers and Charlie Gallagher. Jock was always a great believer in "horses for courses", a phrase that he used a lot in The Celtic View, and in any case it would “gee up” (Jock’s love of horse racing frequently got the better of him) the rest of the squad.

Celtic turned it on that night, winning 4-0 and Gallagher was outstanding, setting the tone of the game within the opening five minutes when he crashed a shot against the bar at the Shed end of the ground. The bar shook visibly for a long time after that, but so too did Dundee United, overwhelmed by the sheer power of this dynamic young Celtic side. John Divers, Joe McBride, Tommy Gemmell and Ian Young with a penalty got the goals while the much vaunted Orjan Persson got himself an early bath from referee Bobby Davidson for taking a wild kick at Tommy Gemmell. And Dundee United’s supporters, normally much praised for their gentlemanly encouragement of their team, dented their haloes considerably by throwing coins at Celtic goalkeeper John Fallon!

It was a token of great things to come. Charlie might have thought that he was in for a long spell in the side, but then John Hughes became available after suspension. Gallagher had been playing on the left wing (nominally, at least) at Tannadice on Wednesday night, but now found himself out of the team when Dundee United played Celtic yet again at Celtic Park on Saturday. Gallagher was not given an outing for the reserves at Tannadice on the Friday night, a game which Celtic won 4-2, because there was a chance that he might have played for the firsts on the Saturday. He was therefore idle, but enjoyed his experience of sitting in the stand watching his team mates demolish Dundee United again.

Gallagher’s role as 12th man was confirmed in the next game against Motherwell. Two League Cup sectional games remained, both of which were away and both of which Celtic simply had to win if they were to qualify. But then Joe McBride called off injured for the game at Fir Park against his old team mates at Fir Park, Motherwell, so John Hughes was put in the centre and the ever willing Gallagher took over on the left wing.

More arguments on supporters’ buses and in pubs centred on John Hughes (Yogi Bear, as he was called) than on anyone else. This had always been the case even before the arrival of Stein. He was brilliant on his day, but he was infuriatingly inconsistent. He could score great individual goals, but had some awful days as well. But at this stage he had a good relationship with and enjoyed the confidence of Jock Stein, so Jock was prepared to tinker with the forward line on occasion to suit him – Yogi could play in the centre or on the left wing, another source of argument on the terracings as to where his best place was – and Gallagher was moved around as a consequence.

A less mild mannered man than Gallagher might well have taken umbrage at all this, but he was quite happy to be in and out of the team. This was, of course, one of his strong points – that he was a good team man with no tantrums or transfer requests or causing trouble. He played at Motherwell on the Wednesday night, and played well in a good 3-2 victory, the margin of victory being a little deceptive for Motherwell scored in the last minute after Celtic had been well on top throughout. Gallagher played a part in the making of the first goal, taking a corner kick and trying to find the head of John Hughes who just missed the ball. But John had taken a couple of defenders with him and the ball came to Chalmers who slipped it to Lennox to finish the job.

All this meant that Celtic merely needed a 0-0 draw at Dens Park, Dundee on Saturday to qualify from the section after they had appeared to be dead and buried. Gallagher travelled to Dundee with the team but was once again he was the forward who had to drop out when Joe McBride reported fit enough to play in the centre allowing Hughes to be on the wing. It was a last minute decision, but Gallagher accepted things gracefully.

It was a great pity, especially for men like Gallagher that the substitute rule was not yet introduced. His versatility would have made him an ideal substitute, but Scotland, conservative as always, resisted the idea of substitutes. It had been introduced on a limited basis in England that year – one man allowed to cover for an injured man – but it would be the following year before Scotland managed to achieve even that. Things were changing though, and it was clear nonsense (and dangerous nonsense at that) to see badly injured players hobbling about lest their team went down to less than 11 men.

Thus Gallagher was a spectator and indeed supporter (he always had been that and would continue to be all his life) in the funny shaped Dens Park stand. As it turned out the three players whom he might have aspired to replace, and whom he had replaced in the past – John Divers, John Hughes and Joe McBride – were the men who scored the goals in Celtic's 3-1 victory, Celtic's best result at Dens Park for many years. John Hughes's goal, in particular, was one of his best ever in that it all happened so quickly. He beat Scotland right back Alec Hamilton on the left wing, charged across the field parallel to the goal and about 30 yards away from him, then suddenly, almost without turning, hammered home a great shot. It was one of these moments when there was a moment of stunned silence before the crowd took it all in, then Dens Park erupted at such brilliance. Celtic duly qualified after Joe McBride confirmed Celtic's victory with a late header.

Happy days, then for Celtic as summer 1965 gave way to autumn. Charlie's next first team game was at Stark's Park, Kirkcaldy in the first leg of the Scottish League Cup quarter final. It was a real thumping for the locals who were mesmerised by the sheer power of the Celtic forward line. Celtic were well served by the guile of Gallagher as they won 8-1 against a Raith Rovers team, now in the Second Division and who had seen better days.

Gallagher however did well to avoid the game at Ibrox in the Scottish League on the Saturday after. He had picked up an injury and the number 8 position reverted to John Divers. The interest in this game was tremendous with the gates at the Celtic End locked, and hundreds compelled to climb the wall! They might as well not have bothered for Rangers won 2-1 in what was a very disappointing sub-standard Celtic performance. Gallagher's injury kept him out of the return game against Raith Rovers and the 7-1 beating of Aberdeen, as the team recovered from their Ibrox disappointment. He did get a game, however, in the Cup Winners' Cup game against the quaintly named Dutch team Go Ahead Deventer and played well in the 6-0 victory in Holland.

The Dutch side were no real problem, but a far more difficult game approached on Monday October 4 against Hibs at Ibrox in the Scottish

League Cup semi-final. It was a game not without its political side however, for when Hibs objected to playing the game at Ibrox because the floodlights were not good enough and that Ibrox was on the wrong side of the city for their supporters to get there, Celtic were only too keen to join in and embarrass Rangers. Those who claimed that this was NOT a Parkhead eccentricity, in a rare piece of collusion with Hibs, designed to discredit Ibrox were naïve in the extreme! However, the Scottish League said no.

50,000 braved the rain to see one of the best ever games played between Celtic and Hibs. Hibs were in fact the better side and with the time running out, they were leading deservedly 2-1. Celtic's efforts began to flag on the sodden pitch and Gallagher, playing at inside right – Divers was now completely out of favour and Bertie Auld who might have played there was injured - was beginning to toil for the heavy ground did not lend itself to Charlie's inch perfect passes, especially in the latter stages when the pitch became all the more churned up. It was Tommy Gemmell who created the equalizer for Celtic when he managed to get the ball into the penalty box, Hibs failed to clear it properly and Bobby Lennox was on the spot to give Celtic and their drenched legions (those who had not yet gone home!) a lifeline so that they were still in the Scottish League Cup.

Extra time brought no resolution although both teams came close, and the replay date caused all sorts of problems with Scotland playing next midweek and Celtic playing their Second Leg of their European tie against Deventer in three days time. In addition, we had the repeated protest from both teams about the venue with no other desire, apparently than to annoy and embarrass Rangers. Celtic supporters joined in, writing letters to newspapers about the lack of parking and how they had to peer to see any of the game under Ibrox's "inadequate" floodlights, but the Scottish League refused to be bullied. The replay was scheduled for Ibrox yet again on Monday October 18 – only five days before the date set for the final. Rangers would be the opponents, for they had now won their semi-final against Kilmarnock. It had been played at Hampden, where both Celtic and Hibs argued their game should have been played.

Gallagher had two games to play before the replay to consolidate his place in the team. He had missed the irrelevant European game – the tie was already well won – but turned out to play against Hearts at Parkhead on October 9. Oddly, as The Celtic View pointed out, although Charlie had played many games this season for both the first XI and the reserves, this was his first home game at Parkhead. The 35,000 crowd saw just exactly what they had been missing, for he was superb that day as Celtic beat Hearts 5-2. Gallagher sprayed passes throughout, had several shots that just whistled over the bar and scored the 5th goal with a 20-yard curler that deceived Jim Cruickshanks. Hearts scored two irrelevant counters late on, but it was truly a great Celtic performance.

Next week, the team was at that bogey ground of Falkirk. This was a great game with Celtic showing all the character in the world by coming back from 2-0 down and then 3-2 down to win 4-3. It was really too fast a game for Charlie to star, but he did well enough to stay in the team for the game that really mattered at this time – the replay against Hibs.

This was a totally different game from the first one, for Gallagher was on song, the pitch was a lot drier than the first game, and Celtic won 4-0 when it could have been a lot more. Charlie would have been upset to see his old team mate John McNamee, now playing for Hibs, being sent off near the end for a piece of petulance and arguing back to referee Bobby Davidson. McBride, Hughes, Lennox and Murdoch scored the goals. Charlie played a significant part in the third goal when he sent over a lovely cross to find the head of John Hughes who in turn headed the ball on to the onrushing Lennox. The 51,000 crowd went home delighted, Celtic were in the final of the Scottish League Cup and no-one said any more about the Ibrox floodlights, which, if truth be told, were not all that bad with European teams like Real Madrid having had no complaints in the past!

Thus six months on from his first triumph in the Scottish Cup final, Charlie found himself in another Hampden Cup final The fact that it was against Rangers was an added dimension of course, but the Celtic community now began to look forward to Saturday's game with a mixture of emotions and apprehensions. The stakes were higher than ever before, far higher than any ordinary Old Firm game (if any such game could be called "ordinary") and far higher even than most League Cup finals.

At the end of the semi-final replay, the Celtic dressing room understandably was in euphoria. Stein coming along the corridor heard the laughter and sounds of triumph, so he decided that they must be taken down a peg or two. Incredible as it may seem, he slapped his own face to make it red and to simulate anger, and then tore into the team telling them that what had happened tonight would count for nothing if they did not win at Hampden on Saturday.

Kerrydale in The Celtic View paraphrased (and presumably sanitised!) what Stein said to the players. "You've done a fine job tonight, but you've not even half completed it. You showed great grit and determination against Hibs as well as much skill, but I want even more – if that is possible – in the final on Saturday. I want the Celtic eleven who play Rangers in the League Cup final to be the most determined team ever to have worn the green and white striped shirts. I want a win over Rangers – nothing less. I'm sure you want that also. So let's concentrate on Saturday".

The new Celtic's credibility was certainly at stake here. The revival of the winning of the Scottish Cup would count for a lot less if they lost this game. The Celtic death wish remained of course very real in the face of Rangers, as was witnessed when Rangers had defeated them at Ibrox only a month ago. Last year at this time, Celtic had been in the ascendancy but they had lost last year's League Cup final and then had collapsed for more or less the rest of the season destroying their League campaign as well. There were however a few differences. One was that they had now actually won a trophy; another was that they now had a Manager who was definitely not prone to believing that Rangers were some sort of supermen. And of course, a major difference as far as Gallagher was concerned was that in 1964 he was not playing in the League Cup final; in 1965 he would be.

He and Bobby Murdoch had picked up leg knocks in the Hibs semi-final, (Gallagher had to move to the left wing for a spell rather than his now favoured inside right position) but after some treatment at Celtic Park on the Tuesday morning, they were pronounced fit. Stein had no hesitation in naming the same team that had beaten Hibs in the semi, with the forward line reading Johnstone, Gallagher, McBride,

Lennox and Hughes. Glasgow now braced itself for a six figure crowd at Hampden on Saturday. Celtic had won the tournament twice, but Rangers had won it twice in the 1940s, had failed to win it at all in the 1950s, but had won four years in the last five, including of course last year against Celtic. The referee was Hugh Phillips of Wishaw, generally reckoned to be one of the better referees, even though he was none too popular at Celtic Park! Only the Stands were all-ticket – as Celtic had only reached the final on Monday, there would have scarcely been enough time to get tickets printed, distributed and sold anyway – and it was pay at the turnstiles (5 shillings = 25pence) for everyone else.

Nerves were a real problem for the players, but Jock played it well. After Sean Fallon, presumably with Stein's approval) wrote a grossly over-optimistic column in The Scottish Daily Express, little more was said, other than what had been said in The Celtic View and everything was decidedly low key. Gallagher and the others appreciated this, for although there was always pressure on someone playing for Celtic, it was not a good thing when the Manager publicly piled even more on by saying things like "must win" and "credibility at stake". Little more was said than "quietly confident". Indeed a few things were said about the League championship being even more important.

The weather was good, a gentle autumn day, and 107,608 (a record which stands to this day and only the second ever six figure crowd for a Scottish League Cup final) turned up. It was not the good, clean game – a "showpiece" as the saying went – that everyone would have liked, although it did not go to the other extreme of an "orgy of crudeness" or the "X Certificate final" that some of the press, The Sunday Post in particular described it as being. It was tough, but credit must be given to Mr Phillips for not letting things get totally out of hand.

The teams were:

Celtic: Simpson, Young and Gemmell; Murdoch, McNeill and Clark; Johnstone, Gallagher, McBride, Lennox and Hughes

Rangers: Ritchie, Johansen and Provan; Wood, McKinnon and Greig; Henderson, Willoughby, Forrest, Wilson and Johnston

Gallagher's name is seldom mentioned in Press reports. This emphatically did not necessarily mean that he did not have a good game, except in so far as no-body had a good game because of the constant stoppings for mainly petty fouls. The tone was set in the first five minutes when Ian Young brought down Willie Johnston and earned a booking. This apparently haunts Young to this day, but it was simply setting out Celtic's stall in that there was to be no more "Mr Nice Guy". Far too often in the past, Celtic had played the game like gentlemen, earning the approbation of Mr Kelly and indeed the Press and all neutrals – but had lost the game. Stein clearly thought that it was more important to win, something which Celtic fans agreed with.

The first half had gone about 15 minutes when Ron McKinnon of Rangers unaccountably and under no apparent pressure stuck up his hand and handled the ball. It was going nowhere but it was inside the box. "Penalty" said Celtic and more importantly Mr Phillips agreed. Up stepped the lumbering, occasionally temperamental figure of John Hughes. (According to his own admission, Hughes had taken the field that day praying that there would not be a penalty kick which would require his services) Behind the goal at the Celtic End, 50,000 fans held their breath, but John slotted the ball home. Celtic were now one up, and the defence which had been hesitant before suddenly gained confidence, McNeill in particular winning everything in the air.

About 10 minutes later, Celtic whose fans had often complained that they did not get enough penalties, got another one. This time there was a degree of doubt about it with Rangers protesting bitterly, but a penalty it was, and once again Yogi did the business, although Billy Ritchie got a hand to this one. Celtic thus went in at half-time 2-0 up, but Gallagher was aware that the next 45 minutes were going to be very long indeed, as he listened to Stein's talk about getting the basics right. Football in essence is a simple game, and if you pass the ball to someone in your own side, you will usually be OK.

This however was no ordinary football game. Charlie's inclination was always to get the ball, beat a man and then pass the ball. He would have loved to have been able to find someone like Jimmy Johnstone or John Hughes to inflict further damage on Rangers. But this was hurly-burly stuff and twice Gallagher was the victim of a rash tackle or what was euphemistically called a "challenge" from a Rangers midfielder. He knew better than to let them know that it hurt and continued as well as he could, making sure that he did not retaliate.

Slowly, painfully slowly the second half wore away. More and more Gallagher was being deployed as an extra defender or at least a "holding midfield" man as Rangers attacks grew ever more desperate. Sometimes only Bobby Lennox was left up in the Rangers half, although Gallagher was very aware that a goal from Celtic would effectively kill Rangers off.

Then with 8 minutes to go Rangers got a goal which even their best friends would have to describe as fortuitous. TV replays did not make it clear but it seems that when John Greig and Ian Young went up for a ball, the ball went into the net off Ian Young's face, as the distant Rangers end which had been contemplating departure now became animated for the first time in the game.

It was what was then called "kitchen sink" time as Rangers threw everything at that King's Park goal with Gallagher now back as an out and out defender, occasionally dribbling the ball out of the penalty area but more often resorting to the tried and tested expedient of howfing the ball up the park or out of play. But Celtic were lucky in that they had all the experience in the world in goal in the shape of Ronnie Simpson, already the proud possessor of two English Cup medals. Ronnie took charge of the situation, giving instructions to everyone including captain McNeill, as 50,000 behind that goal died a thousand deaths every time a blue shirt got the ball.

But full time came at last and Celtic had won the Scottish League Cup for the third time. Amidst all the hugs and kisses from the triumphant, the gentlemanly Gallagher was always careful to shake the hands of the vanquished and to offer them a word or two of encouragement. After all, he had been there himself in 1961, and he knew what it was like.

The drama of that day, however, was not quite over. The Cup was presented, the players received their medals and the team came out to show their trophy to the exultant fans on the East Terracing, some of whom were shedding unashamed tears of joy. But then as they turned to show the Cup to their fans in the North Enclosure, they suddenly saw a cavalry charge of about 100 mentally challenged youths coming at them with hostile intent from the Mount Florida end.

Mercifully, the players and the trophy were undamaged by these people who were showing the world just exactly why they would soon be called the Huns, and equally mercifully, the Celtic fans did not retaliate. They had clearly taken to heart Jock Stein's strictures about hooliganism, and Celtic emerged from that day with the Scottish League Cup and a great deal of credit. Celtic's players also deserve a certain amount of credit for their self-restraint for big powerful well-trained athletes like John Hughes and Tommy Gemmell might have made an awful mess of these undernourished and pitiful specimens of humanity. It was however a nasty example of the ugly and unacceptable face of Scottish football.

It was of a great deal less importance to Gallagher than that he had now won three medals in that calendar year of 1965 as a League Cup medal joined a Scottish Cup one and a Glasgow Cup one. Not at all bad for a man who had entertained serious doubts about any kind of future for him at Celtic Park. In spite of all the unpleasantness, it had been a great day for Charlie. Life had turned for Charlie and Celtic.

It was also very nice to see Ronnie Simpson win his first Scottish medal, and Jimmy Johnstone and Joe McBride win their first ever medals. The team would now go on to greater things starting the Wednesday night after the League Cup final when they team went to Dens Park, Dundee. This venue was never easy for Celtic, and tonight they had to work hard for their 2-1 victory against a team inspired by Scotland internationalist Charlie Cooke. Celtic scored twice in the first half, but Dundee scored from a free kick early in the second half and it was only "inspired teamwork" which saw Celtic through, and made people realise that this Celtic team had the important ability to win games, even when you are under the cosh for long periods of the game. This is the quality which wins League titles.

Charlie was now a regular in this very fine side, as Celtic mounted their first realistic challenge for the Scottish League flag for over a decade. Until Christmas, Gallagher missed only one game, against Kilmarnock in late

November, as they team began to impress. Only one point was dropped – a feckless 1-1 draw against Partick Thistle on a typically dull November day at Parkhead – but on the other hand, there were some very good performances indeed with away victories at difficult places like Dundee, (as we have seen) St Johnstone and on the Saturday before Christmas, Dunfermline Athletic, a team who had been in great form. Progress was made in Europe with the defeat both home and away of Aarhus of Denmark. Joe McBride was scoring prolifically, but it was the consistent opinion of those who watched Celtic in those days that it was a team performance every week. And most of this good run came when captain McNeill was out injured, but there was an excellent depute in John Cushley.

Charlie was one of those who made the team tick with his skilful passing. He was now playing with the confidence that sustained success brings, and it was little wonder that the Celtic crowds were now soaring. Christmas Day brought a good crowd to Parkhead to see Celtic beat the luckless Morton 8-1 as Celtic finished the remarkable year of 1965 on a high note. But the New Year clash with Rangers on Monday January 3 1966 was now looming.

Gallagher had missed the game on New Year's day itself – a 3-1 win at Shawfield – but was back for this game against Rangers, arguably his best game for the club. The game had an early kick-off at 2.00 which was just as well, for the game might not have been completed in the fog which fell late in the second half. Rangers had gone ahead, but this was no longer a Celtic team that was intimidated or would accept setbacks every easily. The second half saw some tremendous Celtic pressure, and the 5-1 win might have been a lot more. Steve Chalmers scored a hat-trick, the first from a well taken Gallagher corner kick, and Gallagher was very much involved in the other two.

One was a tremendous drive from Charlie at the edge of the penalty box after some fine work from John Hughes on the left wing. John Hughes himself describes this goal "I…saw Charlie Gallagher taking up a great position about twenty-five yards out. Charlie could strike a beautiful ball and that was undoubtedly his forte… I beat another couple of defenders before looking up to make sure Charlie was still unmarked and slipped the ball as expertly as I could in front of him". Charlie met the ball cleanly and the ball was in the net via the underside of the crossbar, virtually before anyone realised that he had hit it. It was a great goal, but the other one involved the referee Mr Tom Wharton.

Mr Wharton was huge, and earned the nickname "Tiny" simply because he wasn't! He was a real character on the field, and although widely believed by Celtic supporters of being a Rangers supporter (Celtic supporters always think that, don't they?) he was always strictly fair. If he had any fault, it was that he tended to show off rather too much. One recalls the sight of Wharton and Stein, both huge men, discussing the prospects of play on the field that very day before the start. The gates had been opened and the crowd had begun to trickle in. They were by no means friends and both of them in their heavy overcoats did a great deal of finger wagging at each other with Stein at one point waving his arm round the ground and pointing out that the spectators were already there and would be mightily disappointed if the game did not go ahead. Interestingly, there was no representative form Rangers there, but the two big men eventually agreed that the game was on, and shook hands in mutual respect.

Mr Wharton was very middle class and polite, and always called the players Mr Gallagher and Mr Gemmell and Mr Johnstone etc. On this occasion, Celtic had won a free kick on the edge of the box, to be taken by Charlie. "Wait for the whistle, Mr Gallagher" was the instruction. Charlie slipped the ball to Jimmy Johnstone, got it back immediately and then passed it the other way to the incoming Bobby Murdoch. But the referee was in the way! And Mr Wharton was big! But calmly he simply opened his legs, allowed the ball to run through and Bobby did the rest. It was a remarkable goal, and curiously there was no protest from the Rangers players who might have felt aggrieved at this.

Charlie suffered for this because he left the field at the end having received a none too subtle kick on the ankle from a Rangers defender. He cannot recall who it was, but there were several likely suspects. He recovered though and Celtic were now in dream land, having defeated their rivals by that massive score of 5-1. At the end of that week, following intensive treatment on his ankle, Charlie further proved his worth to the team by scoring the only goal of the game against Dundee

United at Parkhead. The arrival of the Tannadice Terrors to Celtic Park was by no means one of Glasgow's greatest touring attractions, for they were always predictably defensive. Gallagher scored the only goal of the game. It was a mundane, ordinary goal when he was on hand to sweep in a rebound off the goalkeeper after some fine work by Jimmy Johnstone, but it earned Celtic two points in what was otherwise a rather dull game.

But now things became complicated with Dinamo Kiev coming to Parkhead to play in the Cup Winners' Cup. January was an odd time to play a European tie, but in these days, clubs could arrange it between themselves, and Dinamo would not play their return tie in their home city of Kiev but in Tblisi Georgia where the weather at this time of the year would be considerably milder. The game in Glasgow was played on January 12, and it had been hoped that the return match could be played on the following Wednesday of January 19, but Soviet intransigence and bloody-mindedness made this impossible, and the game was played a week later – but with major problems of travel, caused to a very large extent by a prickly dictatorship which was unimpressed by the great Glasgow Celtic and did not take kindly to Westerners coming to their country!

But the Celtic performance on January 12 when the Ukrainians were simply torn apart was something which made all Europe sit up and take notice. Gallagher played his part in this as well, although the hero of the night was two goal Bobby Murdoch, and 64,000 left the ground marvelling at their team's performance (with an added cameo being the display of keepie-uppie and ball control by young reserve George Connelly at half time) while the Kiev coach was left fulminating unconvincingly about the German referee – something that had its origins, perhaps, in the dark days of 25 years previously when so many Kiev players and supporters were murdered by the Germans.

The next game was at Pittodrie on Saturday January 15. Scotland was frozen and it might have been better for Celtic if the game had been called off, but thanks to their proximity to the North Sea, Aberdeen was a fraction milder than other parts of the country and the game went ahead on a snow-covered pitch. Celtic supporters were there in great numbers, marching along Union Street and up King Street with a huge banner on which ran the legend "7-1 5-1 The Untouchables" linking the New Year triumph against Rangers with the 7-1 of blessed memory.

Such optimism was praiseworthy, but it was a little premature. In-fact the game turned out to be a good one, but alas for Celtic it brought an end to their undefeated run which had lasted 24 games since their defeat at Ibrox in September. Celtic went ahead, but a few defensive errors lead to a 3-1 defeat, an indication too of the fact that Aberdeen were slowly beginning to come back after a decade of mediocrity and under-achievement. They had frankly been a very poor team in the early 1960s and it was Celtic's first defeat there since 1960.

Charlie had little to reproach himself for, although he suffered with the difficult surface. For no real accountable reason he found himself out of the team for the next two games – a 1-0 win over Motherwell at Parkhead then the return game against Dinamo Kiev in Tblisi. Bobby Lennox got an outing in his place against Motherwell, something that seemed strange to the supporters for Lennox and Gallagher were totally different types of players, but he appreciated why he didn't play in Georgia. Stein on this occasion, opted to play a double centre half in McNeill and Cushley and had Murdoch in the inside right position. It was successful as well, for the game finished 1-1 and Celtic were through to the next round.

But it took them a while to get home. In circumstances reminding a Classical scholar of Odysseus' return from Troy. Ten years it took the "god-like, much-enduring Odysseus" to reach Ithaca and his worthy wife Penelope. Celtic were a little quicker than that, but certainly would have deserved the epithet "much-enduring". (They always had been god-like!) They were delayed by a combination of bureaucratic Soviet stubbornness and then bad weather at Stockholm Airport when they were diverted there, and the result was that it was nearly midnight on Friday night before they got home – and they had to play Hearts at Tynecastle the next day! A wise course of events would have been to phone the Scottish League from Stockholm and ask for a postponement. As it was, they were in touch with Tommy Maule, the Secretary, but for some reason did not ask officially for the game to be postponed. Nor did Mr Maule offer.

It was then, when they eventually got home that Jock Stein showed that he could be as pig headed as any Soviet bureaucrat, for he ordered a training session at Parkhead late on the Friday night immediately after they touched down at Glasgow Airport! This was understandably resented by the players, including Gallagher, and it would surely have made more sense to let the exhausted and stressed players back to their homes and families and then bring them in for a light training session at 10.00 am on the Saturday before the trip to Edinburgh.

It was not all that surprising, therefore, that Celtic then lost their second game in a fortnight. There were other factors. Hearts indeed played well to the delight of their supporters, and Celtic shot themselves in the foot to a certain extent by dropping Jim Craig. Craig had been sent off in the Soviet Union, and, although there was no automatic suspension, Celtic opted not to play him, Bob Kelly having leaned on Jock Stein to teach Craig a lesson. Thus McNeill was at right back and John Cushley at centre half. It was a move that did not work that day against a nippy Hearts attack which contained Willie Wallace. But the main thing was the exhaustion of the players. Even Gallagher who had not played at Tblisi was well below par, although things might have been different if his first minute shot had gone in rather than skimmed the bar. Celtic lost 3-2. They had seemed virtually impregnable after the 5-1 defeat of Rangers but having lost two games in January since then, now began to look decidedly vulnerable.

A Scottish Cup game now followed in early February against Stranraer – apparently the first time these teams had ever met! – easily won 4-0 before a small crowd at Parkhead, a feature of the game being the first goal scored on the volley by Gallagher following a Johnstone cross, but then Gallagher lost his place in the team for a spell. Indeed, he only played another 6 games that season, but they were all significant.

He did not really deserve to be dropped, but in mid February Bertie Auld who had been injured came back to play at inside left and Joe McBride was moved to inside right allowing Steve Chalmers to play in the middle. Gallagher accepted all this phlegmatically, and watched as the team beat Falkirk, advanced in the Scottish Cup at the expense of Dundee on a cold frosty midweek at Dens Park (the game having been postponed on the Saturday) and then alarming their fans by going down to Stirling Albion at Annfield (an old bogey ground in the past). Quite a few of the disgruntled supporters expressed the view that Gallagher might have made a difference to that dysfunctional forward line which, quite simply, just seemed to have an off day – or perhaps they were upset by the orange jerseys worn by Stirling Albion quite deliberately at the behest of their Manager, ex-Ranger Sammy Baird!

But then a great Scottish Cup tie appeared on the horizon at Tynecastle. Hearts had, of course, beaten Celtic little more than a month earlier and the tie was all ticket. By this time winter had given way to spring, and although Gallagher was in the party, Stein decided to go for Bertie Auld for this game. It was a game marred by serious overcrowding at the Gorgie Road end requiring suspension of play for a few minutes as the crowd spilled on to the track and a few luckless fans were seen to be carried away on stetchers. The problem had arisen out of a well-constructed plot by some ticketless fans to get in. One of their number did have a ticket and duly entered the ground. He then loosened the bolt of one of the exit gates left criminally unguarded by stewards and police who were in any case distracted by other problems caused by the huge crowd. Hundreds of fans then rushed in through the exit gates. Some indeed had tickets, but it was a lot easier in any case to walk in through the exit gate than it was to queue at the inadequate turnstiles which clearly were not coping with the huge crowd.

Mercifully and miraculously no-one was killed or seriously injured in this surge of humanity, and eventually the police were able to direct fans to less crowded parts of the ground. It was frightening, though, for all concerned and Gallagher from his seat in the stand was as concerned as anyone. The players then rewarded the crowd for their patience and bravery with a great game which ended 3-3. Willie Wallace again starred for Hearts, but Celtic showed great skill and composure for twice coming from behind. Indeed they were 3-2 up late in the game, until Hearts scored a late equalizer to earn a replay through the detested Johnny Hamilton whose ability to wind up Celtic fans was legendary. Crucially for Gallagher, both McBride and Auld were injured – McBride's arm injury compelling him to play with his arm as if in a sling, a curious sight!

– and opportunity beckoned for him in the Wednesday night replay.

McBride recovered, but Auld didn't and Charlie was in, as an astonishing 72,000 appeared at Parkhead for the replay. It showed, apart from anything, just what a huge sleeping giant Jock Stein had awakened. Long after the game started, and even allowing for a ten-minute delay, crowds were still trickling in, most of them Hearts supporters thwarted by virtually unprecedented traffic jams all along London Road and its environs. This time Celtic made no mistake and Gallagher played his part in the convincing 3-1 victory. In particular, he made the first crucial vital goal when he picked up a loose ball, fed Joe McBride who in turn fed Jimmy Johnstone. Celtic's very convincing win – Hearts scored their consolation goal very late when the game was virtually over – was much lauded by the fans, particularly when they heard that Rangers had gone down to Falkirk in the Scottish League, and that Celtic were now back on top on goal average.

After that game, however, it was job done as far as Gallagher was concerned as Stein resorted to his traditional belief of "horses for courses" moved Gallagher back to the reserves again, or more commonly, gave him a seat in the stand for he was frequently the "reserve to travel" simply because he was such a versatile character. He was also an emotionally stolid sort of chap who did not throw the toys out of the pram if he did not get a game. He next played in a League match against St Mirren on April 9 when he opened the floodgates by scoring the first goal in what was a 5-0 win for Celtic.

He did not play in either of the games in the European Cup Winners' Cup semi-final against Liverpool – a painful and unlucky defeat. The first game at Parkhead was a 1-0 win – and it should have been a lot more! – but the Anfield game saw Liverpool take a 2-0 lead but then Bobby Lennox scored a great goal, wrongly disallowed by a team of officials who simply could not believe how fast Lennox was! The bottle throwing of the fans that night was deplorable, but, unlike most outburst of hooliganism which are often unpredictable and irrational, this one did at least have some sort of cause.

Some felt that the calming influence of Gallagher might have had a beneficial effect in the cauldron of Anfield, but Celtic had little else to do other than pack up and go home to lick their wounds. It was not as if they didn't have anything important on their plate for the next game was the Scottish Cup final against Rangers on April 23! Bertie Auld was suspended and could not play, and there was also an injury problem with Bobby Lennox. It was expected that Bobby would play but in a last minute decision Gallagher was given the nod in a forward line which read Johnstone, McBride, Chalmers, Gallagher and Hughes. He had, it will be recalled, missed out in a last minute decision before the League Cup final in 1964. This time he was more fortunate.

It was curious however to find that this game – an Old Firm Scottish Cup final - did not receive the hysterical build up in the newspapers which one might have expected. The simple reason was that Celtic had other fish to fry as well. Liverpool had, of course, been a heart-breaking experience for all at Celtic, particularly as most folk agreed that Celtic had been the better team over the two legs. Indeed, it was now agreed by everyone, even the English BBC, that the great goal scored by Lennox late in the game at Anfield had been wrongly ruled out for offside. Now Celtic had the opportunity to bounce back. Would they do this? Or would the Liverpool defeat be an infectious one? Both Celtic and Rangers had won the Scottish Cup 18 times each. Celtic had won the Scottish League Cup, but the Scottish League, like the Scottish Cup itself was still in the balance.

The teams were:

Celtic: Simpson, Young and Gemmell; Murdoch, McNeill and Clark; Johnstone, McBride, Chalmers, Gallagher and Hughes

Rangers: Ritchie, Johansen and Provan; Greig, McKinnon and Millar; Henderson, Watson, Forrest, Johnston and Wilson

Referee: T Wharton, Clarkston

The weather was fine, although there was a breeze blowing towards the Celtic end when Rangers kicked off playing in that direction. The game was even, and neither team was able to claim any decisive superiority, although there were a couple of occasions when Gallagher might, with a bit of luck, have won the game. One was late in the first half when he shot against the wind and the ball, having beaten Billy Ritchie, just rose over the bar at the last second, and the other was early in the second half when The Evening Times talks of Gallagher "shaking his fist in anger" at Steve Chalmers when Chalmers opted to slip the ball to Hughes rather than Gallagher who was in a far better position to score. It was indeed difficult to imagine Chalmers and Gallagher falling out, for they were both players renowned for their gentlemanly and sporting approach to the game!

Rangers had Jimmy Millar playing at left half. This was in some ways a strange move, for Millar was normally a forward. He was however a dangerous player, and Gallagher had to spend a great deal of time and energy to keep him quiet. Rangers had their moments on the game as well, but Press reports tend to stress that it was a "gritty midfield battle" – often a euphemism for it being a dull game. "Two well balanced teams" was a phrase also much employed by the journalists that weekend.

So 0-0 it was in front of 126,552 fans, and the replay was scheduled for the following Wednesday night. For this game, Stein opted to bring back the now available Bertie Auld. This was naturally a bitter disappointment to Charlie, and it is debatable whether the decision was the right one. Maybe Charlie's cool, assured approach might have won the day as distinct from the more aggressive style of Bertie Auld, but Stein made the decision and Gallagher could only sit in the stand and watch the team fight hard but lose out to the Kaj Johansen goal (praised by the Scottish press "not without cause but without end") late in the second half. It was a sad game for all Celtic fans, for Celtic were the better side.

Gallagher may well have been disappointed to miss out on the final, but he would surely have been encouraged by a letter that appeared in The Celtic View that very day, written by a man who called himself "Rob Roy" of Coatbridge in which he says that "He seems to me the present day Scottish inside forward who most closely follows the tradition of Charlie Tully, Ian McMillan (of Airdrie and Rangers) and John White (of Falkirk and Tottenham Hotspur). None of these players was a great back-checker or defender, yet each retained his place in a highly successful team because he could split open a defence with one pass; he doubles the value of the other four forwards. It is not simply the length or accuracy of Charlie's passing which makes him a great player. It is the unorthodox, sudden "wrong" pass made at the right moment which panics a methodical defence and which all Celtic supporters associate with Gallagher's play"

That was an extremely perspicacious comment by "Rob Roy". The breaking down of a packed defence has long been a frustration for Celtic fans of all ages. So often, teams (and we could point out a few in particular) came and continue to come to Celtic Park with a goalless draw the limit of their aspirations. "Parking the team bus" across the penalty box is the current description. In these circumstances, the attacking team must try the unexpected – the shot from a distance, the pass to a man who appears from nowhere, the threading of a ball through a defence rather than the aimless punt for the ball to be headed away. All these things Charlie Gallagher was capable of , and it is of little surprise that we find another letter in the same edition of The Celtic View from a Michael Harte of West Lothian wondering why Mr Stein does not deploy Charlie a lot oftener "as he is the most brilliant player on Celtic's books". That would be some claim, if it were true, and Charlie himself would never have said that. He might even have been embarrassed to read it. He was very much a squad member, even if it meant occasionally that he didn't always get a game.

Now that the Scottish Cup had gone in those heart breaking circumstances, the spectre was frequently raised in the Press and in conversation of whether Celtic could lose the League as well. Did they have the "bottle" to save the League, something that Stein had always said was his priority? Within eight days, they had unluckily lost the European Cup Winners' Cup and now the Scottish Cup, and they really had to concentrate now on the Scottish League in which there were only three games left. They were equal on points with Rangers, but had two advantages in having an extra game and a superior goal average. Nevertheless, nerves began to play on the Celtic supporters when John Hughes, Joe McBride, Jimmy Johnstone and Bertie Auld all reported injuries after the Cup final.

In the event Johnstone and Auld made it, but Gallagher was given a run for the last three games at inside right at the expense of the injured Joe McBride. Bobby Lennox and Bertie Auld made up the left wing. Stein got this one right, for Gallagher brought a degree of calm to the dressing room and the field, (where he showed his virtually unchallenged ability to deliver the best pass) in those last three frenetic games. They could hardly have been more difficult – Morton desperately trying to avoid relegation at Greenock, the talented and determined Dunfermline at Parkhead and then Motherwell at Fir Park.

The important game was probably the first, and it was a particularly poignant game for Jim Kennedy, one-time colleague of Charlie and now playing for Morton in a fight that would determine the future of both teams. Celtic emerged victorious with first Jimmy Johnstone scoring and then late in the game Bobby Lennox, and Morton were condemned to the Second Division. However, the League was not yet secured for Celtic, for Rangers had also won that day at Dunfermline, the team who were due to play at Celtic Park on Wednesday night while Rangers faced Clyde at Ibrox. As The Celtic View pointed out, a win for Celtic would more or less do it, irrespective of the Rangers score, such was Celtic's goal average superiority. If Clyde actually scored and Celtic won, it would be very difficult to see any other outcome than Celtic's first League flag since 1954.

But it was a hard struggle for Celtic that night before 30,000 anxious fans. Alex Ferguson put the Pars ahead on the half hour mark before Gallagher flicked on a Johnstone cross for Lennox to equalise at half time, then Johnstone scored brilliantly in the second half. With the team 2-1 up and so much at stake, Celtic now played a sensible midfield containing game in which the players looked considerably more in control than the panicky fans were. It was in a situation like this that Celtic saw the best of Charlie Gallagher. He could hold a ball, read a situation and pass to the best placed colleague. He also didn't hide. He was always hunting for the ball, permanently mobile, helping the defence if necessary, bolstering up the midfield when required and always willing to try a shot. Full time brought relief and even a sense of triumph, as thousands invaded the park. Their joy was premature as it turned out, for the bad news was that Rangers had beaten Clyde 4-0 that night. One goal from Clyde would probably have confirmed Celtic as champions, but it was not to be.

As it was, all this meant that Celtic could still be pipped, but only if Motherwell beat them 4-1 or more at Fir Park on Saturday May 7. Rangers indeed conceded defeat before this game, and Celtic appeared at Motherwell as Champions in all but name. It was by no means the best game that Celtic played all season. Gallagher played at inside right but it was a tense, nervy affair. Celtic, mercifully, won 1-0 thanks to a late Bobby Lennox goal, something that meant Celtic had won the Scottish League for the first time in 12 years, and Gallagher had won his first League medal.

12 years was the longest period of time (if we ignore 1938-1954, which included the war years) that Celtic had gone without being Champions of Scotland, and the triumph was much celebrated. The winning of the League had been Celtic's no 1 priority, and although there had been disappointments in Europe and the Scottish Cup, the winning of the League made up for most of that. Not even the wildest of optimists, however, could predict that that Celtic would now win 9 Scottish Leagues in a row, beating by three years the record of the great Young, Loney and Hay team of the Edwardian era. Gallagher was in at the very start of that, and remains proud of his contribution.

There now followed a tour of America. Historians enjoy telling us about what a great "bonding" experience it was for the 17-man squad who were in the new world from mid-May to mid-June, but it was not perhaps, if one scratches the surface, quite the idyllic occasion that we are led to believe. John Hughes, for example, tells a story which reflects little credit on Jock Stein when Jock failed to tell Yogi that his wife had miscarried. There was a brawl in a game against Bayern Munich, and Tottenham Hotspur accused Celtic of cheating by using Jimmy Johnstone as a substitute contrary to a pre-existing arrangement. Nevertheless, more good than bad came out of it, unlike a subsequent tour in 1970 (after Gallagher had left the club) which contained little other than disaster.

In playing terms, Celtic played 11 games winning 8 and drawing three – the draws being played out against Bayern Munich, Bologna and Tottenham Hotspur. But they proved their credentials when they beat Tottenham Hotspur twice, playing some sparkling football and impressing the locals and their many supporters in the New World. Jim Craig stayed behind because of his finals in Dentistry at Glasgow University, Ian Young and Jimmy Johnstone left early to get married, reserve centre half Frank McCarron had a bad dose of sunburn in Bermuda, and there were occasions when there was a distinct shortage of players with Sean Fallon and Neil Mochan on the verges of a most unexpected comeback!

These players may or may not have been on the fringes of becoming the greatest team on the planet, but they were still just young lads, most of whom not having had a great deal of experience of life outside Glasgow and its immediate environment. It was therefore, a great learning experience, not least for Charlie Gallagher who had the honour of scoring the last goal of the tour in the 88th minute of the game against Atlas of Mexico in Los Angeles, something that gave Celtic a 1-0 victory and ensured that they could fly home on June 15 undefeated.

There had been one sour note as far as Gallagher was concerned. His wife Mary was in America at the same time, unknown to the Celtic management, and turned up unexpectedly at a hotel where she was given a less than hearty welcome from Jock Stein! This was of course, according to Charlie, quite in character for Jock who did not want women any place close to the players when there was a job to be done. There was a small piece of hypocrisy in all this, for Stein was not above a little flirting with players' wives at club functions, and the occasional attempt to impress them with his singing (he had not a bad voice, according to Charlie). But when business was to be done, he was quite capable of being unpleasant and boorish to members of the fair sex.

It had been a great season for Celtic and for Gallagher. He had played well, but still could not be guaranteed a place in the team – but that said a great deal more about the quality of the team than it did about the ever ready and ever pleasant Charlie Gallagher. Time for a rest for the Celtic squad as they sat back and watched the World Cup in England. 1966/67 would soon be upon them.

CHAPTER EIGHT

INTERNATIONAL RECOGNITION AND LISBON

Season 1966/67 is an immortal one in the annals of Scottish football, let alone Celtic FC. It was the one year in which Scottish football attracted the attention of the world and only a few very churlish people dared to deny the status of Celtic as a world class power. The shame was that it has never yet been repeated, and indeed did not last very long, but anyone who was alive in 1967 will recall the euphoria and ecstasy of it all and will to this day retain the hope, the ever dwindling hope, that it can happen again.

Charlie was of course very much part of all this, but was not, sadly, one of the eleven who won the beautifully ugly big trophy that immortal day of May 25 in Lisbon. But Stein was always very careful to emphasise the idea of it being a squad who won the European Cup and indeed Charlie has his own little piece of private glory, as we will see. Yet it has remained a bone of contention over the past 50 years as to who exactly did win the trophy. Was it the 11 who played in the game, or was it the whole squad? It has to have been the whole squad, and really must include Charlie for, although he did not play in Lisbon, he did have a key role in getting the team there.

But to begin at the beginning, Charlie continued his honourable tradition of winning the Glasgow Cup – his third. The Cup was officially won on November 7 1966, but some would argue that it was won as early as Tuesday August 23 when Celtic beat Rangers 4-0. Lennox scored three goals and McNeill one, but it was a fine performance by a team which had started the season well, and which was still hurting from that unfortunate experience of the Scottish Cup final the previous year. It was also the night that Stein showed his undeniable ability as a Manager in two respects.

Gallagher had not yet played for the first team that season. The team had started well and already included a 4-1 defeat of Manchester United in its portfolio, but Jock was always a great one for giving everyone a chance, and Charlie was drafted in at inside right for the Ibrox game with Joe McBride moving to the centre forward position and Steve Chalmers given a rest. He felt that the craft and calmness of Gallacher would be vital in the cauldron of Ibrox.

But the other thing that Stein twigged was that Kaj Johansen was no real goalscorer. His "wonder strike" of last April was in fact a fluke, (John Hughes will admit that he should have been shadowing him in that Cup final replay and would have done so but for a slight knock) but it had gone to the heads of everyone at Ibrox. Kaj would therefore never be able to resist the pressure from the Ibrox terracings to have another go. He would thus go forward at every opportunity leaving gaps at the back, and making the Rangers defence rely on John Greig to an excessive extent. Greig could not, however, on his own cope with the speed of Bobby Lennox. Stein told Gallagher and Murdoch to feed Lennox at every opportunity. This they did and Lennox scored a hat-trick, the other goal having come from a cute Gallagher through ball to, of all people, Billy McNeill.

Charlie also played in the other two Glasgow Cup games. Against Queen's Park on Monday October 10 along with fringe players like Danish goalkeeper Bent Martin and Ian Young, a fine full back but no longer guaranteed a game in this fine side, Charlie was given a game in a regulation 4-0 defeat of Queen's Park, scoring a goal in the process. The final against Partick Thistle was also played at Celtic Park on Monday November 7.

He owed his selection in this game because Jock Stein was in a bad mood with some of his players! A couple of days previously, Celtic having played superb football all season so far, suddenly decided to have a bad game and could only draw with St Mirren on November 5. It was by any standards a feckless performance but there were extenuating circumstances in that Billy McNeill was out injured and Bobby Murdoch was (wrongly) sent off in what seemed like a case of mistaken identity. In addition, it was the first dropped point of the season! Tommy Gemmell was hardly a success at centre half, but it was the forwards who seemed to lack the guidance of McNeill more than the other defenders.

The draw came a week after Celtic retained the Scottish League Cup in a tight 1-0 win over Rangers. Charlie, sitting in the Hampden stand, no doubt went through all the horrors of hell as Rangers piled on the pressure in the second half, and Celtic were indebted to Willie O'Neill's goal line clearance and a few fine saves from Ronnie Simpson. Then on the Wednesday night, Gallagher had been given a game against Stirling Albion and had played well in the 7-3 goal fest. He sustained a slight injury in the first half and was taken off as a precaution, so was out for the game against St Mirren.

It was by no means a bad performance, or if it was, it was an isolated one. Nevertheless, Stein and the Celtic crowd had come to expect better, and amazingly some so-called fans turned on their players. That makes sense in the context of the Stirling Albion game was well, for to the astonishment of all press and journalists, the crowd turned on them there as well. Celtic were 7-1 up, then Stirling Albion came into the game and scored a couple of well-taken goals to make the score 7-3. Catcalls and boos were heard – and this was with the team four goals up, and having already shown off the Scottish League Cup which they had won on Saturday! The angry Stein shared this mood. He seemed to blame Jimmy Johnstone for it all. Jimmy was dropped, Steve Chalmers was put on the right wing and Charlie, now recovered from his minor knock, was brought in at inside right for the Glasgow Cup final.

31,000 saw a marvellous Celtic performance with another 4-0 victory and Celtic had now already won two pieces of silverware, the Glasgow Cup joining the Scottish League Cup won nine days previously! Gallagher played well – one of the goals came from one of his free kicks – and Celtic were cheered to the echo at the end, with Partick's Manager, the ever gentlemanly Willie Thornton, a Rangers legend and winner of the Military Medal in World War II, joining in the praises of Celtic. It was a shame that the Glasgow Cup had not been contested in season 1965/66 (because they couldn't find dates for it!), for if Celtic had won it, it would surely have meant yet another Glasgow Cup medal.

At the end of January, the ever versatile Charlie found himself playing on the right wing in a Scottish Cup game against Arbroath at Parkhead. He was covering for the injured Jimmy Johnstone. The men from Angus put up a brave fight, but were clearly being overwhelmed with the score at 3-0 half way through the second half. The game was going nowhere special, but suddenly with nothing particular happening on the field, a loud outburst of cheering was heard in the Main Stand. The noise spread round the ground, and with still nothing happening on the field, all of Parkhead was a frenzied cauldron of excitement with people cheering waving scarves, pummelling each other on the back and hugging and kissing each other indiscriminately.

He suspected what had happened, virtually unbelievable though it was, but it was only when the crowd started singing "The Huns are out of the Cup", that he knew for certain. Berwick Rangers had beaten their Glasgow counterparts in a result that stunned all the footballing world! The news came before Celtic's game had finished, for there had been an early kick off in the small town of Berwick.

Charlie did not play too many League games that season but he was quite happy to play in the reserves and to know that he was a very reliable member of the squad. Not that everything was always totally harmonious of course, for as always with fit young men all striving for a place in the team, there was inevitably a certain amount of tension. Charlie tells with relish the time that he actually punched Billy McNeill!

This distinctly uncharacteristic behaviour came about when Stein arranged a few very competitive training games at Barrowfield in which the winners were given a bottle of orange juice (sic) and the losers got nothing! Gallagher was playing against Billy McNeill who was giving him a hard time with niggling fouls and a few verbals. Charlie took it for a while, but then suddenly the red mist came down and Charlie belted his captain! Stein saw it and immediately ordered him off the Barrowfield training ground and told him to come and see him in his office at Celtic Park when they all got back.

It was like a bad boy having to see the Headmaster! Fearing suspension, a transfer to some Third Division English team or even, perhaps the sack for "violence", Charlie approached Mr Stein with dread, knowing that Jock did not particularly like him and that he had maybe been looking for the opportunity. But to his surprise, Stein, while telling him that he was a little out of order and that he shouldn't do it again, said it was good that he was able to look after himself! Aggression was not really a great part of the play of the gentlemanly Charlie Gallagher! And he is proud of the fact that he was never booked or in trouble with referees at Celtic Park.

Gallagher made it up with McNeill – not that that was a huge problem, for McNeill regarded Charlie very highly indeed – and the incident was forgotten about by the next day. Indeed it may even have been a plot hatched up by Stein and McNeill to provoke a little more aggression from Gallagher! It was just as well that the Press didn't get to hear about it, otherwise more would have been made about it than need have been. In later years when spats between Tosh McKinlay and Henrik Larsson, then between Artur Boruc and Aiden McGeady reached the press, an inordinate amount was made of them. There was also the famous occasion when Bobby Evans and Charlie Tully came to blows. A few days later they beat Rangers 7-1!

But if Charlie was on the side lines as far as Celtic were concerned in season 1966/67, there was compensation from a rather surprising source. To this day, Charlie will tell everyone that he supports Ireland rather than Scotland. He is not anti-Scotland as many Celtic supporters sadly are, but has his own reasons for supporting Ireland. His parents were from Donegal, the cradle of Celtic FC in many ways, and he recalls spending many summers in his childhood in Donegal. But the main reason, of course, for his support of Ireland is that he played twice for them. Indeed he is very proud of the little piece of history that he created in becoming the first Scotsman to play for Ireland. People with a sense of humour can compare him with James Connolly in 1916, for he was born in Scotland (in Edinburgh) and "played" for Ireland, as it were, in the tragic circumstances of the Easter Rebellion of 1916.

Charlie's involvement with Ireland's football team started one day in January 1967 at training, when Sean Fallon, Celtic's Assistant Manager and himself of course an Irishman from Sligo, approached Charlie and asked him if he would like to play for Ireland. Charlie's answer was "I can't. I was born in Scotland." Sean then told him that the rules had been changed so that men of Irish heritage could play for the national team. Shay Brennan of Manchester United and John Dempsey of Chelsea had already taken advantage of this ruling. This of course opened the doors to many people of the Irish diaspora, but no Scotsman had as yet been invited. Charlie chuckled at the idea and carried on training. But as he was not at the moment commanding a place in the Celtic team, the idea of playing for Eire seemed remote.

It would probably be true to say that Association Football in the Republic of Ireland was not particularly strong in 1967. It was certainly nothing like the obsession that it was in Scotland, for example, and struggled to compete against Gaelic Football and Rugby Union, a sport incidentally which successfully manages to incorporate both Irelands – North and South – and making people in mainland Britain, who do not understand the complexities of the situation, wonder why this sort of thing does not happen oftener!

A myth used to permeate the Celtic areas of the west of Scotland to the effect that the whole population of the Republic of Ireland spent Saturday afternoons glued to their radio to find out how Celtic were doing. This was not really true. Donegal and some areas in the northern part of the island were recognised as pro-Celtic, but "indifference" would be the best word to describe how many Irish people felt about Celtic. Some supported an English team like Manchester United, and everyone in Ireland knew about Celtic and vaguely hoped that they did well, but the idea that fleets of boats left Southern Ireland to come to see Celtic playing in a Scottish Cup final, for example, is absurd. The European Cup would change that to a certain extent, for that would make everyone sit up and take notice with even Eamon de Valera getting a chance to meet Jock Stein and the European Cup, but in early 1967, Celtic was no big deal for most of Ireland.

Not that Celtic or men with Celtic connections hadn't had their moments in southern Ireland. Jimmy Quinn in 1908 scored four goals for Scotland against Ireland in Dublin and found himself briefly called "the uncrowned King of Ireland", a title more commonly associated with the late Charles Stewart Parnell, and Jimmy Delany almost won an Irish Cup medal in 1956 with Cork Athletic which would have looked good beside his Scottish, English and Northern Irish ones!

It would also be a mistake to in any way underestimate the feelings of "Irishness" which permeated Celtic FC and had done so since the early days of the club. We are not talking here about rebel songs and anthems sung by the support. We are talking about what the club itself did. Michael Davitt, the Irish patriot had on March 19 1892 planted shamrocks on the new Celtic Park, on August 26 1922 the flags at the ground had been lowered to half-mast for a game against Hamilton Accies in remembrance of Michael Collins, the Irish rebel murdered in the Irish Civil war between Free Staters and Republicans, and 1952 had seen the prolonged and successful struggle to be allowed to keep flying the Irish tricolour over Celtic Park when George Graham of the SFA had tried to have it removed.

It was significant that support for Celtic was stronger in Ulster, for in the North, of course, there existed also the opposite. Any action has a reaction, as any scientist will tell you, and because loads of people in Northern Ireland from the Protestant community supported Rangers, it was only natural that the Catholic community would actively support Celtic. The Royal Ulsterman and other ships that crossed to Scotland could be busy and indeed tense places on the Friday night before and the Saturday night after Celtic v Rangers games.

The time was, of course, when there was a Belfast Celtic, but they had folded in 1949 after serious rioting at their ground. This support transferred itself to Glasgow Celtic, although some moved to Cliftonville or some other Ulster team other than Linfield, who were the acknowledged "Orange" team of Northern Ireland! And Belfast

Celtic's best ever player, Charles Patrick Tully, joined Celtic in 1948. This man very soon became a cult figure in Glasgow and was much talked about throughout the late 1940s and 1950s. No Roman Catholic could ever play for Rangers, of course, but Celtic opened their doors to everyone, and one often wonders what the Orange bigots made of Bertie Peacock, a man of a Protestant background from Coleraine who became captain of Celtic and Northern Ireland and distinguished himself with both!

Charlie Gallagher was a squad man for Celtic in 1967. The team were doing well, but the big talking point in Scotland that winter was the unaccountable collapse of Rangers in the Scottish Cup. In a season that would soon bring a Scotsman called Charlie Gallagher to play for Ireland, Rangers went out of the Scottish Cup to an English team. This was to another team called Rangers, Berwick Rangers who played in the Second Division of the Scottish League, and also in the Scottish Cup, rather than in the English League and the English Cup. Their ground, Shielfield Park is however, a few miles over the border in England. On January 28 1967, they beat Rangers 1-0 – one of Scottish football's biggest ever upsets.

Two weeks after that, Gallagher starred for Celtic as they beat Ayr United 5-0, and then a couple of days later, the announcement was made that Charlie had been chosen to play for the Republic of Ireland on the grounds that his parents were both Irish. Johnny Carey of Manchester United fame was the Manager, but what that word "Manager" actually meant, we cannot be sure in the context of 1967. He probably did not choose the team, which was in fact chosen (like Scotland's team) by a committee of Selectors, and it would appear from what we have seen earlier that Sean Fallon was at least consulted and was probably very influential in the decision. Sean would in later years also play an influential part in Charlie's career after he left Celtic, as we shall see.

Charlie's cousin Pat Crerand, who was born in the Gorbals, but considered himself more of an Irishman than a Scotsman, would have loved to play for Ireland, and had the rules been changed earlier, might have done so. By 1967, however he had played 16 times for Scotland – and usually with distinction. In his hard hitting autobiography Never

Turn The Other Cheek he tells an amusing story about his International debut.

As it turned out, his debut was, ironically enough, against the Republic of Ireland at Hampden on May 3 1961, only a week after that dreadful Scottish Cup final against Dunfermline. As the players lined up for the National Anthems, Pat could not bring himself to join in God Save The Queen which was then considered to be the National Anthem of Scotland. Had it been Scotland The Brave (Flower of Scotland, that most dreary of dirges, had not yet arrived), Pat would have had no problem, but the Royal Family and the British upper class conjured up so many negative feelings after what they had done in Ireland. On the other hand, when the band played the Irish national anthem The Soldiers' Song (very familiar, of course, to Pat from Celtic Park), he found himself humming along!

Such feelings however did not prevent him playing a brilliant game for Scotland in the 4-1 win, nor did he ever really play badly for Scotland, his best game being arguably the game at Hampden on April 14 1962 when Scotland put an end to a 25 year hoodoo and beat England 2-0.

Charlie's first International game for Ireland was a qualifier for the 1968 European Nations Cup, and was against Turkey in Ankara in a land even more forbidding and unknown that it is now. The news went down particularly well with Celtic supporters everywhere. There had of course been Ireland (both North and South) internationalists who played for Celtic before, some great ones like Patsy Gallacher, Charlie Tully, Bertie Peacock and Sean Fallon, but Charlie was the first "Glasgow Irishman" to be chosen to play for the country that many still considered to be the land of their birth.

Jock Stein was delighted as well. He was, of course, himself very Scottish, but, understanding the proclivities and sympathies of the Celtic support, was clever enough not to minimise or play down the Irish connection. He exploded in print in The Celtic View to welcome the news, and then to mark the occasion, decided to make Charlie the nominal captain and to give him the honour of leading Celtic out onto the field for the next game against Elgin City on February 18 in the Scottish Cup. The modest

Charlie was overwhelmed by all this, but he was cheered to the echo every time he touched the ball with the Jungle (the covered enclosure which was reckoned to house the real hard liners of the Celtic support) churning out The Soldiers' Song and other Irish favourites like Sean South of Garryowen as Celtic beat the gallant but overawed Highland League team 7-0.

He was due to meet his Irish team mates in a London hotel before flying to Ankara. He duly went there and to his astonishment they were all in the bar, their opening gambit being "What do you want to drink?" Charlie, naturally shy and diffident, was virtually a teetotaller and lived under the stern regime of Jock Stein who tried with an almost obsessive ferocity to prevent his players from touching alcohol. He did not always succeed of course with some of his players, but Gallagher agreed that anything that might impair his fitness was to be avoided. Yet here were his new team mates enjoying a pint before they set off for the game. Jock Stein would have had a fit!

In any case there was another perceived problem. The "Dubs", for example, tended to be a bit exclusive, and there was possibly even a little resentment of this Scotsman who was very much an outsider. There must be in all clubs a certain "esprit de corps", and clannish behaviour and cliques must be broken up. It is very difficult for the Manager to do this when he only sees the team for a few days. Newcomers must be welcomed.

Gallagher had a particular problem in that he had met only a few of his new team mates. In some cases he did not even know their names, although he did team up and make friends with Al Finucane, another "outsider", if that is the right word to describe a man from Limerick! Al was a "Home Irishman" in that he did not play for an English team, so he immediately had something in common with Charlie. He had also at one point, apparently, in the past been watched by Jock Stein and Sean Fallon with a view to joining Celtic.

Charlie uses the word "animals" to describe Turkey's players and their fans, and, although honoured to play in International football, frankly did not enjoy the experience of playing in Ankara. The team lost 2-1 at the 19 Mayis Stadyum. Noel Cantwell of Manchester United scored for

Ireland in the last minute to put a respectable face on the score line, and although Charlie was delighted to have represented Ireland, he was nevertheless glad to return to Glasgow. The team was: Alan Kelly, Mick Meaghan, Noel Cantwell, Charlie Hurley, Joe Kinnear, Al Finucane, Mike McGrath, Johnny Giles, Eamon Dunphy, Frank O'Neill and Charlie Gallagher.

There was an aftermath. It was one of the few occasions on which Jock Stein was actually wrong – something that hurt the big man. The whole incident was caused however by some colossal and indeed breath taking and scarcely believable incompetence on the part of the Football Association of Ireland. A few days after his return to Scotland, Charlie was called in to the Manager's office. The conversation ran along the lines of "Are you not proud to play for your country?" "Yes, of course, I am, Boss" "Then why didn't you pick up your Irish cap?" "But, I did, Boss". "No, you didn't, because here it is here. They've sent it on to me to give to you." "Well, there must be some mistake, Boss, because my cap is at home", and he brought it in the next day to prove it.

Diligent enquiries then followed, and to cut a long story short, it was indeed a mistake, but some mistake! There had once been a Mick Gallagher who played for Hibs and he earned one Irish cap in 1954. This cap was intended for Mick, but questions, surely, have to be asked about why it was 13 years later before it was sent on, and why it was sent to the wrong Scottish club! Admittedly, they both wear green and claim tenuous Irish origins, but they are in different cities, and 13 years is a long time for a cap to be hanging around in an office waiting to be sent on to the man who won it! It is little wonder than Irish football was not held in particularly high regard at this time! It also seems that Mick was none too fussed about playing for Ireland!

But this was not the highlight of the 1966/67 season as far as Gallagher was concerned. He was not in the team which lost to Vojvodina in Yugoslavia, but was given a game in the St Mirren game which followed immediately. This was a fine 5-0 win in the Paisley wind and rain, and then Stein made his fateful and inspired decision to keep Gallagher in the team for the visit of Vojvodina to Parkhead on March 8. This time it was at the expense of Bertie Auld who had limped off at Love Street, but who had apparently recovered. Nevertheless, Stein had a hunch that Gallagher was the man for the occasion.

Once again, Stein got it right. Celtic equalised through Steve Chalmers, and the tie seemed to heading for a play-off in neutral Rotterdam. With very little time left, Jimmy Johnstone forced a corner on the stand side of the field as Celtic were attacking what is now known as the Lisbon Lions end of the ground. Across trotted Charlie to take it. The fans all recalled the 1965 Scottish Cup final when Gallagher took the corner which allowed McNeill to propel Celtic to glory. Could the same happen again? It did. Charlie sent over a high one, the flying angel of destruction arrived yet again in the shape of Celtic's captain, and the ball hit the back of the net to put Celtic into the semi-final!

Yet it might have been different. As he was about to take the corner, he saw Jimmy Johnstone, tailed by two Yugoslavs come across to him. The thought occurred to him to take a short corner, but he decided against it for two reasons. One was that he was not sure how long there was left, and a short corner would inevitably have wasted time. The other was that, as there were two defenders with Jimmy, this meant that there were two fewer in the penalty area! The instructions from Jock Stein had always been in these circumstances NOT to use Jimmy. He was to be the decoy. McNeill started his run, the ball was perfectly flighted, and Parkhead erupted.

Two seconds after the game restarted the referee blew for time up. It had been that close, and Celtic Park went hysterical. "Aye, Jock cut it fine tonight" was the verdict of the Press box, but it meant that Celtic were now in the semi-final to play the Czechoslovak Army side Dukla Prague. Sadly for Gallagher, however, his corner kick would be the last ball he would kick for Celtic in the European Cup, for he would lose out to Bertie Auld for the other games of the campaign.

He did however play a handful of domestic games for Celtic that season, notably in the replay of the Scottish Cup semi-final against Clyde. The team had played dreadfully in the first game, but in the replay, one of the rare games when Bertie Auld and Charlie Gallagher played together, Celtic treated their fans to a superb display of football to put themselves into the final where they would beat Aberdeen, but without Charlie who was, as often a reserve. But what a reserve! And it is surely no disgrace not to manage to command a place in that fine team. But he was always ready, willing and able.

But he had domestic concerns. A big event occurred in his family life on March 25 1967. Celtic beat Hearts 3-0 at Tynecastle that day – Charlie wasn't playing, and the Reserve game at Parkhead was rained off - but, more importantly for Charlie back in Glasgow, Mary gave birth to a boy to be called Paul. This happy event was tempered by severe complications however to Mary who needed to have an operation after the birth for ovarian cysts. Her condition however did not prevent her from going to Lisbon for the European Cup final, even though when she got back, her doctor disapproved! Nor could she deny it, for there were pictures aplenty of all the wives in Lisbon, and Mary was undeniably there!

In the meantime, the International scene had not yet passed Charlie by. The Turkish trip may have been a bit of a nightmare, however much he enjoyed the experience of playing for the country of his parents, but Charlie enjoyed a great deal more his next and last (as it turned out) game for Ireland. This was a home tie against Czechoslovakia at Dalymount Park, Dublin on Sunday May 21, a matter of some four days before the European Cup final in Lisbon. Charlie possibly realised that he wouldn't be in the Celtic 11 for Lisbon, but he was very much part of the squad, and had to be at the ready for last minute emergencies. He was thrilled nevertheless to be given another chance to play for what he now saw as his native country, and was given the blessing of Celtic to go and do so.

It would be impossible to minimise the footballing atmosphere in Glasgow and in Scotland in general in those heady days of May 1967. Celtic and Rangers were both in European Cup finals, and even Kilmarnock had reached the semi-final of what was then called the Inter Cities Fairs Cup and was the equivalent of what is now the Europa League. As important as anything for a Scotsman was the fact that Scotland had defeated World Cup winners England at Wembley as well a few weeks ago, and for Celtic fans, there was the domestic treble of the Scottish League, the Scottish Cup and the Scottish League Cup. It was the first time they had ever done that. But dwarfing them all was the small matter of the European Cup final in Lisbon.

Charlie had not been a regular in the Celtic starting XI which was now generally Simpson, Craig and Gemmell; Murdoch, McNeill and Clark: Johnstone, Wallace, Chalmers, Auld and Lennox. But he had played in a few key games – the semi-final replay of the Scottish Cup against Clyde for example – and had usually done well. But he had played in one very disappointing game – a 2-3 defeat to Dundee United at Parkhead, a few days after the Scottish Cup win over Aberdeen at Hampden and a game in which Celtic might have won the League if they had even earned a draw. Because the team did badly that night, Charlie found himself side lined for the next game, the game in which they actually did win the League against Rangers at Ibrox. Effectively, the team that won the League that day would also be the team for Lisbon.

The atmosphere in Glasgow, as we have said, was electric but considerably less so in Dublin. Dublin had not yet developed into being the vibrant, cosmopolitan centre that it would became in the early years of the 21st century. It had not yet entirely exorcised all the ghosts of 50 years ago, as was seen when Nelson's Column in O'Connell Street had been blown up in March 1966, and it was starkly obvious in any case that Dublin was not really a football-minded city.

A disappointing crowd of 6,257 saw a makeshift Ireland team plagued with injuries and withdrawals go down 0-2 to a strong Czechoslovak team, some of whom were familiar to Charlie for he had experienced Czech football a month previously when Celtic played Dukla Prague in the European Cup semi-final, even though he had not actually played against Dukla. By this time Charlie Hurley was the player-manager, but Eire were outclassed by a fine professional Czech side who scored a goal in each half and ran out 2-0 winners. The Irish side was Alan Kelly, John Dempsey, Mick Meaghan, Theo Foley, Charlie Hurley, Eamonn Dunphy, Ray Tracey, Andy McEvoy, Al Finucane, Charlie Gallagher and Oliver Conmy.

The programme for the game is interesting. Tribute is paid to Johnny Carey who had now resigned from the post of Manager, and the Editor feels it necessary to tell his readers about Czechoslovakia, starting with the strange sentence that "Czechoslovakia is the (sic) socialist country, situated in the very centre of Europe. He then talks about "famous hospitality" "murmuring forests" and "a real paradise for huntsmen". It gives every impression, in fact, of having been lifted straight from a tourist guide!

There is also a mention of the game in May 18 1938 in Prague which ended in a 2-2 draw, which in fact was the first encounter between the two nations. One would have liked to have known more about the political background to this game between two young nations, neither of which had existed 20 years previously and one of which was about to be torn apart by Adolf Hitler!

By the time that Charlie got back to Glasgow on the Monday, he found the city in a state of barely controlled hysteria with some Celtic supporters already well on their way to Lisbon, and a few green and white scarves dotted round the airport. Charlie himself had no time to dawdle either, for the team flew out early on the Tuesday morning, and by Tuesday night they were training hard at the stadium itself, as tension rose inexorably all over Scotland, England and Ireland, which now began to show a distinct interest in the fortunes of the "émigré Irishmen" as they were called in one Irish newspaper.

The next few days passed in a whirl. For the fringe players it can't have been easy, for although Stein had made up his mind who was going to be in the XI or XII (the regulations in 1967 allowed a substitute goalkeeper so John Fallon was named for that job), no-one ever knew when a sudden injury or illness would prevent someone from taking part. In the case of Gallagher who was a utility player for the whole forward line and indeed the midfield as well, there was more chance of a sudden call-up than anyone else.

It is always difficult in those circumstances. No-one ever wants to see a colleague injured, but Gallagher would not have been human if he had not wanted, in his heart of hearts, to play. No-one was injured in the warm up however, and Gallagher watched the game like all the other supporters. He and the other reserves were given a seat more or less on the halfway line at the front of the Main Stand. If any supporter wonders what Charlie's emotions were, all one has to do is examine one's own emotions on that roller coaster of a night, for there was no greater Celtic supporter than Charlie Gallagher. He experienced the disappointment at the early dubious penalty, frustration at the repeated failure to score and then the ultimate glory when we did score. He also had a great view of McNeill fighting his way through the crowd past where the reserves were sitting on his way to collect the Cup! John Fallon and John Cushley however had been detailed to grab the bench on the other side of the field that Stein wanted and before Herrera could grab it!

The hours after the game no-one can remember all that well, but Charlie is given the credit for allowing a female Brazilian journalist to get past the policemen and the jobsworths and then gain access to the Celtic dressing room. Quite a few people who were at the after match dinner stated that the players were all struggling to take in exactly what had happened. The team came home on the Friday night to a deserved heroes' welcome, even though it meant being transported round Celtic Park on what looked like a coal truck! It was in fact a builder's lorry owned by RD Stewart.

Some of the other fringe players talk about feeling a little out of things, but Charlie had no such emotions. After all he was a Celtic supporter in any case, but he also could feel that he played his part in the triumph by his substantial, indeed decisive, contribution to the Vojvodina game. He had played in 20 games in that remarkable season in which the team won every competition it entered into. To be a member of that squad was indeed a great honour, and that fact that he never actually played in the European Cup final in Lisbon is no disgrace, and indeed the pain, if one can call it that, was alleviated by the fact that he was a close friend of all his "rivals" for a place in the team.

It took a long time for the enormity of what had happened to sink in. Celtic, the team that Charlie had loved all his life and whom he had joined almost a decade ago, were now the champions of Europe, joining Real Madrid and a very few others. None of the big English teams that the BBC kept telling us about had ever managed to do that, and yet Celtic, who had never looked vaguely like winning any Scottish trophy until 1965 had now won the European Cup. Charlie had been part of that.

Supporters too were finding this hard to grasp. Was this actually the same team who had had perished miserably to Dunfermline in the Scottish Cup final of 1961, whose supporters had rioted when they had folded to the incredulous St Mirren in the semi of 1962, whose supporters had deserted them en-masse in protest against their feckless display against Rangers in the final of 1963 and who had then managed to succumb five times to Rangers in 1963/64?

The answer was yes and no. Yes, it was the same green and white jersey, yes it was the same ground, the same supporters, to a large extent the same players… but there was one vital and visible difference called Jock Stein. He had taken Celtic by the scruff of the neck and made them the best team in Europe.

Ah yes, Jock Stein! Celtic without him would have been like Hamlet without the Prince! Gallagher, like many other players, must have asked himself how he actually felt about the Boss. There could be no doubt about his technical footballing nous and ability. He was a genius, and he was also painstaking in his research on other teams, his attention to detail and his strictness with his own players about punctuality, keeping fit and, particularly, staying away from alcohol. Yet Gallagher disliked the way that he treated some players, not least himself, for, to the players, Jock was never the "favourite uncle" sort of character that he liked to portray himself to the fans whom he always said were the life's blood of the game. "Football, without fans, is nothing". It would be fair to say that he was a totally different character to his players in comparison to what he was to his fans.

Gallagher also wondered about where he himself went from here. Would he have preferred to try his luck in England with a team who would guarantee him a regular start? Or even in Scotland with a team like Motherwell or Hearts who would have welcomed him and his talents? He was now 26, and not getting any younger. All these considerations must have weighed on his mind, but a look at the terracings that night as the building construction lorry went all round the ground must have answered his question. There was still no team on earth like the Celtic.

But, in any case, the season was not yet over. Less than a fortnight later,

Celtic took to the air again this time to Madrid to play in the testimonial game for Alfredo di Stefano. Some of the fringe players were given a game in Madrid, notably John Fallon in the goal, but Charlie did not take part. Nevertheless he knew that there would be a future for him at Celtic Park when the new season came round in August. Indeed he did not want any kind of future other than a green and white one.

And of course that summer he had a new baby. His wife recovered from the various surgical and medical procedures necessary, but that took a fair amount of time. A new baby is a demanding thing to have to deal with at any time. It looked for a spell, in view of what had happened during the pregnancy and birth that Mary and Charlie would not have any more children. In that, the medics were wrong, as we shall see.

CHAPTER NINE

GALLAGHER'S CHAMPIONSHIP

Things did not look good for either Celtic or Gallagher at the beginning on February 1968. The season already had the look of anti-climax about it, with only the Scottish League Cup won in October to show for their efforts in stark contrast to last season's heroics. South America had been an unmitigated disaster which Charlie had done well to be on the edges of and not in the middle. The European Cup had been surrendered, again without Charlie, at the first time of asking to Dinamo Kiev – admittedly with bad luck in the Ukraine but with little excuse for a supine, sub-standard performance at Parkhead in which some heads seemed to have swollen to an unwarranted extent. That was all in the autumn, and then at the New Year two goalkeeping errors seemed to have given the advantage to Rangers in the Scottish League.

And now on the last weekend of January another disaster had struck. A half-hearted, disorganised sort of Celtic side had deservedly gone out of the Scottish Cup to a professional and clinical Dunfermline Athletic. Celtic had been devoid of luck, but it had been 2-0 and the Press and Jock Stein himself had been under no illusions about things. The team were struggling and as The Sunday Express was not slow to say, "It's a long way from Lisbon".

To a certain extent, there was something inevitable about this. It is difficult to retain momentum at such a high level as Celtic had been at. Maybe a mistake was made in standing still in summer 1967. Maybe another big signing or two was called for to "ginger" up the squad, yet it was hard to even think about replacing any of that great side.

For whatever reason the hopes expressed that Celtic might dominate European football for several years in the same way that Real Madrid had done a decade before were dashed.

Even in Scotland, Rangers were now clear favourites to win the League. They were undefeated, were two points ahead (and even that was assuming that Celtic won their games in hand) and did not have to play Celtic again in the League. It was almost like going back to the pre-Stein era. Reflecting a change of Manager, Rangers were playing with youthful enthusiasm – and annoyingly, with luck.

They had never, for example, deserved their draw at Celtic Park at the New Year. It had been John Fallon's nightmare – and Charlie was distressed at this, for he was a friend of John – but it meant that Rangers retained their advantage. All Celtic could do was hope that someone else could beat them, for teams only played each other twice in 1967/68.

And were was Charlie Gallagher in all this? He had played only a handful of games this season, and was in danger of being forgotten about. Being the unofficial deputy to Bertie Auld was not a great place to be, but he stayed where he was. His normal phlegmatic self would not allow him to throw tantrums and demand transfers, and he had played for no-one other than Celtic, but he must have wondered, yet again, what this future was going to be.

To someone other than Gallagher, the thought of a transfer to another club would have been attractive. His skills were appreciated by other clubs, and even Rangers supporters frequently wondered why in this dark hour of Celtic's season he was not given more of a run. He could not of course have played for Rangers, but many other Scottish clubs admired him. England too possessed many clubs who had been aware of his skills, and in 1968 it was often said that when an English club was in trouble, they merely looked north and came back with someone.

Yet would be have wanted to go anywhere else? Celtic through and through, Glasgow through and through, and now with a wife and baby to think about, he would have been reluctant to move. Besides, he may well have felt that his opportunity might yet come at Parkhead.

Certainly in early 1968 the depression around Parkhead was tangible and the disillusion was obvious among the support who found it difficult to accept that, having had an all too brief taste of the good life, we had to go back to the mundane mediocrity that seemed to be facing us. Yet Stein was not called a great Manager without cause, and there would be no dismal surrender, as we had seen all too often in the early 1960s.

So February dawned with Celtic generally reckoned to be in decline. The usual cliches like "one season wonders" were being trotted out with annoying predictability by those who thought they were being stunningly original, but even the most loyal of Celtic fans had to reckon with the possibility that the Scottish League Cup would be all that Celtic would win in the first post-Lisbon season. Perhaps, some of us reckoned, it would be no bad thing if Celtic did not win the League this season. Celtic could then re-group, bring on some of these impressive youngsters that we had heard about with names like Dalglish, Macari, McGrain and Hay, possibly even buy a player from England and come back fighting next year. This might mean curtains for the career of several players, not least Charlie Gallagher.

Charlie was in danger of becoming one of these players who, when one looks at photographs 20 years down the line, one asks "Who was he?" Yet the perceptive of the support had recognised his worth, and Stein, for all his sometimes boorish and unpleasant treatment of some of his fringe players, (not only Gallagher) obviously agreed, for there had been no attempt to unload him at this stage. In particular, he was recalled with pleasure by fans for his two famous corner kicks against Dunfermline in 1965 and Vojvodina in 1967 – both of which were highly significant in the history of Celtic. But good and important as these corner kicks were, there was more to Charlie Gallagher as a player than his ability to find the head of Billy McNeill from a set piece.

But for this year, the thought of Rangers being champions was a painful one. Rangers had a few months previously staggered the world by sacking their Manager Scot Symon when they were actually top of the League! This had happened when Celtic were in South America in early November, and seemed to be an indication of panic. It certainly lacked any common sense or clear thinking, and appeared to have been brought about by a combination of a bad result against Dunfermline and Celtic winning the Scottish League Cup the Saturday before! Symon's replacement was David White, until recently the very successful manager of Clyde but a man with little pedigree of coping with football at this level. Yet as January turned into February, Rangers were not only top of the League but were also still in the Scottish Cup and in Europe. That could not have been said about Celtic.

In the run-up to the game against Partick Thistle on February 3, Gair Henderson in The Evening Times said that a win for Celtic was a "must", for the players had been told that there might soon be new faces at Parkhead, and "there is nothing like a pistol at the temple to get rapid action – and there will certainly be more effort and more spirit in the green and white jerseys for weeks to come" This message, which seemed to contain some inside information, was backed up in a strongly worded statement in the programme written by Jock Stein himself. New energy was certainly evident in the Partick Thistle game, for Celtic won convincingly 4-1, but there was still no Charlie Gallagher. Fans were a little happier with this performance, but there was still the depressing news that Rangers had narrowly beaten Clyde 1-0. It would be an all too familiar scenario in weeks to come.

The following week saw Celtic beat Motherwell at Fir Park, but none too convincingly. John Hughes scored the only goal of the game, but was then injured and replaced by Steve Chalmers. This was significant for, with only one substitute allowed in those days, Bertie Auld had to limp back on when he was injured – something that did him few favours and led to serious trouble as he aggravated his injury. Charlie was playing for the reserves that day at, of all places, Ibrox in a gloomy 2-0 defeat. Even more dispiriting was the news that Rangers first team had won at Dundee that day.

Legend has it that a meeting with all the players in the table tennis room on Tuesday February 13 changed it all. Stein spoke eloquently, telling the players that they were man for man better than Rangers "but you know that anyway", and there were two other advantages. One was that Rangers were involved in two other major competitions, and the other was that their new Manager was inexperienced. It was Stein's belief that Rangers could yet be "psyched out" and, as it were, compelled to lose the League – as long as Celtic won their games and won them well. There was no margin for error.

Bertie Auld's injury ruled him out for the time being – effectively he would not play again the rest of the season - and thus Charlie made his low key return to the team on the night of Wednesday February 14 for a home game against Stirling Albion, postponed a month previously in the bad weather of January. The weather was still not great, and the disappointing crowd of 17,000 perhaps gave an indication of how highly the support rated Celtic's chances of winning the League Championship. It turned out to be a mundane, regulation and unimpressive Celtic victory by 2-0 with a penalty from Tommy Gemmell and a lob over the goalkeeper by Willie Wallace. Charlie played quite well but his performance was not highlighted in any newspaper reports. Still, the victory narrowed the gap to four points behind Rangers with a game in hand. (There were only two points given for a victory in 1968).

Thus was launched Gallagher's finest hour. There are those who believe that "ilka doggie has his day" or that everyone has his brief moment in the sun. The heroes in the Iliad of Homer all had what was called their "aristeia" when they charged up and down the battlefield killing all and sundry of the opposition who happened to be in their way. Destiny was now calling to Charlie Gallagher.

Tom Campbell in Jock Stein – The Celtic Years has this to say of Gallagher in spring 1968 "…Auld was injured…in came Charlie Gallagher as a direct replacement, fitting into the midfield role which he relished. It was another reminder of the previous regime's in competence as Gallagher, never particularly fast, frequently had been played out of position (as a centre forward or a right winger for example) while the chairman indulged his own version of Fantasy Football. Like Auld, Gallagher could read a game and organise strategies to break down defences. In addition and perhaps surprisingly for one of such a slight build, Gallagher was an excellent striker of the ball and possessed a lethal shot. Those supporters who felt uncomfortable in remembering the barracking Gallagher had received previously from the less tolerant were delighted to see him take full advantage of the recall. From the deep lying position he spread passes all over the field and, more importantly, was the ideal link man with forwards now running freely and steadily into dangerous positions. Bobby Murdoch stated that one key to Celtic's success went largely unnoticed: 'For years nobody twigged that what we were doing – and looking for – was creating space".

All this was in the future however because for the next two weeks Celtic took a back seat. Being out of the Scottish Cup, they had no game on February 17, although they arranged a friendly at St James Park against Newcastle United which they lost narrowly. Charlie did not play in that game, his place going to young George Connolly. Then all of Great Britain turned their attention to the Scotland v England game on February 24 at Hampden (a disappointing 1-1 draw which suited England rather than Scotland), the weather was unpleasant and saw the postponement of a game against Aberdeen in the following midweek and it was Saturday March 2 before Celtic played again. By this time Gallagher was well prepared for his key role in the 1967/68 season.

In the meantime, Stein had told the players that he would manipulate the media. He would leak stories, make sure that Rangers were knocked off the back pages and he asked his players to dazzle the country by their play. He then told them that he would play his master card, although to an extent he had been forced to do this. It was made clear that Charlie Gallagher, that silkiest of passers, would be brought into the team for an extended run. Bertie Auld struggling with bad injuries sustained at Motherwell would later admitted with magnanimous and characteristic candour "I was drappt" but that was not entirely true. He was in fact badly injured and eventually needed a cartilage operation, but even if there had been any chance of him recovering, it would have been very difficult for Stein to drop Gallagher.

The first game back for Celtic after the enforced break was at Rugby Park, Kilmarnock on March 2 on a heavily sanded pitch and in weather which was still cold, (there had been a considerable amount of frost) but providing a little reluctant sunshine. Sunshine was the word too for this fine Celtic performance. Charlie excelled that day with his superb passing, although most of the plaudits went to Willie Wallace for his four goals and Jimmy Johnstone who had his own point to prove to Kilmarnock's trainer

Walter McCrae with whom, when the pair of them with the Scotland squad last week, he had crossed swords. Walter had asked Jimmy to be a linesman rather than play! Jimmy made the remark that his performance was "no bad for a linesman, eh, Walter?" Celtic won 6-0, and one of the goals was scored by a young gentleman with the illustrious name of Jimmy Quinn, the grandson of the great Jimmy from Croy of 60 years ago.

This game was broadcast on the radio, and highlights were shown on TV, so that all Scotland was impressed and, in the psychological battle that Scottish football always is, all of Ibrox began to tremble. Rangers themselves won 6-2 against St Johnstone that day, but the sheer speed and brilliance of the Celtic team as seen at Rugby Park was not lost on Rangers. It would have an effect on them, and caused their Board of Directors to make a distinctly wrong decision.

Both teams played in midweek on March 6 – Rangers beat Dunfermline narrowly and luckily, and once again Celtic turned it on at Parkhead to beat Aberdeen 4-1 in a game that might, with advantage, have been stopped at half-time. Indeed, it was a game which Gallagher and Celtic seized by the scruff of the neck from the very start and they were 4-0 up at half-time with Aberdeen looking as if "they hadn't reached Glasgow yet" in the words of a fan. In the middle of the second half, Stein took Gallagher off, not because he was displeased with him, but rather because he wished to keep his new talisman for future occasions. In any case Charlie's replacement that night was a boy of some promise. He was a debutant by the name of David Hay.

Highly impressive stuff this was, and enough to send more than a few shivers of fear down Ibrox way for it was then that Rangers co-operated with an astonishing own goal. It concerned the Glasgow Cup, a grand old tournament – the third oldest in the world behind the Scottish and the English Cups - which in its day had attracted great crowds and enthusiasm. By the 1960s it was struggling, - it had not been competed for in 1965/66, for example, because no-one could agree dates - but when Celtic were drawn against Rangers in the semi-final (Celtic had already beaten Partick Thistle at the start of the season) at Ibrox, the game was much anticipated.

Celebration after the 3-2 victory over Dunfermline Athletic in the Scottish Cup Final. 24th April 1965

Player having fun in the pool at Seamill Hydro in 1967

Charlie scores the 4th goal in the 5-1 victory over Dundee in January 1967

Scottish Cup Winners 1965

John Hughes, Alec Byrne and Charlie in training at Barrowfield Park for the Scottish Cup Quarter Final against Hibernians at Celtic Park

Charlie shows off his goalkeeping skills to his nephew in January 1967

Charlie, followed by Ronnie Simpson, leads out the team for the Scottish Cup tie against Elgin City on 18th February 1967. Jock Stein made him Captain of the day after Charlie was selected for his first cap (versus Turkey) for the Republic of Ireland.

Celtic team 1960/61

Photograph taken before a League Cup match versus Partick Thistle on 8th August 1964 which ended 0-0

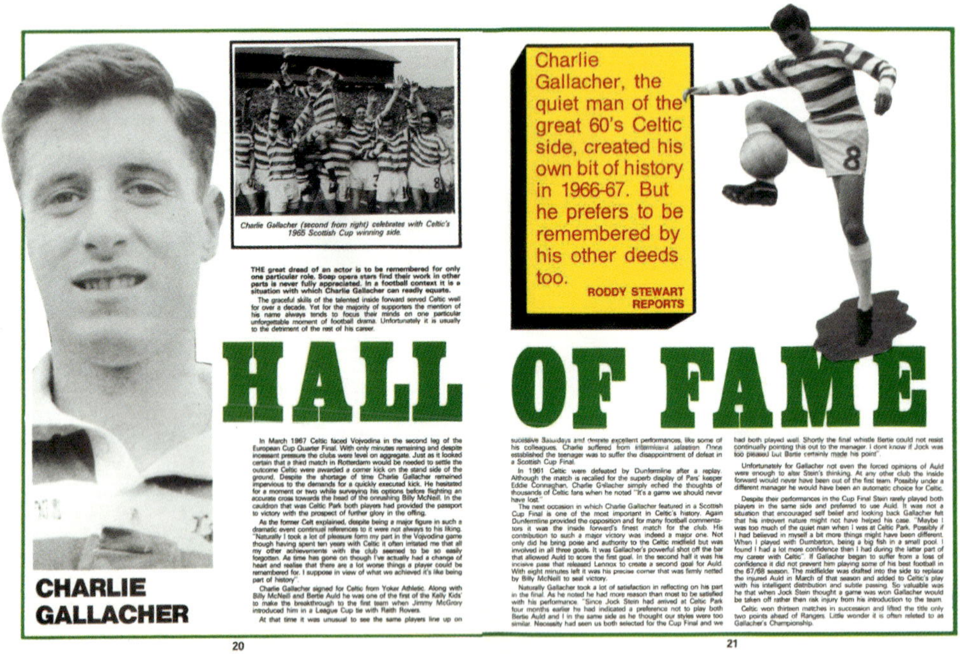

CHARLIE GALLACHER

Charlie Gallacher (second from right) celebrates with Celtic's 1965 Scottish Cup winning side.

THE great dread of an actor is to be remembered for only one particular role. Soap opera stars find their work in other parts is never fully appreciated. In a football context it is a situation with which Charlie Gallacher can readily equate.

The graceful skills of the talented inside forward served Celtic well for over a decade. Yet for the majority of supporters the mention of his name always tends to focus their minds on one particular unforgettable moment of football drama. Unfortunately it is usually to the detriment of the rest of his career.

Charlie Gallacher, the quiet man of the great 60's Celtic side, created his own bit of history in 1966-67. But he prefers to be remembered by his other deeds too.

RODDY STEWART REPORTS

HALL OF FAME

In March 1967 Celtic faced Vojvodina in the second leg of the European Cup Quarter Final. With only minutes remaining and despite incessant pressure the clubs were level on aggregate. Just as it looked certain that a third match in Rotterdam would be needed to settle the outcome Celtic were awarded a corner kick on the stand side of the ground. Despite the shortage of time Charlie Gallacher remained impervious to the demands for a quickly executed kick. He hesitated for a moment or two while surveying his options before flighting an accurate cross towards the head of the onrushing Billy McNeill. In the cauldron that was Celtic Park both players had provided the passport to victory with the prospect of further glory in the offing.

As the former Celt explained, despite being a major figure in such a dramatic event continual references to it were not always to his liking. "Naturally I took a lot of pleasure form my part in the Vojvodina game though having spent ten years with Celtic it often irritated me that all my other achievements with the club seemed to be so easily forgotten. As time has gone on though I've actually had a change of heart and realise that there are a lot worse things a player could be remembered for. I suppose in view of what we achieved it's like being part of history".

Charlie Gallacher signed for Celtic from Yoker Athletic. Along with Billy McNeill and Bertie Auld he was one of the first of the Kelly Kids' to make the breakthrough to the first team when Jimmy McGrory introduced him in a League Cup tie with Raith Rovers.

At that time it was unusual to see the same players line up on sucessive Saturdays and despite excellent performances, like some of his colleagues, Charlie suffered from intermittent selection. Once established the teenager was to suffer the disappointment of defeat in a Scottish Cup Final.

In 1961 Celtic were defeated by Dunfermline after a replay. Although the match is recalled for the superb display of Pars' keeper Eddie Connaghan, Charlie Gallacher simply eched the thoughts of thousands of Celtic fans when he noted "It's a game we should never have lost."

The next occasion in which Charlie Gallacher featured in a Scottish Cup Final is one of the most important in Celtic's history. Again Dunfermline provided the opposition and for many football commentators it was the inside forward's finest match for the club. His contribution to such a major victory was indeed a major one. Not only did he bring poise and authority to the Celtic midfield but was involved in all three goals. It was Gallacher's powerful shot off the bar that allowed Auld to score the first goal. In the second half it was his incisive pass that released Lennox to create a second goal for Auld. With eight minutes left it was his precise corner that was firmly netted by Billy McNeill to seal victory.

Naturally Gallacher took a lot of satisfaction in reflecting on his part in the final. As he noted he had more reason than most to be satisfied with his performance. "Since Jock Stein had arrived at Celtic Park four months earlier he had indicated a preference not to play both Bertie Auld and I in the same side as he thought our styles were too similar. Necessity had seen us both selected for the Cup Final and we had both played well. Shortly the final whistle Bertie could not resist continually pointing this out to the manager. I dont know if Jock was too pleased but Bertie certainly made his point".

Unfortunately for Gallacher not even the forced opinions of Auld were enough to alter Stein's thinking. At any other club the inside forward would never have been out of the first team. Possibly under a different manager he would have been an automatic choice for Celtic.

Despite their performances in the Cup Final Stein rarely played both players in the same side and preferred to use Auld. It was not a situation that encouraged self belief and looking back Gallacher felt that his introvert nature might not have helped his case. "Maybe I was too much of the quiet man when I was at Celtic Park. Possibly if I had believed in myself a bit more things might have been different. When I played with Dumbarton, being a big fish in a small pool, I found I had a lot more confidence than I had during the latter part of my career with Celtic". If Gallacher began to suffer from a loss of confidence it did not prevent him playing some of his best football in the 67/68 season. The midfielder was drafted into the side to replace the injured Auld in March of that season and added to Celtic's play with his intelligent distribution and subtle passing. So valuable was he that when Jock Stein thought a game was won Gallacher would be taken off rather then risk injury from his introduction to the team.

Celtic won thirteen matches in succession and lifted the title only two points ahead of Rangers. Little wonder it is often releted to as Gallacher's Championship.

20

21

Charlie with former team-mate, goalkeeper, John Fallon supporting the Bhoys at Easter Road in 2012

Charlie and former rival, Davy Wilson, join Dumbarton FC in the early 1970s

Charlie with Jackie Stewart (manager) and Kenny Wilson at Dumbarton FC

Charlie (top row, second from left) with the 'old guard' at Dumbarton FC

Charlie and John Fallon visit two Celtic fans in their home (a Celtic shrine) in Dundee in 2007. This mother and son were both seriously ill and, sadly, passed away shortly after this visit.

Charlie on a recent visit to Celtic Park, reminding us of the worldwide support the Bhoys enjoy!

The game had been scheduled for some time in February, but the bad weather which had delayed Rangers replayed Scottish Cup tie with Dundee meant that it was postponed until Monday March 11. Rangers with their fixture problems – they were also in the European Inter Cities Fairs Cup and of course the Scottish Cup - asked for a further postponement because both teams would also be playing on Wednesday. It would therefore have still been a level playing field in the sense that both teams would be playing three games in a week, and for this reason the Glasgow FA, fed up of being pushed around, dug in their heels and insisted the game should be played on that Monday.

There is a common Celtic perception that authorities, be they the Glasgow FA or the Scottish FA, are in the pay of Rangers, and will invariably back up Rangers and do Celtic down. Not so! History does not really support this assertion. In fact if anything, the SFA, the Scottish League and other organizations resent the arrogance of Rangers who often give the impression that they are above everyone else. On this occasion the Glasgow FA, a body who had seen better days but who boasted correctly that their tournament was older than the Scottish League, showed here that that they were not going to be bullied by a mighty financial organisation like the men from Govan, still less were there any secret deals made by men who rolled up their trouser legs in private and shook hands in a strange fashion!

The wily Stein realised that all he had to do was stay silent and Rangers would be isolated. Celtic of course had always been willing to play. But now Rangers suddenly announced that in view of their other commitments in the Scottish League, the Scottish Cup and the Inter Cities Fairs Cup, they had decided that they would not fulfil the fixture and that they were to be withdrawing from the Glasgow Cup! It was an even more astonishing decision considering that the game was to have been played at Ibrox.

To a neutral observer, to Celtic supporters, to the Press and to even some of Rangers own fans, this looked like cowardice and fear of facing Celtic in the only competition left this season in which the two teams would meet. Clearly Celtic's dramatic return to form against Kilmarnock and Aberdeen was having its effect. Celtic fans certainly thought this was the case, and were not slow in letting Rangers fans know their point of view.

It was a clear insult to the city of Glasgow, and Rangers' pleas that the winning of the Inter Cities Fairs Cup would bring great glory to Glasgow cut little ice. As it was, it was a gift for Celtic, who were now in the final of the Glasgow Cup and they had clearly gained the moral high ground and the support of neutrals. A cruel joke went round Glasgow that Rangers for their next game were to have the unlikely letters IRA embroidered on their shirts, standing for I Ran Away!

Even given fixture congestion, there were at least two things Rangers might have done. They might have approached Celtic to suggest that both teams fielded a weakened team – but would Stein have agreed? – or they could have declared their pitch unplayable because of all the frost and/or rain than bedevilled Glasgow that spring. As it was they meekly surrendered – and this from a team whose supporters sang a song that they would do no such thing!

Two days after the Monday when the Glasgow Cup game ought to have been played, Rangers were deservedly punished for their craven behaviour. Clearly smarting from the abuse and ridicule heaped on them, Rangers went out of the Scottish Cup to Hearts, to a late Donald Ford goal at Tynecastle, thereby, as their critics were not slow to point out, easing their own fixture congestion! But as far as Celtic fans were concerned, this was only the icing on the cake, for they heard the news on their way home from Celtic Park having just seen their own team beat Airdrie 4-0. The Tynecastle game had been delayed because of serious over-crowding, so car radios and pub TVs had the honour of passing on the good news.

Willie Wallace scored a hat-trick, and Jimmy Johnstone was outstanding, but discerning spectators noted the quiet and unspectacular performance of Charlie Gallagher with his inch perfect passes and wonderful understanding with Jimmy Johnstone and Bobby Murdoch. On that same day came the sad news for fans of Bertie Auld that he was going into hospital for a cartilage operation and would be out for the rest of the season. This clearly put the onus on Gallagher to deliver the goods, but it also gave him a sense of security that his position was not under any immediate threat. He did not pass up the opportunity.

Indeed, a glance at Celtic teams for the months of March and April will show that virtually the same team took the field every game. This was good, for players knew each other, the camaraderie was excellent and they all knew each other well enough to cover for each other's mistakes and to forgive each other the occasional blemish. It was actually a fine time in Celtic's history as the support, realising than something was happening, rallied round after all the "I'm no comin back" sort of rubbish in January, and it was visibly a collective effort.

The position at the top of the League was that Celtic and Rangers had both played 25 games. Nine games remained. Celtic had by far the better goal average over Rangers, and the way they were playing meant that they were likely to steadily improve it, but the problem still remained the two points. Goal average, we remember, meant dividing the goals for by the goals against, rather than goal difference which is simply the crude method of subtracting goals against from goals for. Rangers were undefeated in the League, and Celtic needed someone to beat them, or at least two teams to draw with them. And it had to be someone other than Celtic, for the two teams would not meet again this season in the League or indeed any other competition.

Charlie might have been unsettled by the rumours going around at this time that Stein was making a bid to sign Jimmy Smith from Aberdeen. This would have been a direct threat to Charlie's place in the team, but by the time that Celtic travelled to Brockville on March 16, nothing had happened. It was claimed that Stein did in fact make an offer to Aberdeen, but it seems to have been a fairly half-hearted one, and it was turned down by Aberdeen, if indeed anything was offered.

It is hard to believe that this move would have been a success. Smith was talented, sharing with Jimmy Johnstone the nickname of "Jinky" and was certainly a Celtic sympathiser, but he was a proven discipline problem with both his Manager and with referees. He had publicly disgraced himself with a dreadful tackle of Stevie Chalmers in last year's Scottish Cup final – for which he had been booked – and too often found that the Aberdeen fans turned on him for his attitude which did not always appear to be as committed as it should have been. If Jock had gone for him and failed, he would have consoled himself in that he had Charlie Gallagher who was not only a talented player in the first place, but was also steadily improving with the added responsibility thrust upon him. And there was certainly no problem with his attitude. Indeed, Charlie would prove that Celtic did not need Jimmy Smith.

A run in the team was what was needed. This Celtic team was superb – everyone knew that – but that did not mean that it did not require some time for Gallagher to bed in, as it were, in match conditions. It was one thing on a training ground and quite another in a game in front of ever-demanding fans. Bobby Lennox for example was so fast that he preferred the ball a few yards in front of him so that he could run on to it, whereas Johnstone preferred it at his feet, and as long as you managed to get the ball to Wallace or Chalmers in or near the penalty box, there was at least a chance of a goal. Charlie, never an extrovert in the dressing room, was nevertheless quite assertive on the field and fitted in fairly seamlessly as the team gradually moved into top gear.

Much had been made of the psychological aspect of all this, and anyone who ignores this aspect is ignoring the truth. As long as Celtic won their games, Stein and the fans knew that there was at least a chance that Rangers would crack. Rangers knew they had been lucky not to lose to Celtic in the two League games that season – the New Year game in particular – and they probably knew that in their heart of hearts, Celtic were a far superior side. Rangers had now exited from the Scottish Cup after clearly losing out in the psychological warfare resulting from their Glasgow Cup decision. Their young Manager called Dave White had done a brilliant job for Clyde but was this job too much for him? Clearly out of his depth at this level against Jock Stein, he must have wondered what he was doing. Rangers, in fact, began to look like a man going down a dark alley and expecting to be mugged.

Rangers' adequate but no-more-than-that squad would clearly have doubts as they looked over their shoulders at the approaching Celtic juggernaut, which, for all their failings this season, had, last year, won the European Cup – a fact that everyone reminded Rangers of. And Celtic were now on a Gallagher-inspired roll, playing superbly and not looking as if they were going to make any errors.

Saturday March 16 was one of the worst days, weather-wise, that one could imagine with a howling wind and heavy torrential rain. Celtic were at Falkirk. Brockville, now thankfully closed down, was grossly inadequate at the best of times and out-of-date even in 1968, when it was called "Broken-downville" by visiting supporters. Falkirk had of course been a graveyard for Celtic in the late 1950s and early 1960s, and they could always be guaranteed to put up a good game against Celtic, whatever their current form was against other teams.

This particular day saw the BBC TV crew, there for their highlights programme at night, deciding to abandon their position on top of the enclosure roof! In addition, a piece of roan pipe blew off and hit a poor girl on the head. The exposed terracings were sparsely populated, and those who were there, were clustered under a few umbrellas and hoped in their heart of hearts that referee Mr Anderson of East Kilbride would abandon the game, and allow everyone to go home or to the pub. Indeed, when he extended the half time interval to about 20 minutes to allow the players to change their gear, we suspected that he had done just that!

But a good player in a good team can play in every type of weather, and Charlie rose to the occasion. Celtic led at half-time through a soft penalty as everyone tried to adjust to the conditions, but in the second half, even with large puddles beginning to form on the park, Celtic began to take a grip of the game, adapting their style to a short passing sort of approach, and Wallace and Lennox scored the goals to give Celtic a 3-0 win. The only fly in the ointment was Rangers 5-0 win over Stirling Albion at Ibrox, but Gallagher felt that it was a good day for Celtic the game with a win at a ground which had so often in the past provided a huge hurdle.

Similar weather was in place for the next game, this time a 5-0 beating of lowly Raith Rovers at Parkhead. Ron Trevorrow of The Evening Times says quite unequivocally that "there is no team in the land that could live with these modern day soccer gladiators in green and white". Willie Wallace scored a hat-trick and Bobby Lennox and John Hughes scored one each. Charlie played superbly that day but was substituted near the end, and we feared that he had picked up some kind of injury, but if it was, it was a very slight one. More might have been expected of Hibs that day, but they capitulated 1-3 to Rangers which meant that now with only 7 games left, the gap was still that gnawingly annoying two points.

But now Celtic seized the initiative. The game v St Johnstone at Perth, originally scheduled for early January but postponed through bad weather, was going to take place on Wednesday night. Rangers were involved in the Inter Cities Fairs Cup against Leeds United on the Tuesday, so Stein realised that Celtic could actually be on top of the League if they won at Muirton Park, the then home of St Johnstone. (The Saints moved to McDiarmid Park in 1989). A further opportunity to unsettle Rangers occurred when Willie Ormond, the Manager of St Johnstone, suggested to Celtic that he would rather play the game on the Monday because St Johnstone were in the Scottish Cup semi-final next Saturday against Dunfermline Athletic, and would prefer more time to prepare.

You could almost imagine Stein's eyes gleaming when he heard this. Not only was there now a chance to be top of the League even BEFORE Rangers took on Leeds United, but Stein also twigged that for a team like St Johnstone, a Scottish Cup semi-final was a huge occasion. They had only been there once before in 1934, and therefore the focus would very definitely be on Saturday's Scottish Cup semi-final rather than a League game of lesser (for St Johnstone) importance. Opportunity was knocking for Celtic.

The now recently re-energised Celtic support, there in huge numbers that mild dry spring evening, saw Celtic and Gallagher take command from a very early stage. Lennox scored 4 goals in a 6-1 victory in which Gallagher sprayed passes throughout. Conditions were a lot better than in recent games, and Muirton Park was often reckoned to be the best surface in Scotland for football. This was tailor made for Charlie whose inch perfect passes frequently drew gasps of admiration from the crowd and even the occasional ripple of applause from the traditionally sporting St Johnstone supporters in the main stand. It was indeed a marvellous exhibition of football, reported in detail in the newspapers, and causing all sorts of distress at Ibrox.

Tommy Gemmell tells an interesting story about this game. St Johnstone's only goal came from a free kick. Stein gave the players a day off training the following day, but after that, pretended to be furious and the next few days at training were spent in doing nothing other than clearing free kicks! This of course is an indirect compliment to Charlie Gallagher and the rest of the team, for he clearly felt that everything else was going well. Further evidence of the "quivering" of Rangers came when feckless forward play prevented them from scoring at Ibrox against Leeds United, but every one of the huge Ibrox crowd knew that, given their obsession with Celtic, in their heart of hearts that the problem really was the six goals scored at Perth the previous night! A crack was not far away.

Everyone – even sports psychologists – will deny that what happens at a different ground on a different day in a different competition has any effect on another game. But anyone who has ever taken part – even as a spectator – in the claustrophobic atmosphere of the Old Firm will appreciate that there is a great deal in nerve games. It has happened too often that a triumph in one half of Glasgow will have its effect on the other. Stein certainly realised that.

As the spring came (or seemed to), Celtic moved up a gear. March 30 was a big day in the Scottish football programme, for it was Scottish Cup semi-final day. How odd it was to see neither Celtic nor Rangers involved in the Scottish Cup at this stage! But the League programme continued with Celtic and Rangers playing difficult games at Dundee United and Airdrie respectively.

The weather clerk seemed to have taken an interest in the destination of the Scottish League and the Scottish Cup. He, apparently, wanted to watch the football as well. At long last we had a good, sunny day to see Celtic at their best, as they went to Tannadice Park (not always the happiest of hunting grounds in the past) and put five past a Dundee United side which had beaten us twice last year and drawn at Parkhead in December. Once again the forward play was superb and the local Press even went as far as to say that it was the best display of attacking football seen on Tayside for many years. Dundee United Manager Jerry Kerr was compelled to agree. Indeed, veteran Celtic supporters had never seen anything like it either.

Jimmy Johnstone scored a wonderful individual goal to open the scoring, and the biggest surprise of the first half was that Dundee United had survived until half-time having conceded only two goals. It was an absolutely devastating performance, and it was difficult to imagine anyone on earth living with Celtic. There was a confident jauntiness about the team with Jimmy Johnstone occasionally verging on the unstoppable, Charlie Gallagher spraying passes, Willie Wallace and Bobby Lennox interchanging at speed and John Hughes thundering down the left wing. Not for the first time, did supporters regret that awful game at Celtic Park on September 20 last year which effectively put Celtic out of the European Cup! Interestingly, immediately after the 3rd goal went in, Charlie was taken off and replaced by David Cattenach. It was as if Jock Stein decided that it was "job done" and the time was now ripe to take off the star man and keep him for future occasions.

Gallagher had indeed had a fine game in what was football at its best. He received one of the greatest compliments possible from an elderly fan who, either by a genuine mistake or what was called a Freudian slip, said "Well done, Patsy (sic) Gallagher!" It was one of the best games played by the team in this great epoch. The fans loved it, and the Press and TV reported it all with adulation and jaw-dropping astonishment. And Rangers quivered even more.

They may have quivered, but they still were winning, today getting a late lucky winner to get the better of Airdrie after a poor performance. Both Scottish Cup semi-finals were being played that day as well. Both Dunfermline v St Johnstone and Hearts v Morton ended up in 1-1 draws and were rightly slated as "dreadful" and "boring" in most newspapers. Neither game looked good on the TV highlights, and it was so frustrating to see one's team playing so well, but, at this stage, looking still as if the Scottish League Cup, won away back in October was all that we were going to have to show for their splendid efforts.

But Celtic's performance in Dundee did have one side-effect. The local Press now played a part. The Dundee Courier, The Evening Telegraph and even The Sunday Post naturally enough supported the two local teams, but were basically pro-Celtic. (Odd, considering that their politics were blatantly pro-Tory!) Spearheaded by Tommy Gallacher, son of the illustrious Patsy of long ago, a campaign was launched in the knowledge that Dundee United's next two games were against Rangers – at Tannadice in a postponed game on Wednesday and then at Ibrox on the Saturday. Basically, it admitted that Celtic were good, but also told United that they would have to improve. Pressure was put on the Dundee United players, and the Wednesday game at Tannadice in particular was pointed to as a game to show their fans that they weren't as bad as Celtic had made them seem on Saturday.

But before that, weather once again played a part. The problem about Scotland's weather, particularly in the spring was its unpredictability. It had been pleasantly warm on Saturday but now Scotland suffered a rash of snow storms and blizzards – by no means unprecedented in late March or April – and early on Wednesday morning Aberdeen woke up to several inches of snow. Celtic were due there that night but were alerted and told not to travel. The bad weather however had not reached as far south as Dundee (or Glasgow for that matter) and Rangers' game at Tannadice was on.

So for Charlie and indeed for all the Celtic fans, it was an anxious night waiting for the news from Tannadice. It turned out to be the night in which the first real crack in the Ibrox edifice became visible, because to the delight of their own fans and to those of Celtic, Dundee United stiffened their defence, played the boring defensive football for which they were notorious and earned themselves a goalless draw on a cold, wintry night. The contrast between Saturday and Wednesday could not have been more acute both in terms of the weather, and in the standard of football. The bad news was that Rangers had now played the same amount of games – there were now only five left – but they were a point ahead. Still, given Celtic's far superior goal average, one more point lost by Rangers would do it, as long as Celtic didn't lose any games.

This particular night also saw Dundee, a good team in 1968, reach the semi-final of the Inter Cities Fairs Cup, and Dunfermline and Hearts reach the final of the Scottish Cup. Hearts were thus upbeat for their home game at Tynecastle on Saturday April 6 when Celtic arrived. Hearts had of course been in a fairly obvious decline for a year or two since they threw away the Scottish League in 1965, on the same day as Celtic's win over Dunfermline in the Scottish Cup final. In fact, one often felt that April 24 1965 was the day that symbolised the reversal of roles of the two clubs, for Hearts had prior to 1965 looked like the side that would provide the most consistent challenge to Rangers, while Celtic had been the permanent disappointment, failing on key occasions to believe in themselves. Now the roles were reversed and it was changed, changed utterly.

On this day it was like old times again with a 27,000 crowd at Tynecastle. The Hearts supporters were buoyed to hysterical proportions with their win over Morton in midweek and relishing the prospect of a Hampden Cup final – something that they were not slow to remind us of. In truth it was their first Scottish Cup final for 12 years.

But Celtic played things low key, scored two good clinical goals from Johnstone (in which this tiny man outjumped the whole defence to head home) and Lennox and then kept good possession of the ball during a somewhat lethargic second half. It was in situations like this that Celtic saw the benefit of Charlie Gallagher. Whatever else he could do, he could read a game. He could tell when to slow things down and when to speed things up. He sensed on this occasion that the situation, with Celtic 2-0 up at half-time, needed only sensible possession of the ball against a team which had certainly done well on the Wednesday night but were now suffering from the emotional effects of it all. In any case, Hearts were not quite as good as their some of their more optimistic supporters felt they were.

One recalls the scene just as the players came out for the start of the second half with all eyes still glued on the half time scoreboard at the Gorgie Road end of the ground. The Gorgie Road terracing presented the amazing sight of all heads facing away from the field and the Celtic players themselves also facing the board as they waited for the referee to re-start the game. This was of course the only way in which the score at Ibrox could be conveyed, for there was no radio coverage until 4.10 pm and the BBC could not be guaranteed to give scores of games other than the one they were broadcasting.

The scoreboard operators clearly relishing the occasion put up all the other irrelevant scores ignoring the importunate cries of "It's these bastards from Ibrox we want to hear about", and even, for a laugh, putting up a few fake scores like 5-0 or 0-5. With both teams now back on the field, a "0" at last appeared for the home team at Ibrox, and with everyone now shouting for "3" or "4" to appear for Dundee United, another "0" was put in place. Goalless at half-time! Still, it was something!

It didn't last, however. Celtic's good and deserved victory was somewhat tarnished when the radio at 5.00 pm us told the grim news that Dundee United had been unable to repeat their heroics of Wednesday night and had imploded, fairly predictably and depressingly, at Ibrox (as indeed they often did). Rangers had won 4-1 with Alex Ferguson having one of his rare good days in the blue shirt of Rangers. So, four games each to play, and Rangers still one point ahead.

There was a pop song going the rounds in spring 1968 which always reminded one of Charlie Gallagher. It was called "Me The Peaceful Heart" and was sung by the Glaswegian pop star Marie Lawrie, better known as Lulu. In particular, the last two line of the chorus just seemed to sum up Gallagher's approach

"...wondering why the stormy weather

Always finds me, the peaceful heart."

There was indeed something very calm and re-assuring about Charlie. Everything else might be exploding in frenzy round about him, with some of Charlie's team mates guilty of losing the place now and again, but there was always the reassuring presence of Charlie, now and again seen to have a "quiet word" with some of this colleagues who were giving signs of beginning to get riled by an opponent.

There was a picture which appeared in several periodicals of Charlie with an easel doing some painting. This also typified the man. Peter Marshall describes him as "exquisite" in everything that he did. In the same way as he used exactly the right colour for his painting, he knew exactly where to place his pass, and precisely the right weight to put on it.

Midweek once again gave Celtic the temporary lead in the League. Rangers were playing in Europe on the Tuesday night, losing to Leeds United at Elland Road, so Celtic had the chance on the Wednesday to gain the initiative in their postponed game at Pittodrie. Rangers fizzling out at Leeds – they lost 0-2 - was once again, one felt, a symptom of the strain they were under because of the pressure from Celtic, but the official Celtic line was "it's of no consequence to us" (as Jock Stein said to a supporter as he boarded the train for Aberdeen that morning – but he had a twinkle in his eye!). Everyone knew that Celtic would get a further boost from Rangers travails.

Indeed the Ibrox world was now crumbling like a cake. They now ONLY had the League to play for, having lost everything else. In the space of a few weeks, after they had run away from Celtic in the Glasgow Cup, they had exited the Scottish Cup and the Inter Cities Fairs Cup. Celtic were already the possessors of the League Cup, and they were now desperately hanging on to their one-point advantage in the Scottish League. But Rangers problems would count for nothing if Celtic could not win at the toughest ground, other than Ibrox, on the Scottish circuit – Pittodrie.

Aberdeen, who had disappointed this season, had nothing to play for other than pride, which had of course been badly dented by their 4-1 defeat at Parkhead a few weeks ago. Celtic still had the luxury of an injury free squad, so the team once again picked itself – Simpson, Craig and Gemmell: Murdoch, McNeill and Brogan: Johnstone, Lennox, Wallace, Gallagher and Hughes – a few changes since Lisbon of a year ago, but changes for the better, it was felt. Once again we must call into question the statement apparently attributed to Stein in 1965 that he wanted to get rid of Johnstone, Gallagher and Hughes. They were not only still there, they were starring, all three of them! Indeed, it was the opinion of many supporters that they were now playing better football and with more confidence than last year. And as at Tynecastle, another aspect of their play came into view – the ability to soak up pressure.

Amazingly well supported in the 25,000 crowd considering that it was a Wednesday night 150 miles away from home, (although what does "home" mean for Celtic, considering the support that they have in all parts of Scotland, including the surprising size of the pro-Celtic faction in the North East?). Celtic had what was probably their hardest game since the New Year, being indebted to Ronnie Simpson for at least three good saves from Davie Robb, one of which at least seemed net-bound. Celtic's goal was a regulation Johnstone to Murdoch to Lennox in the 60th minute, and after that, Celtic were forced to defend, with Gallagher detailed to support the midfield and not venture too far forward. Referee Eddie Thomson's final whistle came as a huge relief, meaning as it did that Celtic were top of the League by one point with three games to go.

Rangers had four to play, but, now still coming to terms with their failures in other competitions, the pressure was intensifying.

Saturday 13 April saw the repetition of a pattern that we had seen on many Saturdays this season – a convincing Celtic win and a scratchy Rangers one, and more frustration for the Celtic crowd. At Parkhead Celtic beat Dundee – no mean opponents under Manager Bobby Ancell (himself a football purist) for they were now in the semi-final of the Inter Cities Fairs Cup – 5-2 playing sparkling football to the delight of the 41,000 crowd, whereas at Stark's Park, Kirkcaldy, Rangers had to hold on against a tremendous late Raith Rovers onslaught to edge home 3-2 before a huge crowd which delayed the kick-off by 12 minutes. Thus the environs of Parkhead had the phenomenon of Celtic fans clustered round cars to hear how the game at Kirkcaldy was going. No-one in Kirkcaldy didn't believe that Raith Rovers shouldn't have had at least one penalty, but Rangers were still holding on. The full time whistle came to predictable groans and curses.

Writing in the following day's Observer Hugh McIlvanney has no doubts about what was the main cause of Celtic's superiority. "Most of Dundee's difficulties stemmed from the killing accuracy of Gallagher's passing. Gallagher's languid air, his reluctance to become embroiled in any robust activity, masks a genuine menace. His eye for an opening is flawless and the sureness of his touch enables him to curve passes round defenders into the path of the running forward. He could release Lennox from apparently hopeless positions and when Lennox breaks, no defence is safe".

Strong words indeed from a fine journalist who didn't often try very hard to hide his love for the Celtic! Rangers, annoyingly, however were still that point ahead. But there are times in life when one's faith in an all-loving deity are reinforced. Celtic who had now scored 100 goals that season were still waiting for someone to beat or even draw with Rangers in order to give the team the break and the League title that their play had so richly deserved. More and more people, not all of them of the Celtic persuasion, were beginning to say that it was time for justice to be done, and for the side that had so dramatically electrified the Scottish season since February to step up and claim the title.

Charlie Gallagher's role in all this was crucial. In 1968, it often seemed like blasphemy if someone said that a team played in a 4-2-4 formation, the tradition of the 2-3-5 M or W set-up dying hard. 4-2-4 or 4-3-3 was seen as a sign of defensive mindedness, so beloved by the Continentals. But to a supporter, it did seem very much as if this was what Celtic were playing, and doing so with conspicuous success. The back 4 would be Craig, McNeill, Clark (or Brogan) and Gemmell, the middle 2 would be Bobby Murdoch on the right and Charlie Gallagher on the left, with Johnstone, Lennox, Wallace and Hughes in the front. Murdoch would tend to bring the ball forward himself before releasing it, whereas Charlie would beat one man and then deliver a silky, visionary pass to one of his eager front runners, the combative and talented Willie Wallace, the speedy greyhound called Bobby Lennox, and the two loose cannons in Jimmy Johnstone and John Hughes, both of whom, Johnstone in particular, capable of winning any game virtually on his own.

But of course there were two other great strengths in the team. One was the fact that, notwithstanding what the perceived team formation was, the team was fluid. Great Celtic teams in the past – the Jimmy McMenemy inspired team of 1908, and the Jimmy Delaney and Malky MacDonald team on 1938, for example, both had this in common, that they could interchange almost at will and render themselves almost impossible for the opposition to man-mark. In any case, a 4-2-4 system, the pure undiluted 4-2-4, seemed to exclude wingers. Celtic's system emphatically did not do that. In fact Johnstone more than once asked at pre-match team meetings what was expected of him. Jock would say "You? We'll get the ba' tae ye and then ye can just dae whit the hell ye want!"

The other thing was the great team spirit. Everyone knew that Jimmy Johnstone was, on his day, the best in the world – the old timers even permitted him to be included in the same breath as Patsy Gallacher and Jimmy Delaney! – but he was emphatically not a prima donna, at least as far as the rest of his team were concerned! Emotionally insecure on occasion, Jimmy would sometimes go on to the field saying things like "Ye heard fit the Big Man said. Gie me the ba'!"

In this respect Charlie Gallagher was the perfect foil for him. Totally different characters, they nevertheless understood each other and fed off each other in an astonishing display of mutual symbiosos. Jimmy liked being told that he was the best in the world, he did on occasion fall out with Big Jock, he could on occasion fall out with a referee and he certainly put Walter McCrae of Kilmarnock in his place when Walter tried to bully him with the Scotland squad – but he never considered himself above his team mates or indeed the Celtic supporters. He needed his ego massaged from time to time, but Jimmy was astonishingly like "an ordinary man", as they used to say about Jimmy Quinn.

And this could be said of them all. They all talked to supporters without ever giving the impression that they were talking down to them, they got on well together and they were all proud to be playing for the team that they loved. Some like Simpson, Gemmell and Wallace perhaps had not been born as Celtic supporters – but they were now! They may have been well paid professionals, but they were never anything other than the man on the terracing – except that they had been blessed with the ability to play football. This was certainly true of the unassuming Charlie Gallagher, now recognised by most of the support as the man who was producing the "tick" in Celtic.

So now we come to the dramatic events of Wednesday 17 April, and enter Greenock Morton, where Rangers went that fateful Wednesday. This was Rangers game in hand over Celtic, and as it happened, Morton were due at Parkhead on Saturday. Celtic on that same Wednesday were at Hampden playing Clyde in the Glasgow Cup final, the trophy of course which Rangers had scorned in early March. Ironically, now that Rangers were out of the Scottish Cup and the Inter Cities Fairs Cup, they would have had all the time in the world to play their Glasgow Cup fixtures!

Celtic had no such problems about the trophy that was actually older than the Scottish League and only a few years younger than the Scottish Cup itself. In fact, they were the holders for the past three years in 1964, 1965 and 1967 (it had not been played for in 1966 - because of fixture congestion!), and were proud to list this venerable old trophy among their 5 successes of last season! Stein paid Clyde and the Glasgow Cup the compliment of sending out his best available side.

Celtic delighted their fans with a great 8-0 victory at Hampden, in a game made remarkable at half-time by the movement of fans from one end of Hampden to another on the running track, the better to see more goals going in after the break! They were already, by half time, 7-0 up! Gallagher was substituted in the second half because the job was so obviously done and Stein wanted to give John Clark a run out in the team. Clyde supporters stood and clapped this great Celtic side, as their players simply shook their heads with that "What can we do?" look about them. Jock Stein paid tribute to Clyde for their sportsmanship and Gair Henderson in The Evening Times makes the astonishing suggestion (presumably, one hopes, as a joke) that if Celtic played continued to play like that, it might be an idea to introduce a handicapping system in football! The 8-0 victory equalled the record score in the Glasgow Cup set by Queen's Park in 1889!

Those Celtic fans who moved from one end of Hampden to another were already buoyed up by encouraging news from Greenock, for Queen's Park, no lovers of Rangers, were broadcasting score flashes with a certain amount of glee. Morton were 2-0 up at half-time, and shortly after the restart, both sides scored to make the score 3-1. The news was spreading around Hampden, where Celtic having done all their work and with no desire to humiliate any further their part-time opponents, most of whom were Celtic supporters in their spare time! Chants of "3-1" and "Morton" left the players in no doubt either, but there was still some time to go. Rangers scored on the hour mark through John Greig, and then fifteen minutes later, Willie Johnston headed an equalizer.

An eerie silence now descended over Hampden. Little of interest was happening on the pitch, as the game was being played out. All thoughts were with the gallant Morton defence at Cappielow, or even if they could just slip up and score another! Their two full backs were Laughlan and Sweeney – and they didn't sound as if they were Rangers supporters, and there was also Preben Arentoft in the midfield, and he was a great player.

John Fallon, the "villain" of the New Year – it had been he who in one of his rare outings for the club who had conceded two goals to Rangers, tells the story of how he was playing in a reserve game at Parkhead against Raith Rovers that night in a virtually deserted stadium and was told the score at both other grounds by a friendly ball boy. He left the field totally unaware of what the score had been in the game in which he was playing (Celtic Reserves beat their Raith Rovers equivalents 2-1), but hit the roof with delight when he learned that Morton had held out for a draw.

The full time whistle at Cappielow came more or less at the time that the magnificent old Victorian trophy the Glasgow Cup was being presented to Celtic, and thus there was a double celebration! Two trophies had now been won this season, and Celtic were now in the lead in the Scottish League on goal average (significantly better) with two games left – Morton at home and Dunfermline away as distinct from Rangers who had to go to Kilmarnock before finishing off with Aberdeen at home.

Rangers then lost even more friends by another crazy, arrogant, superior decision – and one which cost them dear. The last games of the season would have seen Celtic at Dunfermline and Aberdeen at Ibrox. Celtic's game could not be played on that day as Dunfermline were in the Scottish Cup final against Hearts at Hampden. Dunfermline and Hearts, Dunfermline in particular, suggested ever so nicely to Rangers that it might be an idea to bring forward or to postpone the Rangers v Aberdeen game. This would mean that the Scottish Cup final (which would be struggling to fill Hampden given the comparative lack of support for both East of Scotland teams, neither of whom had a huge fan base in the West) could have the city of Glasgow to itself. The suggestion was sound and backed up by the Press.

Rangers however seemed to resent being dictated to by someone like Dunfermline and refused to move their fixture, clearly believing that there was the possibility that they could now have had all their games completed before Celtic did, and so that Celtic would therefore have to go to Dunfermline the following midweek needing to win to capture the League. This line of thinking backfired on them spectacularly, as we shall see.

But there was more to it than that. Rangers' attitude created the impression that Rangers were more important than the Scottish Cup final and that Rangers were, in some ways, superior. They had given that impression before, notably in 1954 when they took their players on a tour of Canada rather than let them play for Scotland in the World Cup! It was an attitude that did them no favours, and Stein, always with his ear to the ground to find ways to capture the morally higher position announced that he was taking the whole Celtic team to Hampden on April 27 to watch the Scottish Cup final. Not only that, but he suggested that the whole Celtic support should do likewise. It was an important day, he said, and everyone realised just exactly who he was getting at here. He still of course was not without his hankerings for Dunfermline, for it had been he who had created them out of virtually nothing.

But that was the following week. In the meantime, Celtic now scented blood, but Morton now fancied themselves for an Old Firm double on April 20. They were given a great reception by the cheering, chanting, triumphant 51,000 Parkhead crowd for their efforts of Wednesday night, and such was the pressure on the Parkhead turnstiles that the kick-off was delayed. This would be significant in the late drama that was to come. After Willie Wallace scored early on with a brilliant flying header from a Hughes cross, Morton equalized on the stroke of half time.

Celtic had seemed a little edgy, but this was all put down to nerves, for of course it was even possible that Celtic could win the title today if they won and Rangers lost at Kilmarnock. The pitch was a little uneven and fiery, for after a very wet spell, the weather had suddenly turned dry and a few bare patches were visible. At half-time with both games level, anything could happen. On this occasion there was a radio broadcast starting at the traditional time of 4.10 (ie the last half hour) coming from Rugby Park – but everyone was aware that because of the delayed kick-off Celtic's game would finish at least 5 minutes later than the Rangers one. However, with news coming through on the transistor radios that Rangers had scored and were edging it over Kilmarnock with about 20 minutes to go, Celtic had to get another goal to win the game.

The second half was agony as Celtic in their all green strip pressed and pressed towards the Railway End where most of the fans were crammed but could not break down Morton's stubborn defence. The goal scoring machine was simply not working today. Minutes passed but the goal would not come. Celtic changed their formation more than once, trying Hughes on the right wing and Johnstone on the left, Gemmell surged forward repeatedly but the goal would still not come. Gallagher moved all over the forward line in an attempt to force the issue but still nothing happened. A few chances was missed, a few corners were forced, and we all, behind that Railway End goal tried to suck the ball into the net, for it began to look as if Celtic would have to settle for a draw.

We screamed and shouted, begging for penalties where there wasn't even any contact between the players, and looked at our watches as the minutes rocketed by. The radio now gave the baleful tidings that Rangers had, in fact, beaten Kilmarnock 2-1 (we accused Kilmarnock of "collaboration"!) and unless Celtic got a goal, Rangers would be one point ahead going into the last game. The ninety minutes had now, apparently, come and gone at Parkhead. Referee Mr Paterson of Bothwell, looked at his watch ostentatiously and histrionically and the final whistle was expected when Murdoch in desperation sent a high cross into the box, Hughes made partial contact, the ball broke to Wallace who miskicked and the ball came to Lennox. The ball took a funny bounce on the hard pitch and Lennox too miskicked, but the ball hit off his shin and went into the net!

Phrases like "Parkhead erupted" did not quite cover it. Many of us were simply overwhelmed by the surging of the crowd, but the memory remains of the Morton player hanging on to the back of the net in sheer anguish and chagrin at having come so close to a famous double over the Old Firm. On the field the players went mad. Tommy Gemmell tells us he toyed with the idea of stealing a policeman's helmet, but fortunately thought better of it. Even the phlegmatic Charlie Gallagher was jumping about hugging his team mates.

The full time whistle went immediately afterwards but amidst the bedlam no-one heard it. We just saw the players shaking hands and walking off the park, the Celtic ones doing a few jigs on the way. Celtic were back on top, ahead of Rangers on goal average, and only one game remained. No-one knew it, but Celtic were now destined to win the League without kicking another ball.

The story is told of the train back from Kilmarnock to Glasgow that afternoon. Rangers had beaten Kilmarnock and when the train left Kilmarnock, Celtic were still drawing, so Rangers supporters thought they were back in front. Now in 1968, when one was on a train, one was virtually out of touch with the outside world as there were no mobile phones or texts and even transistor radios could not pick up a good signal because of the noise of the train. So happy was the atmosphere with how great Rangers were and songs were heard about "Follow! Follow!" and references to obscure incidents in Irish history about guarding walls and grassy slopes. The train reached Glasgow Central, someone bought an Evening Citizen and the atmosphere changed to "We need to buy better players!" "White disnae hae a clue" and how Greenock Morton were in a Jesuit plot to give Celtic the League!

Next Saturday, April 27, was the date for the Scottish Cup final between Dunfermline and Hearts. Celtic of course had no game, and had urged their supporters to go to the Scottish Cup final – well they weren't likely to go to Ibrox to see Rangers v Aberdeen, were they? - and Stein had repeatedly announced that he was organizing a bus party to take all the players. Sadly, there was loads of room at Hampden, for the crowd failed to come close to anything like its full capacity, although quite a few Celtic supporters took Jock's advice and went along to cheer the Pars.

Gallagher thus watched the Scottish Cup final (Dunfermline won 3-1) while at the same time hearing titbits of information about the Rangers v Aberdeen game. With 30 minutes to go, Aberdeen equalized to make it 2-2. This would have been good enough news for it would have meant that a draw would then have been enough for Celtic at Dunfermline on Tuesday night. The players thus watched the Cup being presented to Dunfermline, and then an uncertain rumour began to spread that Aberdeen had scored late in the game. Communications were still not great in 1968 and the players were all sitting on their bus before Stein came in with the final score from Ibrox and told them that Celtic were the Champions, Aberdeen having scored in the 89th minute. Rangers, shell shocked by last week's events, and now convinced that they were not going to win the League, surrendered their unbeaten record on the last day of the season, and had now lost everything. They had been comprehensively "psyched out", even on a day when Celtic were not playing!

East End Park on Tuesday was thus a celebration for both teams. It was the Scottish League Champions v the Scottish Cup winners. The crowd was vast, too big for the ground. The game should have been all-ticket, but as it was, the overcrowding at the city end of the ground was terrifying, and the youngsters who climbed on the roof of the enclosures did so taking their lives in their hands. Some 49 supporters were injured but there was no malice in it, simply overcrowding.

It had been obvious from an early stage that there was going to be crushing. From about 6.00 pm an hour and a half from the kick-off time, the road from the Kincardine Bridge to Dunfermline had been jammed with traffic, and the town of Dunfermline itself was virtually impossible to drive in that night. Many cars and buses were parked in the Dunfermline Glen on the other side of town, as supporters then walked all the way to East End Park.

The problem had arisen when an exit gate was forced open and thousands rushed in. It was not necessarily that they grudged paying, more than they were frustrated at the long queues at the turnstiles. Not for the first time did we see a provincial ground, normally adequate for its purpose, unable to cope with a large Celtic crowd. Before the teams came out, already the packed crowd was swaying dangerously.

Twice the game was stopped in the first half by Mr Wharton to allow police and ambulance men to deal with the injured, as both Managers tried to appeal to the fans to come down off the enclosure roof. On both these occasions, Mr Wharton signalled the players to go off, but he himself, bravely, stayed in the middle with his two linesmen talking to police men. Had he gone off as well, it might have seemed to the crowd that the game was being abandoned and that might have caused more problems, but the fact that he remained indicated that he, at least, was still hoping that football could be played.

Slowly the police managed to ease the problem, decanting some spectators to the Halbeath end of the ground and allowing others to sit on the grass behind the goal. It was a mercy that, although 49 were reported injured, no-one actually lost their life, and it said a great deal for all concerned that this was the case. Both teams were cheered by both sets of supporters, Jock Stein tried to steal the Scottish Cup from George Farm when the trophy was being paraded, everyone laughed and the game itself finished 2-1 for Celtic with Lennox, inevitably perhaps, getting both goals, one early and one late. Both teams however deserve a great deal of credit for playing in such difficult circumstances. But it was a lesson in the problems created by such enthusiasm and passion for Celtic.

For Charlie Gallagher this represented his apogee. Cheered every time he touched the ball and even now and again getting a look of something like approval from Stein, who still apparently did not like him, he had now climbed football's Olympus. He was never the most flamboyant of players in the way that Johnstone or Gemmell were, but the more perceptive of the support appreciated the part he had played in this championship, Celtic's 23rd and the 3rd in a row. He had indeed come a long way since February – so had the team, but he had been the man who took them there. He himself would never have said so, but to many of the more thoughtful and studious of the support, 1968 was Gallagher's championship.

There was of course more to it than that, and Charlie was embarrassed when people use the phrase "Gallagher's championship". Tribute must also be paid to other great members of the team, to Stein's masterly use of psychology (never let anyone tell you that football is not played in the mind as well as on the pitch) and the role of the supporters in all this. They weakened in February, it would have to be said but rallied in March and April and played their own part in carrying the team through. No-one however, either in the support or in the Press underestimated the part played by the modest and unassuming Charlie Gallagher.

There was a brief tour of the New World in the summer. It was nothing like as successful as the longer tour of two years earlier which had done so much to build up the esprit de corps which played a large part in the European Cup triumph. Only three games were played but Charlie played a part in the goal scored by Celtic in the 1-1 draw against AC Milan in New York on May 28 when goalkeeper Belli could not hold Gallagher's shot and Wallace netted the rebound. He then scored when Celtic beat the same opponents in Toronto a few days' time on June 1. So Celtic returned with their reputation enhanced. The horrors of late 1967 in South America had now been forgotten about, and summer 1968 was a happy one. Gallagher was happy and looking forward to a lot more of this. He did not know that his Celtic career was virtually over.

CHAPTER TEN

THE END AT PARKHEAD

Ironically, after all his fine exploits in spring 1968, Gallagher played only one more competitive game for Celtic in Scotland. Gallagher had played well in the games of the American tour, but when the serious business came round in August, Stein introduced George Connelly at the expense of Charlie Gallagher.

We do not know at what stage or for what precise reason Stein decided that Gallagher, still regarded as the hero of last year by many supporters and pundits, should give way. For the high prestige friendly against Leeds United, Gallagher was named as one of the substitutes, but the very fact that Celtic lost that game 1-2 made one feel that Gallagher might yet be preferred for the first real game of the season against Rangers at Ibrox. But it was Connelly that got the nod.

To an extent, we cannot blame Stein because the claims of the immensely talented young George could not really be ignored, but most supporters felt that this was hard on Charlie. Most supporters had been waiting for Connelly to break through. He had first come to their attention in January 1966 at half-time in the Dinamo Kiev game when he had entertained the crowd with a demonstration of keepy-uppy and ball control. It had been thrilling stuff and consistent good reports filtered through about his performances in the reserves, and it was certainly in character with Stein to keep introducing youngsters. Any objections were easily squashed with the undeniable fact that the team were off once again to a great start.

Every single game of the League Cup section was won, and won well, with Willie Wallace in a particular in great goal scoring form. Partick Thistle and Morton were swept aside, but the games that really mattered were the ones against Rangers. Celtic opened the season on a lovely sunny day at Ibrox with a 2-0 win and two weeks later beat them again 1-0 at Parkhead.

Charlie had opened the season at Celtic Park, playing in the Reserve League Cup against Rangers. The team contained quite a few experienced men – Chalmers, Craig and McBride for example as well as Gallagher – but there were also talented youngsters like David Hay, Jimmy Quinn and Lou Macari as well. Celtic won 2-1, but in the next Old Firm reserve game, Gallagher was missing. It may have been a coincidence, but Celtic lost 2-5.

It was a valuable role for Charlie, even though he would have been a great deal happier playing in the first team and indeed, many supporters, recalling his great days of early in the season, thought that he should have been there. Youngsters, however talented, need mentoring and supporting, and Charlie was ideally cut out for just that job. He was sympathetic, kind and understanding, for he recalled his own apprenticeship of ten years ago, and how men like Willie Fernie helped him along. In addition, he was a model professional showing a perfect example to the youngsters in his habits of training hard, abstinence from anything that might do him harm, and that sheer fact that he was Celtic through and through.

But in August 1968 something happened on the world stage which at one point threatened major repercussions, and it was something that Celtic, enjoying their new major role in European football, involved themselves in. The Soviet Union, with its Warsaw Pact allies, on the night of August 20/21 invaded Czechoslovakia. This was because they feared that the "liberalising" tendencies of Alexander Dubcek, who had already done things like allow the freedom of the Press, might encourage Czechoslovakia to defect from the Warsaw Pact and join the West. So, they sent in the troops.

This high-handed action, by no means dissimilar to what Hitler had done to the same country thirty years before and very like what the Soviets had done to Hungary in 1956, was of course roundly condemned by the West, but short of provoking nuclear war with a counter invasion, what could they do? In any case, the USA were hardly, themselves, squeaky clean as they were raping Vietnam at the time. But Celtic now intervened.

Celtic had been drawn in the European Cup to play Ferencvaros of Hungary. Mr Kelly felt that it was unfair that in the prevailing circumstances Celtic should be asked to play a game in Hungary whose troops were now invading another country. He approached the European authorities and asked for a re-draw of the European Cup. He canvassed hard for support, and won his point. The draw was scrapped, re-done and Celtic now found themselves playing St Etienne of France instead of Ferencvaros.

There were those who questioned Mr Kelly's motives. Cynics felt that when he won his Knighthood on New Year's Day, it was for this very political stand, but he certainly won his point and it was an indication of just how far Celtic had come in the past few years. In 1952, Celtic and Kelly had won their point over flying of the Irish tricolour at Celtic Park; now they were able to make their effect on world politics!

The one first team game that Charlie Gallagher played that season was in a game that didn't matter. It was a Scottish League Cup quarter final second leg against Hamilton Accies at Douglas Park on September 25, and Celtic had already won the first leg 10-0! Celtic, fielding virtually a reserve side, won 4-2 in pelting rain, and the only real factor of historical relevance in the game was that Charlie was substituted in the second half and replaced by a young man called Kenny Dalglish, another example of Stein's willingness to bring on youngsters if and when they were good enough.

Soon after that, Charlie began to have problems with his cartilage and ligaments, and an operation was necessary at Bon Secours hospital in November 1968. Jock Stein was notoriously bad at visiting injured players in hospital, particularly those who were now deemed to be on the fringes. Other players and backroom staff visited regularly and there were loads of well wishers among the support, but only once, and then under pressure from people like Sean Fallon, did Stein come to see him. His words were less than totally encouraging "I've signed Tommy Callaghan to replace you!"

He had indeed done just that. Stein had bought Callaghan from Dunfermline. Having managed Callaghan from his time as Dunfermline boss, Jock knew he was good. It would not be entirely true however to state that Callaghan was a direct replacement. He was merely an addition to the very rich pool of Celtic talent available to Stein. In effect, Tommy was mainly used as a substitute, at least for the rest of the season.

What this incident proves however is that the relationship between Stein and his players was not always all that it could have been. No-one would ever dare to doubt the tactical nous and sheer managerial ability of Jock Stein. His record speaks loudly for itself. There are some players who will not have a bad word said about him – Billy McNeill for example – but others, mainly those on the fringes carry a legacy of bitterness. John Hughes, for example, could not bring himself to go to Stein's funeral after several humiliations at his hand. John Fallon has recently told his story of Jock Stein, and it is one from which Stein does not emerge with credit. Fallon was also treated very poorly by Stein when he was injured and in hospital with one churlish visit during which he said to Fallon that he should get a hair-cut!

These stories sit ill with the fans who worshipped Jock Stein, but it is clear than his tremendous record as a trophy winner must be balanced against his lack of sympathetic man-management skills. Stein was born in 1922 into a tough Lanarkshire mining background. It is often fashionable to describe in romantic terms these coal mining villages where everyone looks out for each other. There is a certain truth in that, but there is also the other side of it. One has to be tough and competitive to survive, and sometimes sheer nastiness can be looked upon as a virtue.

This is certainly true of miners who play football. Jock made his debut in the middle of World War II for Albion Rovers. Neither in the mines, nor on the football field was life easy for him, and he was little more than a solid centre half. He himself described himself jocularly as a "passable" centre half – something that can of course mean two things! When he moved to Wales, it appeared than his footballing career was coming to an end, but then by a happy set of chances, he found himself at Celtic Park – absolutely not where his family would have wanted him to go – became captain, won the Coronation Cup in 1953, then a League and Cup double in 1954, but sustained a bad ankle injury in 1955 which compelled him to give up the playing side of the game. His sole International honour was in a Scottish League International game against England at Stamford Bridge – and England won!

His managerial career before he came to Celtic in 1965 was a success, and this continued. But he had seen the hard side of life too. He had lost games – in particular the 1955 Scottish Cup final against Clyde gave his a deep-seated distrust of goalkeepers – and competitions, (any Manager, player or supporter will have a few disappointments in his life) but there was still very little in Stein's background to justify the paranoia that he sometimes seemed to suffer from as far as some players were concerned.

As to why he did not like Charlie Gallagher, we cannot tell. One could find reasons why he did not like some of his other players, but the inoffensive, hard-working, never-complaining Charlie was a man to whom it would have been difficult to take a dislike. Perhaps Stein wanted him to show a little more of the devil in him, because, ironically, he sometimes seemed to like some of his bad boys. Jimmy Johnstone, for example, did enough on several occasions to earn himself the sack or a transfer to some English club, but Stein went the extra mile for him. Tommy Gemmell more than once asked for a transfer, and to an outsider, it often appeared that he and Stein were at daggers drawn. Yet the mutual respect was there. Bertie Auld likewise could get himself into trouble on and off the field, but always managed to keep the affection of his Manager.

Perhaps it was the sheer inoffensive nature of Charlie Gallagher that made Jock Stein not like him. There was certainly no rational reason, other than perhaps that Gallagher was one of the few of the Kelly Kids that had been unknown to Stein when they met up at Celtic Park. But Stein's dislike of Gallagher would be shown up in an incident when Gallagher was playing for Dumbarton. We shall read this story in due course, and it is a story that shocks and horrifies those who profess a liking for Jock Stein.

And yet, even the players who do not speak highly of Stein as a character all unanimously admit that they would have been nothing without him. Had Stein not been appointed in 1965, the subsequent history of Celtic would have been a lot less pleasant. It is difficult to imagine Celtic winning a European Cup, for example, and indeed the likelihood is that Celtic would have ended up in perpetual decline, not unlike the English example of Newcastle United who have now not won an English trophy since 1955. Yet Newcastle's fans have stayed loyal. Celtic's might not have. In January 1965 there were ominous signs that a lot were not coming back.

The truth is that Celtic, to survive as a major Scottish power, had to appoint Stein in 1965. It is also true that most successful men, not only in football but also in every other walk of life, have to have a ruthless streak. This Stein certainly did. Whether it can be used to justify the way that he treated men like John Hughes, John Fallon and Charlie Gallagher is open to question, to say the least.

So what would have happened to Gallagher without Stein? He might have retained his place on the Celtic staff, he might have even won back his first team spot, but without Stein there probably would have been no, or very few medals. He might have departed to Dumbarton or Partick Thistle or Kilmarnock a lot earlier than he eventually did. It would have depended on who the new Manager might have been. He might have been just as ruthless and nasty as Stein – but with a lot less of a football brain. Who is to say what might have happened with a new Manager, or in the real nightmare scenario of Mr Kelly keeping the status quo?

Certainly, if what Stein was reputed to have said about wanting rid of Charlie Gallagher along with Jimmy Johnstone and John Hughes is true, we have to face facts and point out that he did NOT actually do it. He may have SAID it (although never in public) but he certainly did not DO it. Charlie may have been heading for the exit in summer 1965 along with men like Hugh Maxwell and John Divers (who survived summer 1965 but not summer 1966) but he saved himself, in Stein's eyes, by a fine performance in a few games, notably the Wednesday night of March 31 when he starred in the replay of the Scottish Cup semi-final against Motherwell. Gallagher had been brought in on the Saturday but Celtic, with Gallagher still a little nervous and unsure of himself, had been feckless, unimaginative and possibly lucky to get a draw; with Gallagher on song on the Wednesday night, Celtic had booked their final spot soon after half time. Possibly more pointed were the games against Hibs. Without Gallagher, Celtic were well beaten at Parkhead; with Gallagher Celtic "attuning themselves for the Cup final", beat Hibs (who were still challenging for the Scottish League) 4-0.

His successful Cup final was the high point of his career, and 1965/66 saw him in and out of the team, good enough to win a Scottish League and a Scottish League Cup medal, but noticeably he did not play in the games against Liverpool not the replay of the Scottish Cup final. He had played in the first game, a disappointing 0-0 draw, but Bertie Auld came back for the replay. Gallagher's silky passes might just have made a difference on that awful night when Celtic, with most of the pressure, failed to breach the Rangers defence, then lost the one goal of the 180 minutes.

Stein certainly considered him worth keeping before and after Lisbon, and Stein's trust of the player was rewarded in Gallagher's glorious spring of 1968. But then he was hardly used in 1968/69 even before he went into hospital. In truth, even after Charlie's complete recovery from his cartilage operation, there was now no way back for Gallagher at Celtic Park. Not only had Tommy Callaghan been bought from Dunfermline, as Stein had said he would, but it was difficult to spot any chink in their armour.

The team was doing remarkably well, it has to be said, lifting a domestic treble in April 1969 and but for one uncharacteristic error from Billy McNeill against AC Milan in a European Cup quarter final, they might have won that trophy as well. Indeed, many people think that the way that the team played in 1968 and 1969 was better than how they did in 1967. Gallagher was back playing for the reserves by the spring of 1969, a role he accepted in the circumstances, and thus he was not involved in the remarkable month of April 1969 when Celtic, playing devastating football managed to win all three Scottish trophies in one calendar month, including two memorable Cup finals – 6-2 against Hibs in the Scottish League Cup final and then three weeks later 4-0 against Rangers in the Scottish Cup final.

On the Tuesday night after Celtic had won the treble, the Reserves made it trophy no 4 for the season as they beat Aberdeen Reserves 2-0 at Hampden in the Scottish Reserve League Cup final. The team is interesting – Wraith, McGrain and Gorman; Dalglish, Connolly and Cattenach; Gallagher, McMahon, Macari, Callaghan and Davidson. Charlie was back on his old stamping ground of the right wing, the team had two experienced players in Charlie and Tommy Callaghan, a few of the others had played a first team game or two (notably George Connolly who had won the Scottish Cup a few days previously) but most of them were callow youths, clearly learning a lot from Charlie Gallagher. Young Kenny Dalglish, for example, playing at right half, is described as a "carbon copy of Bobby Murdoch", and there could be no higher praise than that!

Gallagher was retained in 1969 for the following season – although it would have been fascinating to see what would have happened if some English team had shown an interest. Charlie trained hard all over the summer. He was still only 28 and felt that he had a certain amount of football left in him, but he must have felt that his chances of playing first team football for Celtic must have diminished. Harry Hood had also joined the club, Davie Hay was now a first team regular, and there were other men in the queue as well. But he never complained. Indeed he still enjoyed a good standard of living, and he also rather enjoyed playing for the reserves, acting as a kind of mentor to young men like Danny McGrain who continually sang his praises.

In the year of 1970, Celtic did in fact make it to the European Cup final again. This had followed the two games against Leeds United and a distinctly unfortunate Scottish Cup final against Aberdeen in which the refereeing of Bobby Davidson played a disproportionate part in the proceedings. But by the time that the European Cup final was played, Charlie had been given a free transfer. His wife and he made jokes about it, for now there would be loads of time for painting the house!

But before that happened, a weird event occurred. Sometime in early 1970 when it was obvious that Charlie would probably not get back into the Celtic side, however well he played in the reserves, Stein told him one day that there was a Manager of a "north of England club" wanting to talk to him. Stein refused to say who it was, but gave Charlie an address of a disused warehouse in the Manchester area so that he could go and talk to the Manager concerned.

Charlie duly travelled down to the place concerned and waited for the man to appear. He had a long wait and no-one turned up. An hour or two passed, and eventually Charlie gave up and headed home. He told Stein about it the following day, but Stein just shrugged his shoulders and still would not tell Charlie who the Manager was nor which team he represented. Charlie heard no more about it!

What was behind this? Was Stein sufficiently insecure and vindictive to send Gallagher on a fool's errand of this nature? If so, it reveals an almost sadistic side of Jock's nature which we find hard to accept. Many other players will testify to the vindictive side of Stein's character, but would he go so far and be so nasty as to do something as bizarre as all that? Yet if not, and if Jock was simply wanting rid of Gallagher, why did he not tell him who the Manager was? He might have earned the club some money instead of simply giving him a free transfer. The truth of this strange matter will never be known.

It was on Friday May 1 1970 that the axe fell, and even then there was more than a touch of nastiness about. With all of Celtic Park agog with the prospect of the European Cup final in Milan, and Celtic preparing to take all their playing staff to see the game, Charlie was looking forward to the trip. Two planes had been chartered, but the first inkling that Charlie had to the effect was that he was getting the boot came when Sean Fallon came to him and said that he could not see Gallagher's name on the list for either plane. The announcement was then made that the playing staff had been reduced from 32 to 31 with Charlie Gallagher given a free transfer. He was the only one, for everyone else was retained. There would thus be no trip to Milan for Charlie and no future at Celtic Park.

The handling of this situation was shoddy, humiliating and, frankly, not worthy of the fair name of Celtic Football Club. It may have been realistically the best decision for both Celtic and Gallagher himself. Gallagher had after all hardly played in the first team for two years, new players had been brought in and things had moved on from Gallagher's great spring of 1968. Things can and do change very quickly in football as we have seen, but this hardly excuses the insensitive way that Stein handled the situation.

A more humane Manager (even Stein himself perhaps in his early years) would have sought the player out for a quiet word before any brutal announcement, explained the situation and offered to do his best to get him another club (Stein had considerable influence in Scottish football). Things could have been amicable and friendly, even though the situation was difficult. But then again, as events in the next few weeks would indicate, Stein seemed to be under a great deal of pressure in spring 1970 in spite of all the obvious success that the team was achieving. There was very little in Milan or the USA that reflected any kind of credit on Jock Stein.

Charlie's departure itself was curt and brief. The conversation went along the lines of "Charlie, I'm releasing you" to which Charlie said "Good" and left Stein's office to find Sean Fallon waiting for him. Sean was not always liked by all players, for he had a tendency to tell the truth, but he was efficient and reliable. He also had the ability to provide a shoulder to cry on. He and Charlie got on well together. He had already used his influence, it was believed, to get Gallagher capped for Ireland, and on this occasion he was able to fix him up with another job. "Don't worry, Charlie", he said. "I'll get something fixed up for you". He would be as good as his word.

In the meantime, Malcolm Munro of The Evening Times was sympathetic but realistic. "Odd man out Charlie shouldn't wait long for a club. He is one of the most accurate passers of a ball in the game and had a big say three or four years ago in forming the present European Cup team. He lacked the pace required by Celtic and fell out of the reckoning. In fact, Charlie played only once for the first team in the last two seasons and seldom for the reserves. No matter. Charlie is an inside forward of quality and if he wasn't just good enough lately for Celtic, then there are a lot of other clubs in the country who aren't either".

It was a sad end to a Celtic career, but Charlie's departure was very quickly overtaken by other and sadder events as far as Celtic and their supporters were concerned. Celtic departed for Milan, seriously optimistic about their chances of a second European Cup. They were, in fact, too optimistic. Bertie Auld wrote a ghosted piece for The People entitled "Why Celtic Will Win", and other players made similar pronouncements. Indeed, given their success against Leeds United in the semi-finals, very few people betted against them.

According to Tommy Gemmell, Stein's team talk was dismissive of Feyenoord, and it is now generally reckoned that the team selection and the team formation, particularly in the midfield, was wrong. To be fair to Jock, most of that criticism came with the benefit of hindsight and very few people stated it before the game, but there was a certain complacency about Celtic as they took the field.

Perhaps they might have taken their defeat by Aberdeen in the Scottish Cup final a little more to heart. They were in the throes of their Leeds United games at the time, and the other factor was of course three awful decisions given against them by referee Bobby Davidson – a penalty when Murdoch was hit in the chest, a disallowed goal and a penalty refused. But Stein and Celtic hid behind these decisions and made them the excuse, in apparent contradiction of Stein's much quoted dictum that "if you are four or five ahead, then refereeing decisions don't matter". Perhaps a long hard look at themselves might have been a better idea, but a few days later they beat Leeds United in the European Cup semi-final and we were all swept away in the euphoria.

The atmosphere in Milan was dominated by the Dutch claxons and in spite of scoring first, Celtic were outplayed, going down in extra time in the most heart breaking of circumstances. It was one of the saddest nights imaginable for a Celtic supporter. A less gracious and less gentlemanly person than Charlie Gallagher might have felt entitled to gloat or a quiet "serves him right" in the direction of Jock Stein, whose biggest failure this was, but Charlie was still a Celtic supporter. He grieved like everyone else.

Indeed it must have been hell for all the players, however much they tried to pretend otherwise. The press took a malicious delight in their discomfiture, highlighting for example a consortium arrangement to handle the money that they had earned – something that went down distinctly badly with their supporters who had impoverished themselves by going to Milan. Things were made a lot worse when they were taken on a pointless, squabbling, unhappy tour of the United States of America after that. Charlie did well to miss all that, as he pondered the re-orientation of his life now that Celtic, that huge component of his existence, had been taken away.

For Celtic, too, this wasn't exactly the end of an era, but it was certainly a watershed in the great years. The tour of America saw Tommy Gemmell and Bertie Auld being sent home by Sean Fallon, and that was after Jock Stein himself had suddenly walked out of a game and gone home! He may have been suffering from some sort of nervous breakdown after the Milan fiasco, for which he knew that he himself was at least partially responsible. Rumours abounded that he was going to Manchester United, but he decided to stay and rebuild a new Celtic. Indeed, the pressure that Stein was under may help to explain some of the crazy things that he did.

The departure of Gallagher must be seen in this context. Simpson had already retired in any case, and Gemmell, Clark, Wallace, Chalmers, Auld and Hughes would not last much more than another season as new players like Lou Macari, Danny McGrain, David Hay and Kenny Dalglish began to appear more regularly. One of Stein's claims to greatness was this ability to create a second great team out of the first one. There can be no argument about Stein's tactical acumen. It was a shame however that his way of doing this lacked tact and diplomacy. It was even more of a shame that the ever likeable Charlie Gallagher was the victim of his insensitive behaviour. Even if Gallagher never again played for the first team, he would still have been able to play in the Reserves, acting as guide, philosopher and friend for the all the talented youngsters who were beginning to appear.

But it was not to be. Gallagher and Celtic parted company. Nothing lasts forever. It was time for a fresh start somewhere else. Time to move on.

CHAPTER ELEVEN

A SON OF THE ROCK: 1970-1973

Charlie may have felt just a little miffed about the way that he had been treated by Celtic when he was shown the door in 1970, but there was still a wonderful postscript to come. It was Second Division football and the invitation came from Dumbarton. He was not yet 30 and he would serve them with distinction for three years until he hung up his boots in 1973.

Dumbarton were one of the pioneers of the game in Scotland. They were founded in December 1872 according to their excellent official history book "The Sons Of The Rock" written by Jim McAllister and Arthur Jones, and they were one of the leading lights in the game up to the legalisation of professionalism in 1893 which of course worked in favour of the big city clubs with their greater resources. They won the Scottish Cup in 1883, the third team to do so after Queen's Park and Vale of Leven. They beat Vale of Leven in the final, and were themselves defeated finalists of four other occasions, one of them being the one that was so significant in the founding of Celtic FC , the defeat to Hibs in February 1887 – something that showed the Glasgow Irish that, if the Edinburgh Irish could do it, why couldn't the Glasgow Irish?

Situated on the north bank of the Clyde, in many ways the cradle of Scottish football given the proximity of Vale of Leven in Alexandria and the mighty Renton, Dumbarton were founder members of the Scottish League and indeed were the winners in the first two years, sharing with Rangers in 1891 and winning it outright in 1892. Since then, success has proved a little more elusive, but they deserved their good reputation and that of the ground which was called "Fatal Boghead" because Rangers,

Celtic and Hearts all had a habit of coming a cropper there on its slope and tendency to get wet in winter, as its name would suggest.

Relegated in 1922 to the Second Division, they had stayed there. Possibly they had more good seasons that bad ones, but only rarely did it seem that they were going to make any sort of challenge for promotion. Like most industrial areas, the suffered from economic depression in the 1930s and there was an additional factor as well. They were one of the many clubs who suffered from being too close to Glasgow, and their town saw many buses and trains every Saturday leaving for Celtic Park. Fewer went to Ibrox, because Dumbarton is a Celtic supporting area with a large percentage of their population being of Irish descent.

In 1970, there were two Divisions in the Scottish League which had 37 teams in all.The First Division had 18 teams and the Second Division 19, something that led to the anomaly of each team in the Second Division having no game on two Saturdays per season, when they were the odd man out. Funnily enough this system seemed to work without any huge complaints, although there was a growing groundswell of opinion that the League structure would have to change some day because the Leagues were simply not competitive enough, and attendances had been falling steadily throughout the 1960s. Rangers had tried in 1963 to remove five teams from the Second Division, something that earned them few friends. Ironically, one of the teams that they wanted to remove was Berwick Rangers, who delivered their own special pay-back day to Rangers in 1967!

As a general rule, and with a few exceptions each way, the First Division was full time, and the Second Division was part time. This led to a few difficulties. A team who were relegated had to prune the staff to reduce the wage bill, whereas there was occasionally a certain apparent reluctance on the part of some teams to go for promotion. No-one ever refused promotion, but there was frequently a certain visible and suspicious loss of form in the months of March and April with odd team selections, missed penalties and goalkeeping errors. Newspapers hinted, supporters muttered, and many people knew in their heart of hearts what was going on, but no-one really seemed to mind. It was just accepted that the necessity to go full time was simply beyond some clubs, as indeed was the necessity of Second Division clubs to sell their promising youngsters to First Division ones or to English teams.

Charlie's colleague Willie Wallace hints at this dark side of Second Division football in his book Heart Of A Lion. He was playing for Stenhousemuir in season 1958/59 and the team was doing well, but then he says "Towards the end of that season, we met the league leaders Arbroath at Ochilview. Much to my delight we beat the "Red Lichties" 7-0 and pulled up to within a few points of them, with Greenock Morton one point behind. Promotion seemed very much on the cards, and I was excited. Strangely, however, things did not work out in our favour in the final few games of the season, during which there were a lot of mysterious team changes. Of course, promotion could have been a financial disaster for the club, which would have found it very difficult to maintain a first division place. The ground would have required considerable upgrading and the support base was only small. Anyway, for whatever reasons, we played some very unusual team combinations in those remaining games of the season, results didn't go our way and the promotion that had seemed more than likely only a few weeks earlier didn't come about".

Jackie Stewart was Dumbarton's manager in 1970. Not to be confused with the racing car driver of the same name, he had been there since 1968 and, ambitious and progressive, he was slowly building up a good side aided by an energetic Secretary by the name of John Hosie. When they heard that Gallagher was available, they moved quickly and offered him terms. As Charlie had been given a free transfer from Celtic, there was no problem. Possibly Sean Fallon who would in later years become a Director of Dumbarton was influential in all this, but on June 18 1970, without any great fanfare of trumpets other than those of the British General Election and the Mexican World Cup, Charlie Gallagher joined Dumbarton and became a Son of the Rock, the nickname given to the club because of Dumbarton Rock which was the obvious landmark which dominated the geography of the area.

This was part of Stewart's plan to rebuild Dumbarton. Quite a few players had been dispensed with, and a few efforts had been made to bring in big name players. The attempt to lure Denis Law was, unsurprisingly, a failure. A more realistic target was Davie Wilson, once of Rangers but now with Dundee United. Stewart did not succeed the first time but kept trying and eventually, a year later, got his man. Wilson and Gallagher from different sides of the Old Firm would team up very well together. Both indeed were tremendously talented players and had a tremendous mutual respect for each other.

Dumbarton's first challenge in the 1970/71 season was the Scottish League Cup. Drawn in a section against Berwick Rangers, Alloa Athletic and Brechin City, Jackie Stewart's new look team surprised even their most devoted of their small but loyal support by winning all their games except for a draw with Brechin City at Boghead and found themselves in the two legged quarter final against Partick Thistle. The first leg was played on September 9 at Firhill on a night of high winds and torrential rain, and the Sons did well to come back from being 2 goals down, and to bring it back to 2-2, then went behind again, before a Gallagher shot was deflected home to earn a 3-3 draw which was much appreciated and enjoyed by the 4,000 crowd huddled under what shelter there was at Firhill.

The second leg two weeks later at Boghead was Dumbarton's best night for many years as the team qualified for the semi-final of the Scottish League Cup for the first time ever. Two men called Gallagher, Brian and Charlie, won the game 3-2 for Dumbarton before an excited crowd of 7,000. The Evening Times says that Charlie is "not as sharp as he used to be but he uses his experience to full advantage" He scored the first goal, beating the Partick Thistle goalkeeper called according to The Evening Times "Bobby Rough" when he became better known as Alan! Full time came to tremendous scenes of excitement among the Boghead faithful who had had little enough to cheer about over the past few years.

The other semi-finalists were Celtic, Rangers and Cowdenbeath. Dumbarton would have wanted Cowdenbeath, but as luck would have it, it was Celtic who came out in the draw for the game to be played on Wednesday October 7 1970. 25,838 (the biggest crowd that Dumbarton had played in front of for many years, if not all their history), came to Hampden to see a game in which Dumbarton might well have provided one of Scottish football's biggest ever giant killings. The crowd contained a fair amount of black and gold scarves, showing the effect that this game had on the town.

But before the game began, Charlie was amazed and shocked to overhear his old Manager Jock Stein tell Davie Hay who would have been Charlie's direct opponent in a voice loud enough to be heard by Charlie himself to "break that wee bastard's legs". It is, of course, by no means uncommon for such things to be said before a game. Charlie had heard it from Bobby Shearer of Rangers and a few other coarse defenders that Scottish football produced on an all too regular production line. But this was Jock Stein!

Charlie, of course, knew that Jock was frequently wound up to an unhealthy extent before a game and often said things that he didn't really mean, but it was still shocking to hear that. It was particularly shocking to hear that sort of nonsense coming from a man who was a legend in the Scottish game and who would continue to be so until his death. It would also have been nice to have thought that Charlie's contribution to Celtic's successes in the late 1960s, 1968 in particular, had not been entirely forgotten! Davie Hay, always a scrupulously fair and immensely talented player, and a good friend of Charlie in any case, was quite embarrassed to hear this and thankfully did not carry out his Manager's instructions!

Charlie however had a piece of retaliation. At one point while clearing a ball, Charlie kicked it straight into the Celtic dugout. Both his own Manager Jackie Stewart and the referee looked at him in disapproval as if he had done it deliberately, especially when Jock Stein in trying to avoid the ball, hit his head against the roof of the dugout! It was one of the few times in football that Charlie, who could boast about never having been booked on senior football, was given a talking to by the referee.

The game contained a rarity of both goalkeepers being called Williams – Evan for Celtic and Laurie for Dumbarton – and it was Laurie who earned all the plaudits with a double save of a penalty kick from Willie Wallace in extra time, but before that Dumbarton had more than held their own with The Glasgow Herald singling out Gallagher ..."and their own forwards, master-minded by Charlie Gallagher, a former Celtic player of 12 years' experience, had the Parkhead defence under pressure for spells" The 0-0 draw marked a great display from Dumbarton, even though Celtic had had to play for a long period of the second half without the influential Bobby Murdoch who was taken off injured.

If anyone thought that this game was a fluke – and it certainly looked that way when Dumbarton managed to lose 1-3 to Alloa on the following Saturday, while Celtic had been lucky to scrape through 1-0 against St Johnstone - such thoughts were dispelled in the replay on Monday October 12 again at Hampden played (most unusually) before an increased attendance of 32,000. After Celtic had taken a 2-0 lead, Gallagher once again took charge of the midfield of the park and inspired the part-timers to score twice and take Celtic to extra time before inevitably succumbing to full time training in the added 30 minutes.

Jock Stein was both much relieved and furious with his own men for their lacklustre performance. He ignored his own team – even though they were now in their seventh consecutive Scottish League Cup final – and made a beeline for the Dumbarton dressing room to congratulate the gallant Sons of the Rock for their brave and unlucky performance. It is, of course, easy to be magnanimous and charming when your team have won, but it would have been interesting to know what exactly he said to Charlie Gallagher whose legs he had wanted broken at the start of the first game!

Dumbarton had less success in the Scottish Cup with an early exit before Christmas at Stranraer. Indeed, apart from the League Cup run, Dumbarton's form before the New Year had been nothing to get any too excited about with away form particularly poor.

New Year 1971 saw Scottish football in shock because of the Ibrox disaster when 66 Rangers fans were crushed to death at the end of the Old Firm match on January 2. In truth, it was no real surprise given the lack of any real concern (as distinct from repeated pious platitudes about safety being paramount etc.) about the welfare of spectators at football matches. Anyone who was ever at an International or a Cup final, for example in the boom years of the 1960s, will testify to the appalling dangers of overcrowding. Nevertheless, it was a dreadful tragedy, and had its effect on everyone.

As far as Dumbarton were concerned, things improved after the New Year, for there was a carrot held out for those who finished in the first four of the Second Division in the shape of a sponsored pre-season tournament called the Dryburgh Cup. Quite a lot of people disapproved of this kind of sponsorship particularly when it came from a firm which brewed beer (a beverage which caused a great deal of bother to so many football fans!) but it did provide money for the poorer teams, giving them something to play for. The top four of the Second Division would play the top four of the First Division in the quarter finals of a tournament which would be held in the two weeks before the start of the 1971/72 season in late July and early August.

There was even more to it than that. The top goalscorers in each Division would play each other in the quarter final. The top goalscorers in the First Division would clearly be Celtic, (who won the League for the 26th time in 1971) so if Dumbarton could reach fourth spot and be the top goalscorers of the top four, another game against Celtic beckoned. The last four games yielded 20 goals as the Sons went for it. First Stirling Albion were hammered 7-0, then Arbroath were defeated 3-0 in heavy rain, both of these games being at Boghead, and then the Sons went to Albion Rovers on Tuesday April 27 to win 6-2 and then, two days later in the last game of the season at Boghead, Dumbarton won 4-0 over Queen's Park. In each of these games Gallagher's contribution had been crucial. The team finished fourth and but for their poor form before Christmas, they might well have won the League. But they had scored the most goals, so a trip to Celtic Park beckoned.

Peter Coleman, Kenny Wilson and Roy McCormack were the men who attracted the attention with their goal scoring, but Charlie Gallagher was the man who made it all happen. The pace was a little slower in the Second Division and this suited Gallagher all the more, for he was thus better able to judge his inch perfect passes. He himself scored nine goals, and enjoyed himself all the more for he was under less pressure to produce the goods. He knew that, barring injury, he was guaranteed his place every week, and this made a huge difference. He was also enjoying playing his football in a more relaxed atmosphere away from Celtic's demanding fans, and the constant, overwhelming and stifling presence of Jock Stein!

The fans too appreciated the subtlety of the play of Charlie Gallagher. There were fewer of them than there would have been at Celtic Park – 1,000 would be considered an acceptable, even a good crowd – but they knew good football when they saw it. Dumbarton supporters, by definition, are not glory hunters. If they had been, they would have been at Celtic Park every week! They were more patient and in a real sense, supportive. The fact that their team finished fourth in the Scottish League Division Two was considered a triumph. And they had a visit to Celtic Park to look forward to at the start of the new season which would indeed turn out to be a remarkable one.

In the meantime, Celtic had won the Scottish League and Scottish Cup double, beating Rangers in a replayed final in the latter tournament. The team had been in the throes of transition, and the Lisbon men were now being shaken out in a novel form of diaspora to teams like Morton, Crystal Palace and Nottingham Forest. Symbolically, in the last League game of the season, Stein had played them all for one last time, except for Ronnie Simpson who had now retired, but who nevertheless came out with the rest of the team before the start.

Dumbarton's game at Celtic Park was played on July 31 1971, and Celtic Park was a strange sight with the main stand still out of commission as it was being redeveloped. Pre-season Micky Mouse tournament or not, the Dryburgh Cup persuaded 22,000 to appear and Charlie was given a great reception by the crowd as Dumbarton came out. It was however another Charlie who was the main focus of attention, for the great Charlie Tully had died a few days previously in Belfast and was given a very impressive minute's silence. Gallagher had of course known Tully, for their careers had crossed briefly in the late 1950s.

It was a young Celtic side captained by Jim Brogan, and Dumbarton looked as if they were in with a chance especially when they scored first through an excellent Charlie Gallagher free kick from the edge of the box. Davie Hay had brought down Roy McCormack on the edge of the box, and Charlie showed the Celtic crowd just what they had been missing with a fine strike from the free kick which eluded the defensive wall and Evan Williams.

The reaction of the crowd was interesting. There was of course a cheer from the small band of Dumbarton supporters, and stony silence from the Celtic crowd, but then realisation grew that the free lick had been scored by Charlie Gallagher. A ripple of applause ran round the Jungle with appreciation at a great goal scored by an ex-Celt, and he was given reluctant approval for all the other good things he did in the game. When he was substituted late in the game, the crowd would have risen to him if they had been sitting down, but of course there was no sitting accommodation! Celtic in the event won the game very comfortably 5-2 with a youngster called Kenny Dalglish catching the eye.

It was however a good start to the season for the Sons of the Rock in that it gave them a taste of the big time atmosphere that the team now aspired to. Yet the team got off to a very poor start once the season started officially, explained to a certain extent by the injury to Charlie Gallagher, but the League Cup this year would provide no opportunity for glory as it had done the year before. Home defeats to Queen of the South and Stenhousemuir, quite apart from ruining any chance in the League Cup, also gave the Boghead faithful little cause for optimism for the League campaign.

The League campaign itself also got off to a bad start with a poor run of form which included a 6-1 defeat at the hands of Raith Rovers at Stark's Park in late September, but gradually things improved and by the time that winter came, Dumbarton settled down to some sort of form, especially when their ranks were supplemented by the arrival of Davie Wilson from Dundee United. Wilson had of course been an Ibrox legend with Rangers, and Wilson and Gallagher brought a wealth of experience with them to Boghead, something that was most noticed on days when things were difficult for the team.

Gallagher had always been a good "bad weather" player in that wet or hard pitches (unless excessively so) were less of a problem to him, and his value became more apparent in the months leading up to the New Year. Kenny Wilson was on form scoring goals, and there were several high scoring victories – 6-2 for example at Douglas Park, and 7-1 over Alloa the week before Christmas at Boghead. The year 1971 finished with Dumbarton handily placed in 4th position following their 2-2 draw with St Mirren at Love Street.

The County Reporter (Dumbarton's local paper) is ecstatic about the team, particularly in the context of the 7-1 defeat of Alloa, using phrases like "Sons were brilliant" and singling out Charlie Gallagher of whom it says "I doubt if Charlie Gallagher has contributed as much genius to a game in a Dumbarton jersey as he did on Saturday". Not only did he score with a penalty kick, but he also had a hand in every other goal! The County Reporter also praises Alloa for their sporting acceptance of their defeat but, tellingly, criticises the Dumbarton crowd for not turning up in greater numbers to see this feast of football. Only 1,300 were there and the "Sons deserve better than that".

In the domestic front, 1971 had seen an addition to the family when Kieron was born. Charlie and Mary had had plans to adopt a baby girl, but the imminence of Kieron had put paid to that. The following year, a girl did arrive when Claire was born. It was a happy time of Charlie's life. He had recovered from his injury of a few years ago, and was enjoying playing for Dumbarton where he had already become a cult hero.

The bad weather of January and February 1972 affected the Sons more than any other team, for the weather was rainy rather than frosty, something which had an adverse effect on the appropriately named Boghead. But sometimes a fixture pile up can help a team and some teams, in the months of March and April once the weather turns a little better, can prosper once they play a game in midweek and then on the Saturday. The games come thick and fast, and players thrive as they never get bored waiting for the next game. Older players, far from being tired by their exertions, do all the better for they have the experience to know how to pace themselves, something that is occasionally lacking in younger men. The Sons Of The Rock history of the club is at pains to stress the value of the two experienced Old Firm players of Davie Wilson and Charlie Gallagher. "Neither was in the first flush of youth, but they used their brains rather than their legs to rally their troops for the final assault".

The second half of the 1971/72 season saw troubled times for Great Britain. The end of January saw the major incident in Ireland known as "bloody Sunday" when the British Army managed to gun down unarmed protesters, but there was also a major coal strike with effects on electricity supply and power cuts. When it happened again in 1974, Sunday football was allowed as a side-effect of it all, but the 1972 strike (so unnecessary and able to have been stopped at an earlier stage through negotiation) inflicted a great deal of damage on the Conservative Government who were forced to surrender. But that was only the first round, as it were. A great deal more had yet to happen in future years.

Raith Rovers put the Sons out of the Scottish Cup in February. One has to be very wary of statements like "a Cup exit gives the team more of a chance to concentrate on the League" but in this case it happened to be true. In March, the team started to play really well, and took revenge on Raith Rovers for the two defeats inflicted on them earlier this season with a sparkling 5-0 victory on April 18 1972 in which Kenny Wilson scored all five goals.

But then Dumbarton wobbled and were heavily dependent on Gallagher to win 1-0 at Alloa and 2-1 at Brechin City as Kenny Wilson's goals began to dry up. Then on Saturday April 29, when promotion might have been secured at home against St Mirren and TV cameras paid a rare visit to Boghead to join the huge 9,000 crowd, Gallagher scored yet again from the penalty spot to put the Sons ahead. But then sadly defensive frailties conceded two goals and put a serious spoke in Dumbarton's chances of both the Championship and promotion. Celtic supporters in the area went to that game rather than to their own game at Tynecastle where there had been complaints of discriminatory treatment, and in particular the parking of buses a huge distance away from the ground. They made a good choice going to see Dumbarton v St Mirren for Celtic, the League having been comfortably won two weeks ago, went down 1-4 to Hearts, an extremely rare occurrence in 1972!

The position had been complicated for the past few weeks, but Dumbarton now had a game in hand – an advantage gained from having had so many games called off in the winter – and that was against lowly Berwick Rangers at home. Things were now simple. Dumbarton were two points behind Arbroath but had a far better goal average. This produced the very simple formula that a win would get both the Championship and promotion, a draw simply promotion in second place behind Arbroath and a defeat would bring nothing at all, the beneficiaries to be Stirling Albion.

9,000 came to Boghead on Wednesday May 3 1972. In some ways it was a historian's dream. It was their Centenary Year for they were founded in 1872, and halfway through these hundred years had been 1922 when Dumbarton had been relegated to the Second Division where they had stayed ever since. It was a great occasion with Charlie's two thunderbolts from a distance, one in each half, contributing to the 4-2 victory. The scenes at the end were a sight to behold and even a revelation for Charlie Gallagher and Davie Wilson, both of whom thought they had seen it all with Celtic and Rangers.

Bob Patience of the Daily Record was more than a little impressed. "... the man who can have the freedom of Dumbarton this morning is ex-Celt Charlie Gallagher. It was Charlie who laid on Dumbarton's opening third minute goal for winger Peter Coleman. It was Charlie who took the pressure off with a spectacular goal after Englishman Jerry Coyne had equalised. And it was Charlie who finally paved the way for a night of sheer nostalgia with an equally great third goal in the 57th minute. Little wonder a "delirious" Jackie Stewart said later "Charlie was magnificent as he had been throughout the last few matches. He pulled us up by the bootlaces tonight. What a player! What a team! What a night!" Quiet hero Gallagher said simply "One of the greatest nights of my life. At Parkhead we were expected to win. This is something different. It's just great."

If 1968 had been Gallagher's Championship for Celtic, the same could be said about this one for the Sons of the Rock in 1972. He scored 19 goals, 9 from the penalty spot and another few from free kicks outside the box, but there was so much more than that for it was he who made all the ammunition for Kenny Wilson and Roy McCormack. He was recognised now as one of the best kickers of a dead ball in British football with his corner kicks particularly accurate and sharp. A future in the First Division now beckoned for Dumbarton, and Charlie would be part of it once more. Summer 1972 was a particularly satisfying one for Charlie Gallagher and his young family.

And where were Celtic at this point? A mixture of good and bad it would have to say, with most of it good, some of it outstandingly good. The Scottish League had now been won for the 7th time in a row, beating the team's own record from 1905-1910, but the end of the season centred on the controversial Dixie Deans. Dixie had been bought in October after the loss of the League Cup final to Partick Thistle, and had been a great success. But he had had the misfortune to be the only player to miss a penalty kick in penalty shoot-out of the European Cup semi-final against Inter Milan. Almost immediately however he bounced back and scored a hat-trick in the Scottish Cup final, something that only Jimmy Quinn had done before!

In the course of the 1972/73 season Charlie Gallagher celebrated his 32nd birthday and now in the First Division, he would find the sheer pace of the game a little too quick for him. Never the fastest of players in the first place, he decided that summer 1973 was a good time to hand up his boots. He had his moments for the Sons in that final season. To begin with there was another visit to Parkhead in the first round of the Dryburgh Cup. It was the first day of a strange experimental rule in which a player could only be offside in his opponents' penalty box or its lateral extension.

There was thus a line drawn from the penalty area to the touchline, and the linesman would have a very easy job indeed as he only had to worry about offside when it was close to the goal. It was a laudable effort to introduce more goals to the game, but after being used in the Dryburgh Cup this year and the Scottish League Cup the following two years, the idea was abandoned. In this game, it did not make a great deal of difference. Nor did it generally, and it was one of those well meaning but short lived experiments to make the game more interesting.

Dumbarton were given a good reception by the Parkhead crowd, particularly Charlie Gallagher and John Cushley who had been McNeill's deputy in the mid 1960s but had departed to play for West Ham United and Dunfermline Athletic. The crowd were a great deal less welcoming of ex-Ranger Davie Wilson, but Wilson played well for the Sons, as indeed did Gallagher before he was substituted in the second half. Celtic won 2-1 in a close game which made everyone realise that Dumbarton had won the Second Division on merit and would be no-one's pushovers in the First Division.

In fact they finished third from bottom of the First Division. In the course of the season another ex-Celt joined the Sons. This was Willie Wallace, who had been offloaded rather too early by Jock Stein to Crystal Palace in 1971, had not really been all that happy at Selhurst Park and returned to Scotland to play for Dumbarton in October 1972.The team however were struggling but rallied at the end after a dreadful run of form in February and March which included a 6-0 beating from Aberdeen and 5-0 from Hibs. Indeed, even in April Celtic, going for the title, showed no mercy as they beat them 5-0 at Parkhead, but the Sons managed to beat Motherwell at Fir Park and then Dundee United at home to save themselves just edging ahead of Kilmarnock and Airdrie. They lost in the League Cup to Airdrie at the start of the season, and went down to Partick Thistle in a replay in the Scottish Cup in February.

In the meantime, the world continued. The incredibly bloody Vietnam war continued, as the USA tried with increasing desperation to find a face-saving way to get out of it. And there was an added complication in Washington in that President Nixon seemed to have authorised the burgling of his opponent's headquarters before the 1972 Presidential election. The place was called Watergate, and this problem would simply not go away.

Charlie suffered from injuries throughout this tough 1972/73 season and when his Manager Jackie Stewart left in January to manage St Johnstone, he began more and more to drop from the picture, his last game for the club being against Airdrie on March 7 as he was substituted in a 3-5 defeat. In summer 1973 he decided that enough was enough and that it was time to hang up his boots. He had entertained hopes that he might have found for himself a job on the backroom staff at Dumbarton when one became available, but the job in fact went to Davie Wilson. What the reason for this was, no-one can say for certain, but we can all guess.

Celtic meantime had a less than totally successful season. Out of Europe before Christmas, they lost the League Cup final to Hibs and the Scottish Cup final to Rangers, in both cases rather unluckily. But they did hold on to their League title for the 8th year in a row, after a prolonged struggle in which, at several points it appeared that Rangers would prevail. But Celtic held firm, and won the League in an epic game at Easter Road against the strong going Hibs. Generally speaking, it had not been a great season for Scottish football with major problems of hooliganism and falling attendances. Scotland lost to England for the third year in a row at Wembley, but a revival was forthcoming in that quarter.

Charlie Gallagher, his career now at an end, would now have loads of leisure to watch Celtic, except for the fact that he had three young children. More pertinently however, he would have to find himself a job – always a problem for a footballer at the end of his career.

CHAPTER TWELVE

RETIREMENT AND REFLECTION

All football players have the problem of what to do after they have given up the game. In Charlie's case, this was when he was nearly 33 – the time of life when in any other job, things are beginning to take off. Football had been his life. He had had the opportunity to be an apprentice as an electrical engineer in a firm in London Road, not all that far away from Celtic Park, but had decided against it, preferring to concentrate on his football.

He was unfortunate in that he arrived before the era of the super-rich footballers. His remuneration from Celtic was always adequate, and above the national average, but it would be wrong to say that footballers in the 1960s lived in the lap of luxury. Today on the other hand, players earn an exorbitant amount from the revenues which accrue from TV companies. It is probably true to say that a player for Dumbarton in 2016 will earn as much proportionately as Charlie Gallagher did in 1972; at Celtic on the other hand, players earnings give every sign of getting out of hand with a great deal of money being paid out to some players whose ability is questioned. And it is a great deal worse in England and Europe. Some think this is a good thing; others beg to differ.

Where this can be seen to be a bad thing is in the attitude of some English clubs who state quite openly that they would rather be fourth in the English League than win the English Cup. This is blasphemy to anyone with any respect for the traditions and history of the game, but then again fourth in the English League gets you into the Champions League and megabucks! We may shake our heads at all this, but that is the sad reality of the situation.

Yet football was talked about just as much in the 1960s as it is now, and it is an open question as to whether or not it is better. As far as Celtic are concerned, there is no doubt that the 1960s were the two extremes. Things were, frankly, very bad until 1965 when Chairman Robert Kelly swallowed his considerable pride and appointed Jock Stein to the Manager's job. Things took off almost immediately, and Charlie is proud to have been part of that. Naturally he is disappointed not to have played at Lisbon in 1967, but he was very much part of the squad, and he had his other compensations as well with his medals in other competitions. All in all he played 171 times for the club and scored 32 goals, won a Scottish League medal in three successive seasons from 1965/66 to 1967/68, a Scottish Cup medal on the day that history changed against Dunfermline in April 1965 and a Scottish League Cup medal in October of that year.

He suffered to a certain extent by being played in different positions. His versatility was not always beneficial to him. In the 1950s when he started to play, positions were fairly rigid, and of course there were no substitutes until the mid-1960s. (In Scotland, one for an injury from 1966/67 onwards and one for any reason in 1967/68 onwards). This tended to mean that wherever the Manager told you to play, that was it. And when, as at Celtic, the decisions were made by a man who, frankly, knew little about the tactical side of the game, players often had a problem. Charlie's deployment on the right wing was by no means a total failure in 1961; yet discerning fans questioned whether he had the pace for that role.

When Charlie began, the formation of most teams (not just Celtic) was a firm and apparently unshakeable 1-2-3-5 with the forwards in a W or an M formation. The wingers and the centre forward were to be supplied by the "fetch and carry" men known as the inside right and the inside left. To a lesser extent, the wing halves did this job as well, but they were further back and had the additional task of keeping the opposing inside forwards quiet. Full backs marked the wingers, and of course centre halves marked the centre forwards. There was no law that said that all jerseys had to be numbered (Celtic, eccentrically, refused until 1960 – and even then the numbers were put on their pants! They carried out this revolutionary move for the first time in a friendly against Sparta Rotterdam in May 1960 and then it became common practice) but budding young mathematicians noticed, for example, that in the mid-field a player and his marker always added up to 14! The inside right was 8, he was marked by the left half who was 6, the centre forward was 9 and the centre half 5, and the inside left was 10 and the right half 4!

For a long time, this system prevailed without anyone objecting. Indeed a feature of the game in the 1950s was the prevalence and indeed the excellence of wingers. England had Stanley Matthews and Tom Finney. Scotland had Willie Waddell, Gordon Smith and Billy Liddell. In domestic football, there was reckoned to be no finer sight that a winger charging down his wing, beating his man, reaching the dead ball line, crossing and in the centre there would be the centre forward waiting patiently to finish it off. Celtic had had great wingers in the past like Alec Bennett and Jimmy Delaney who was often described as "dashing down the wing like the fire brigade"! More recently, there had been Charlie Tully and Neil Mochan. Charlie Gallagher was simply not of that ilk as a right winger.

But the position of right winger itself was now under threat. Under continental influence, a few teams began to send out formations which did not seem to contain any wingers, either on the right or on the left. There was of course no law against this, but the Press seemed to detect some sort of subversion in the 4-2-4 formation with a flat back four, two midfielders and a flat front four. Hearts and Dundee seemed to deploy this formation, and the annoying thing was that it seemed to bring them some success, even at the expense of a few sneers for playing defensive football!

It all depended, of course, on the quality of the players that one had. Team formations do not win matches; players do. And yet to a certain extent, there does need to be some shape as well. The Celtic teams in the early 1960s took the field with the forward line often looking as if it had been simply thrown together whimsically by Mr Kelly. Little wonder that success was not achieved.

One day in 1963 when Jock Stein and Willie Waddell were still Managers of Dunfermline and Kilmarnock, they went to Italy to study Italian team formation. Jock came back from that trip convinced that the old 2-3-5 system was now dead, and that the much maligned 4-2-4 system (wrongly accused of leading to defensive football by some who should have known better) was the answer, even if in a modified way. He realised that the pivotal characters were the midfield men through whom everything was channelled. When he was with Hibs he used a man called Willie Hamilton (whom he often said was the best player he ever managed) for this purpose. When he came to Celtic, it was to be Bobby Murdoch.

So where did Charlie Gallagher fit in to all this? To start with, he was an old fashioned inside forward – that was his position in the 1965 Scottish Cup final – but as the team formation evolved (good team formations evolve gradually over a period of time, they are not created overnight) he was more and more the left sided midfielder who balanced Bobby Murdoch on the right. That was certainly the role he played to devastating effect in the great charge for the League Championship of 1968.

A lot of this was due to the fact that Gallagher covered for Bertie Auld, and that was the role that Bertie had played in Lisbon and in the great season on 1967. It was a shame that Gallagher and Auld were so seldom deployed in the same team – the 1965 Scottish Cup final being an obvious exception - for they were both great players. Stein however did have a point that they were a similar type of player, although markedly different in character. Bertie Auld was more "in your face", more cocky, altogether more aggressive and more sure of himself. Gallagher was more thoughtful, more accurate in his passing, more apparently laid back. One uses the word "apparently" because he could give the impression of being languid and half-asleep for large stretches of the game, but then suddenly he could unleash an inch-perfect pass, or fire for goal.

As important a skill as any was his sociability and facility for getting on with everyone. The Celtic team of the 1960s, like many great sides, had a few firebrands and hotheads who could all get into trouble with referees. Murdoch, Craig, Gemmell and Auld all had their "moments". Never Charlie Gallagher. Yet his good nature and sociability did not mean that he was in any way "soft". Beneath it all, there burned the same sort of the love of the club and determination to do well that there was in any of the others. An ideal team man, one would have thought. So why did Stein, apparently, not like him?

It was more to do with Jock Stein than it was to do with Charlie Gallagher, and it is important to realise that Gallagher was not the only talented player to be, apparently, on the wrong side of Jock Stein. It is important to distinguish between Stein and his relationship with fans on the one hand and Stein and his relationship with his players on the other. Stein was famously charming with fans at supporters' functions, answering all sorts of questions with tact and diplomacy. A hostile question would be dealt with disarmingly, a question put by a nervous, tongue-tied youngster would be listened to patiently and answered with kindness.

The Press were a different matter. He could court them and help them out with stories, knowing that Celtic always needed the Press to be on their side. On the other hand, a columnist who had penned something that he took exception to, could be held up to scorn and ridicule. What no-one could do with Stein was ignore him. More than one journalist had testified to the fact that even when you had your back to the door, you could always tell when Stein had entered the room from the demeanour of everyone else.

With his players, however, there is hardly a man who will give Stein a 100% endorsement of love. Bobby Murdoch is generally regarded as one of his favourites, but he tells the story of how, when he was now playing for Middlesbrough, he and Kathleen met Mr and Mrs Stein on holiday in Majorca. Bobby was sipping some beer, and Stein gave him a dressing down! The fact that he was no longer a Celtic player did not really matter! Steve Chalmers scored a hat-trick against Rangers and was immediately taken down a peg or two when Stein said that he thought John Hughes was the man of the match. Jim Craig, a dentist to whom hands were important, was not allowed to wear gloves; John Hughes had seen fit to query why he had been dropped and was taken to Kilmarnock with the Reserves the following night and publicly humiliated in the dressing room by not being given a game. John Fallon has recently written a book featuring all his many complaints about Jock Stein. And wouldn't we all like to know what really went on between Stein and Dalglish before the disastrous transfer to Liverpool in 1977?

All this seemed designed to show potential rebels who was Boss, but we are still at a loss to answer the question about Charlie Gallagher. He was the model profession, keeping his head down and playing uncomplainingly wherever he was put, whether in the first XI or in the Reserves. What could he possibly have done to earn Jock Stein's disapproval? We will never know, but Charlie has the consolation of knowing that he was not alone. And of course, he is the first to admit that without Stein, that talented Celtic team would not have won very much.

Gallagher always retained his popularity with the fans who would cheerfully greet him on the street to tell him how good he had been. After retirement, he did have one job in football and that was working as a scout for Celtic. This he did from 1976 until 1978. It was a job he enjoyed, going all over the country to spot talent. It was a job which by its very nature led to more than a few disappointments, if the man concerned was injured or not playing that day or simply having an off day. He did, however, recommend one particular centre forward. This player was an undeniable Celtic supporter and had great talent, but had a reputation of not being a particularly nice character and had a propensity to get into trouble off the pitch. Charlie's recommendation was not acted upon by Johnny Higgins (the Coaching Co-ordinator) or Jock Stein, but this particular player went on to have a sparkling career in both Scotland and England.

His first job after football was in "slot television". When colour television first appeared in the early 1970s, not everyone could afford one. A way of circumventing this problem was by a television firm selling a colour television set at a cheap price and if the customer wanted to watch a programme, he paid for it by inserting money, on the same principle as an electric meter. This involved someone going round to empty the "meter" from time to time, and Charlie did this job along with his old adversary Bobby Shearer.

He also, when he lived in Dumbarton, had a General Store in that town. It sold groceries and newspapers – something that necessitated getting up early in the morning but it was a job that he enjoyed every much for about 5 years. It was there that his wife Mary, who worked in selling houses, began her hobby as a singer in Gilbert and Sullivan opera. By this time the family of Kieron, Paul and Claire were beginning to grow up, all of them proud of their father.

Mary's operatic commitment began after being invited to sing at a Celtic function when she sang an old favourite like Danny Boy. Someone suggested that she should join the Dunbartonshire Operatic Society, and she duly did so. Her roles were many and various. She played Elsie in "The Yeoman of the Guard", Tessa in "The Gondoliers", the Maid in "The Pirates of Penzance", Katisha in "The Mikado", Phyllis in "Iolanthe" and Princess Ida in the opera of that name. She often played opposite a man called John Mulvenna who had impeccable Celtic connections!

Mary became an Estate Agent and they later moved back to Bishopbriggs. Charlie sat his test as a taxi driver, a job he did for many years until the bad winter of December 2010. Occasionally he had the melancholy duty of rescuing one particular ex-team mate, sadly no longer with us, when this fellow had had rather too much to drink. Glasgow taxi drivers are of course a breed apart. Famously sociable and knowledgeable about the city, but usually coming down firmly on one side or other of the football divide with trenchant opinions on Managers and players. Naturally they are reluctant to advertise which side they are on for fear of antagonising or alienating the other side or even provoking some unpleasant or even violent reaction, but once engaged in conversation, the guard usually drops!

His job as a taxi driver sometimes curtailed his ability to visit Celtic Park and support the team that he still loved. But he recalls the time when the late Bobby Murdoch phoned and asked him if he wanted to go to Celtic Park with him, for the Directors were keen to use their famous ex-players for Hospitality purposes. It seemed a good idea until Charlie asked how much they were prepared to pay for this service. Jaws dropped, for there had been no plans to pay the players! Charlie, needless to say, was not engaged even after the Directors offered to pay the players some remuneration!

Charlie seldom went back after that until Martin O'Neill managed to ensure free admission for ex-players. He is however now a regular attender, sometimes along with his friend John Fallon the goalkeeper, and has his own views of how the game should be played. His advice to any young player would always be to train hard and to become as fit as he possibly could. The bad training regime – or even the lack of anything that might reasonably be called a regime – at Parkhead in the late 1950s and early 1960s still haunts him, for frequently Celtic were not as fit as other teams and suffered as a result. The much improved training after the arrival of Neil Mochan in 1964 showed him how important fitness actually is. Therefore his advice always would be to a young player to get fit and stay fit.

Charlie and Mary now have 8 grandchildren. Paul has two boys – Matthew and Aaron, Kieron has triplets – Jack, Lewis and Lindsay, while Claire has three girls, Niamh, Eilidh and Cliona who is now a budding gymnast. Now not far from his 76th birthday, Charlie remains the charming, modest chap that he always was. He was proud of his Celtic career and it is hoped that Celtic should be equally proud of him.

Mike Maher currently living in New Zealand sends this testimonial of his recollections of Charlie Gallagher.

"The name Charlie Gallagher takes me back to my first days of being a Celtic Supporter. I look upon the month of October 1960 as the time I became a real Celtic fan. Up until then I was interested in Scottish Football in general rather than any one team in particular. At that point I had no inkling my father was a Celtic man. Although Celtic Park was only a short distance away I had no recollection of him ever talking about going there. At school many of my mates claimed to be fans of St Mirren, Clyde, Motherwell, Hearts and the like. In those more competitive times these were teams who had more recent success than Celtic. However my best friend-Peter Dickson – was a Celtic fan and one day he told me excitedly that Willie Fernie had returned to Celtic. I had never heard of Willie Fernie but Peter's excitement was enough for me and a couple of days later for the first time in my life I made a point of looking out for the Celtic result as soon as possible on a Saturday evening. That turned out to be a 4-2 win over St Mirren. I was off to a good start! For the next few months I avidly checked the Celtic scores and reports and even saw a few highlights of their games on Saturday night Scotsport. Not that the results were always positive. By the end of 1960 Celtic were sitting 12th in an 18 Club division. Not in the hunt for the title. That was for big teams like Rangers, Hearts, Dundee, and Kilmarnock. So it was with some concern that I awaited the result of our game on the last day of the year at home to the Ayrshire side.

When the score came through I was delighted (at least at the time). We had won 3-2. When I read the reports I found out that Killie had been 2 goals up at one stage but Celtic had staged a comeback and that Charlie Gallagher had scored the winner in the 85th minute. One report told how his shot was so powerful it had torn the net. Another said he might be the "New Patsy". As I had never heard at that point of the old Patsy the reference was lost on me. Anyway I had not even heard of Charlie Gallagher. As a relatively new fan I was only getting to know the usual line up but this was a new name to me. I found out he was only 20 and he had played a couple of times before but not with this impact.

That Kilmarnock result gave me hope for the next game 2 days later – Rangers at Ibrox. My first Old Firm game. No live coverage so I gathered with uncles, aunts and cousins in my granny's prefab to watch the highlights on a special edition of Scotsport on the evening of 2nd January 1961. Despite his goal against Killie Charlie dropped out and his place at inside-left was taken by the more experienced Willie Fernie. The game was typical of the times. Celtic scored after 28 minutes. They had a goal disallowed and missed a few chances. Rangers then took advantage of Celtic errors and score twice in the second half to win 2-1. I would get used to this type of performance over the next few years!

Five days later Charlie returned to the team for the home game with Third Lanark. For me though there was another reason to remember this match. My first ever Celtic game. Up until then I had got my football fix by either playing with my friends or watching the St Bridget's Boys Guild team. Peter's father helped run the team and often Peter and I "assisted" him. On Friday evenings we would "dubbin" the balls and on Saturdays was the job I loved. We would go down to a local joiners and pick up a big bag of sawdust which we would use to line the park. However on that bitterly cold January morning Peter's father told us the Boys Guild game was off. Would we like to go to see Celtic instead? Would we?!?!? I could not believe it. At last I was going to see Celtic. I ran home to tell my parents. Nobody was home so I left a note on the sideboard. Nowadays it would seem incredible but in those days I usually went out after breakfast and came back whenever I felt hungry or tired. I never had a key. The back door was always left open. Anyway after leaving the note in the empty house I raced back to Peter's. His uncle was there with his wee van and soon the 4 of us were making the short trip to Paradise. Peter and I were lifted over and we made our way around the Rangers End. We took a spot beside the green iron railing that separated that part of the ground from the Jungle. Beside us was a cinder track leading to a large sliding door which was opened to admit invalid cars into the ground and at the end was used as an exit gate.

Then the teams came out. I was stunned! Up until then I had never seen Celtic in colour. Newspapers and television were in black and white. I knew Celtic wore green and Thirds wore red but that did not do justice to the hues I saw that day. It was a dark, cold day and the floodlights were on. Celtic's shirts were of dazzling emerald, Third Lanark wore a vivid scarlet. It was like Technicolor! I realised then how football transformed the lives of ordinary people. My Glasgow and Lanarkshire were monochrome places. Grey skies over grey roofs. Grey buildings on grey pavements and grey roads. Grey people wearing grey clothes. But for a couple of hours on a Saturday our lives were full of colour.

On this occasion Charlie played outside right but my first game did not have a happy ending. Although Celtic scored first the Hi Hi won 3-2. I have often wondered if anyone in the 22,000 crowd that day could have imagined that in little more than 6 years Celtic would be champions of Europe and Third Lanark would be out of existence!

Charlie retained his place in the team after that and results started to pick up a bit. We defeated Falkirk at Brockville in the first round of the Scottish Cup which gave us a home tie with Montrose. Peter and I decide we had to be there. After our "debut" against Third Lanark we had not been back to Celtic Park. Peter's father had other duties on a Saturday. We knew our parents would not allow us to go a game unaccompanied so there was only one thing to be done. We would have to lie! Another friend – Phil Dolan- joined us in our deceit and it was to his house we went first. Phil told his parents we were going to the afternoon matinee at the Shettleston Odeon and he needed some pocket money. No problem. Next stop was Peter's and the same result. Finally to my place. Initially I spun the same line to my mother but then my conscience butted in. I blurted out the truth. We were actually intending to go to Celtic Park. "Well I will need to tell your father about this" she said as she left the kitchen. The other 2 scowled at me. Now we were in trouble. Not only would we miss the game but our parents would find out about the lies. A few moments later my father came in. "So you were planning to go the Celtic game?" We nodded solemnly. 'Well come on then- let's go" he said. For a few seconds we were stunned and then gleefully getting into the little Ford Anglia to head to Paradise.

My father could not lift us all over so he waited inside while we came through the Boys Gate. He took us into the enclosure in front of the main stand. That cost an extra sixpence each but it meant he could keep an eye on us easier and the incline there gave a better view than from the terracing. We were almost in line with the goal line and thus had a great view of the goals. Almost from the kick off Celtic won a corner on the right. Tactics were simple then. A corner in that area was taken by the outside right. We had a close up view therefore of Charlie Gallagher sending in the corner. He flighted the ball so well that it caused confusion in the goalmouth with a Montrose defender knocking the ball into his own net. Celtic had a comfortable 6-0 win.

That trip seemed to re-kindle my father's interest and we started making regular trips to Parkhead. During the next few months we were regulars in Paradise and I even got to my first away game at Dens Park. Celtic were fielding a more settled team with Charlie a regular at outside right. We ended up 4th in the league table behind Rangers, Kilmarnock and Third Lanark. The Ibrox outfit had finished 1 point ahead of Kilmarnock. I could not help but thinking now that maybe I should have not celebrated that comeback win over the Ayrshire team on the last day of December!

It was with the Scottish Cup though that our hopes of glory rested. We had reached the final and only lowly Dunfermline stood in the way of silverware. However things did not go as planned and the Fifers lifted the Cup. That was the first time I had heard of Jock Stein and we would need to wait another few years before he returned to Paradise to lead us to glory.

In April 1965 my trip to Hampden for another Cup Final against Dunfermline was much different from the 1961 version. Instead of being taken by my father I went on a football special train with schoolmates. We took our spot on the terracing just in front of the floodlight pylon at the Celtic End on the Sommerville Drive side of the ground. Over the next decade we would get used to this spot. We were very confident but after 15 minutes the Pars scored and doubts were beginning to creep in. Then just after the 30 minute mark Charlie Gallagher stepped in. He drove forward from midfield and hit a fierce shot from distance. It thudded the crossbar and went straight up in the air. When it came back down Bertie Auld knocked it into the net for the equaliser. Dunfermline regained the lead just before half time but Celtic equalised 7 minutes after the break. And then with 9 minutes to go Celtic won a corner on the left. Our tactics had changed from that first Scottish Cup tie I had witnessed. Instead of the outside left taking the kick it was entrusted to someone with real accuracy. Charlie stepped up, delivered the perfect cross for big Billy and the rest as they say is history.

Over the next few years Charlie Gallagher was one of the squad who took Scotland and Europe by storm. And yet he did not play as many times as I thought he should. He did figure in lots of games in 1965/66 and I recall yet another of his great corners letting Steve Chalmers put us in the lead in the Ne'erday Old Firm game which we went on to win 5-1. In our great 1966/67 season his appearances were down and he only played in 2 European games. One of those would give him most famous place in Celtic history. In the dying seconds of our second leg quarter final against Vojvodina Novi Sad with the teams tied at 1-1 Celtic won a corner on the right. By now I had graduated to the Celtic End as part of the Celtic Choir. Despite the distance from the far side of the ground I could see Charlie's accurate cross pick out Billy McNeill who headed home to put us into the semi-final. In the 1967/68 season Charlie only played 2 League Cup games in the entire first half of the season. He did not get a real run in the team until the following February.

I seem to recall Bertie Auld picked up an injury and Charlie took the chance to get a regular place. For the next few months he played some of his best football and was a main reason for Celtic clinching the title.

Despite those performances Charlie dropped out of the picture the following season rarely appearing in the first team and after no games at all in the 1969/70 season he left on a free transfer just a few days before the European Cup Final in Milan. However that was not the last experience I had of Charlie Gallagher.

He went to second division Dumbarton and almost inevitably came up against Celtic a few months after his departure. This was in the League Cup semi-final at Hampden. Celtic were expected to win comfortably. However Charlie gave a man of the match display that helped the part timers secure a 0-0 draw. In the replay Celtic were 2 goals up when Charlie scored from the spot and inspiring the "Sons" to equalise before Celtic sneaked through 4-3 after extra time.

Charlie had picked up a couple of Irish caps and this along with his performances meant he was always popular with the fans. I sometimes heard him referred to as "Bridie" (after the popular Donegal singer Bridie Gallagher whose song "the Boys from the County Armagh" was often heard on Celtic buses in those days). However I always thought that nickname was one of endearment rather than an indication of his lack of strength. I did wonder though if big Jock had reservations about Charlie's "frailties". Despite his ability he never seemed to be a real regular and even in that great run he had in 1968 he was still often substituted. Indeed I think Charlie's problem may have been he was too nice. I have never played professional football but I suppose it is not too different from the amateur game insofar as no one likes to be substituted. I often thought that coaches would pick the easiest going guy to come off rather than have the hassle of dealing with a moaner!

I often thought too that maybe Charlie should have left Celtic sooner. If he had opted to leave at the end of the 1967/68 season he would easily have got into any other of the top Scottish sides (apart from one of course although their lack of interest in him would have had nothing to do with his ability!) As a regular choice his confidence would have grown and so therefore would his performance levels.

On the other hand he was a Glasgow boy with a proud Irish background. That resonated with so many of the Celtic Supporters. Would they have walked away from Celtic? Charlie certainly didn't and that is why after all these years he is still considered one of the Celtic legends."

The late Bob Crampsey who taught Charlie at Holyrood and then had a wide and varied career in football journalism and punditry had this to say about Charlie

"a quiet lad, perfectly behaved and a little bit shy...a footballer more typical of the 1940s and 1950s, very talented but a little too self-effacing to be a star...a superb striker of the ball...a credit to the sport in every way"

Tom Campbell, using his knowledge of American football and also Celtic in the 1950s, explains the similarities and the differences between Auld and Gallagher

"both were used by Stein in much the same way as American football teams employ quarter backs; the organiser, the brains, the schemer, the planner, behind all attacking play. It is imperative that the quarter-back (always the highest paid player) be protected at all times. Auld and Gallagher were quarter-backs and had to be given extra protection – but for different reasons: Auld, competitive and aggressive, latterly needed a little more time to work his magic; Gallagher, more intellectual and perhaps artistic, required physical protection... Auld, intelligent as he was, was always a scrapper (like Bobby Collins), Gallagher, equally intelligent was much less so (like Willie Fernie)

The late Angus Potter (a veteran supporter of the 1920s) would allow Charlie Gallagher to be mentioned in the same breath as Patsy Gallacher and Tommy McInally, and described him laconically but effectively

"Charlie Gallagher? Now he IS a football player!"

Pat Woods, a renowned Celtic historian and collector of Celtic memorabilia says,

"If Charlie has a fault, it lies in his modesty about his football ability. In the decade or so that I watched him playing for Celtic, he always impressed me both as a fine passer and a peerless striker of the ball, attributes which gave the appearance of being effortless in their achievement. His contribution to Celtic ending their trophy famine by winning the Scottish Cup in 1965 has been a shade undervalued. I can still recall standing high up on the King's Park End terracing at Hampden and being gobsmacked by the sheer drama of it all as his ferocious 30 yarder cracked off the crossbar, the ball soaring into the air before coming down for Bertie Auld to bundle it over the line for Celtic's first equalizer. That memory of the Final against Dunfermline Athletic tends to be supplanted (pardonably so, perhaps) by the fairy tale Billy McNeill winner fashioned by Charlie's corner taking expertise, a "routine" that was repeated in the dying seconds against Vojvodina in the European Cup quarter final second leg at Parkhead two years later. Believe me, no Celtic fan present that night would have been happy with a play-off against those tough Yugoslavs in Rotterdam. I recent said in jest to Charlie that there should be plaques at the appropriate spots in both grounds to commemorate these feats. Charlie just smiled, but who would question an assertion that his prowess effectively opened the doors to both the greatest era in the club's history and to its greatest triumph?"

Danny McGrain, arguably Celtic's best ever full back says

"One of the benefits of Charlie Gallagher playing in the reserve team so often was that he was able to be our mentor. His presence was re-assuring, and he always had the ability and willingness to help us out. We owe him a great deal"

Maureen Andrew, Spanish teacher and supporter of many years says

"Charlie Gallagher? What a player!"